BUSINESS INFORMATION TECHNOLOGY MANAGEMENT

Business Information Technology Management Alternative and Adaptive futures

Edited by
Ray Hackney
and
Dennis Dunn

palgrave

Published by
PALGRAVE
Houndmills, Basingstoke, Hampshire RG21 6XS and
175 Fifth Avenue, New York, N. Y. 10010
Companies and representatives throughout the world

PALGRAVE is the new global academic imprint of
St. Martin's Press LLC Scholarly and Reference Division and
Palgrave Publishers Ltd (formerly Macmillan Press Ltd).

Outside North America
ISBN 0–333–79253–X

Inside North America
ISBN 0–312–23181–4

This book is printed on paper suitable for recycling and made from fully managed and sustained forest sources.

A catalogue record for this book is available from the British Library.

Library of Congress Catalog Card Number. 99–059234

11 10 9   8   7   6   5   4   3
10 09 08 07 06 05 04 03 02

Printed and bound in Great Britain by
Antony Rowe Ltd, Chippenham, Wiltshire

In memory of Margaret

Where is the wisdom we have lost in knowledge?
Where is the knowledge we have lost in information?

T.S. Eliot, *The Rock*

Where is the information we have lost in technology?

Ray Hackney and Dennis Dunn

Contents

Contents

List of Figures

List of Tables

Acknowledgements

The editors would specifically like to acknowledge those individuals who assisted in organising and participating in the BIT Conference, held annually within the Manchester Metropolitan University, UK, from which many of the chapters for this text were selected.

The editors and publishers wish to thank the following for permission to reproduce copyright material: *Information Systems*, for Figure 11.1, from K. Pohl, 'The three dimensions of requirements engineering: a framework and its applications' (1994); *Sloan Management Review* for Figure 13.9, from N. Venkatraman and J.C. Henderson, 'Real strategies for virtual organising' (1998); Faber & Faber (Worldwide), Harcourt Inc. (USA), for the extract on paye vi from T.S. Eliot's *The Rock* (*Collected Poems, 1909–1962*); John Wiley & Sons Inc. for Chapter 8 by Hidding and Williams from *Competitive Intelligence Review*; and Blackwell Science for Chapter 18 by Hackney and Hancox.

List of Contributors

Carl Adams Southampton Business School, UK.

Paul Beynon-Davies University of Glamorgan, UK.

Janice Burn Edith Cowan University, Austriala.

Tom Butler University College, Cork, Ireland.

James Callaghan University of Cambridge, UK.

Claudio Ciborra University of Bologna, Italy.

Dennis Dunn Manchester Metropolitan University, UK.

Guy Fitzgerald Brunel University, UK.

Brian Fitzgerald University College Cork, Ireland.

Melanie Fretwell AstraZeneca Ltd, UK.

Petter Gottschalk Norwegian School of Management, Norway.

Gareth Griffiths Manchester Metropolitan University, UK.

Ray Hackney Manchester Metropolitan University, UK.

Martin Hancox Manchester Metropolitan University, UK.

Ole Hanseth University of Oslo, Norway.

Gezinus Hidding Loyola University, Chicago, USA.

Najmul Huda Tallin University, Estonia.

Ben Light University of Salford, UK.

Michael Lloyd Williams University of Wales, Cardiff, UK.

Claudia Loebbecke Copenhagen Business School, Denmark.

Nazmun Nahar Jyvaskyia, Finland.

Ian Owens University of Glamorgan, UK.

Vaios Papaioannou UMIST, UK.

Nancy Russo Northern Illinois University, USA.

Pascal Sieber University of Bern, Switzerland.

Erik Stolterman Umea University, USA.

Charles Snyder Auburn University, USA.

Mark Stubbs Manchester Metropolitan University, UK.

Jaak Tepandi Tallin University, Estonia.

Babis Theodoulidis UMIST, UK.

Dave Tucker Manchester Metropolitan University, UK.

Jeffrey Williams University of Pittsburgh, USA.

Larry Wilson Learner First, Inc., Birmingham, USA.

Dave Wainwright Durham Business School, UK.

List of Abbreviations

AT	Agency Theory
BITM	Business Information Technology Management
BPR	Business Process Re-engineering
CASE	Computer Assisted Software Engineering
CGI	Common Gateway Interface
CI	Competitive Intelligence
CIO	Chief Information Officer
CIT	Communication and Information Technology
CRM	Customer Relations Management
CSF	Critical Success factors
DOS	Disk Operating Systems
DRAM	Dynamic Random Support Memory
DSS	Decision Support System
E-commerce	Electronic Commerce
ECS	Executive Calling System
EDI	Electronic Data Interchange
EPSS	Electronic Performance Support System
ERP	Enterprise Resource Planning
FA	Flexibility Analysis
4GLs	Fourth Generation Languages
GEC	Global Electronic Commerce
HERE	Hypermedia Environment for Requirements Engineering
ICT	Information Communication Technology
IM	Information Management
ISA	Industry Structure Analysis
ISD	Information Systems Development
ISP	Internet Service Provider
ITC	Information and Communications Technology
KBS	Knowledge Based Systems
KM	Knowledge Management
KMS	Knowledge Management Systems
MOA	Mass-Observation Archive
ODC	Online Delivered Content
PH	Planning Horizon
RAD	Rapid Application Development

R&D	Research and Development
RE	Requirements Engineering
SA	Sustainability Analysis
SIFT	Sorting Information for Tomorrow
SISP	Strategic Information Systems Planning
SME	Small Medium and/or Manufacturing Enterprises
SSADM	Structured Systems Analysis and Design Methodology
TCE	Transaction Cost Economics
UoD	Universe of Discourse
VAM	Virtual Alliance Model
VOCM	Virtual Organisation Model
VSP	Virtual Strategic Positioning/Perspective
VVM	Virtual Value Model
Y2K	Year 2000

Introduction

Ray Hackney and Dennis Dunn

As Bernard Shaw suggested, prophecy is a dangerous thing. This book explores this notion through a collection of contemporary topics in the field of *Business Information Technology Management* (BITM). It attempts to represent a coherent overview of current and future international BITM research illustrated through a set of recently identified themes.

BITM is usefully classified as a range of systems which are enabled by technologies that support decision making for improved business performance and/or service delivery. This book is fundamentally about these so called *organisational systems* which are recognised to involve the majority of senior managerial activities. This is a consequence of the well documented dynamic and competitive nature of the business environment and the evidence that BITM may provide for effective organisational solutions. BITM is invariably comparable with studies in information systems (IS), information technology (IT) and information and communications technologies (ICTs). It represents the combined view of these fields including the management processes involved. A number of analysts have suggested that an exploration of the features of BITM, or indeed an adequate definition, is also highly problematic. The motivation for the text is, therefore, the realisation of the need for a more eclectic treatment of BITM research. It recognises the multi-disciplinary, multi-faceted and multi-methodological approaches associated with an increased awareness of the *realities* within the interaction of BITM and organisational management. This includes both practitioner and academic interests where the wider, diverse and complex issues associated with BITM exploitation are considered.

There are many texts on IS and IT where the importance of the field is demonstrated in the pervasive and expanding management literature. However, these is evidence, through recent attention to the so called *productivity paradox*, which suggests that even as organisations continue to invest heavily in systems and technology the comparable returns in relation to improved managerial decision making may be marginal. This remains a critical factor for BITM analysts as

1

they explore the need for definitive generic frameworks, within the individual context of organisations, and to produce more appropriate and sustainable strategies. It is from this perspective that the objectives for this book emerged. It is intended to incorporate a holistic treatment for the discipline of BITM which has been identified and articulated by the researchers themselves. In this way invitations from research topics within BITM were sought through an initial call for contributions which was not prescribed. The subsequent submissions were therefore a reflection of current research without the constraints of an imposed theme. It is believed that this is a collection of the best contemporary efforts to communicate, exploit and manage these systems and technologies which collectively represent BITM. The book is intended to reflect the complexity and diversity of approaches for the analysis of BITM within organisational change management processes. From this perspective BITM can be argued to *make a difference* to both theory and practice within the field.

BITM is widely taught in universities where a variety of texts is adopted. The main focus for many of these books is often highly specific and detailed within a narrow topic area, for example, electronic commerce. While these features of BITM are important they do not offer the opportunity to report a variety of concepts. This book attempts to avoid such prescription through its combination of chapters which reflect a consideration of *alternative and adaptive futures* for BITM research.

The structure of the book is illustrated through the topics identified, as follows;

- Research and Methodologies
- Strategic and Global Management
- Knowledge Management and Learning Organisations
- Internet and Intranet Systems
- Millennium, Organisational IS and 'Humpty Dumpty'.

These themes emerged from the invited contributions, representing important research perspectives within the field.

A clear definition of BITM, as noted, is problematic. This is highlighted through the complexity of various approaches to the so-called, technical, organisational and emergent imperatives which various researchers have imposed upon the field. Historically, the nature of BITM has its foundations purely within the former, or technological imperative. This provided a clear prescription to functional areas for supporting organisational activities with IT-based systems. More recently they have usefully been differentiated into notions of IS and IT into a combined view of information management (IM). The added-value of IT to organisations is limited in contexts where its core applications have not been initially and fully defined. There is evidence that an IS strategy should be conceived before the IT strategy is introduced. In this way it is argued that the *what* in terms of business objectives requires attention before the *how* of technology is provided. The identification of IS and IT is often represented by researchers as interchangeable and is commonly noted as IS/IT. In addition, the concept of the *hybrid* manager has been promoted for many years within university course programmes. These individuals, through education and professional development, enable the exploitation of IS/IT through a combination of experience in business *confidence* and technical *competence* for BITM.

Within the foregoing activities there is also a spectrum of BITM applications, ranging from database, decision support, knowledge base, executive, Internet, Intranet and Enterprise-wide systems. Clearly, this multiplicity of *systems* will provide for different contributions to business performance and each may individually be significant to the overall organisational strategy. This is to suggest that BITM relates to the systems and technology which emerges, over time in context, and that invariably supports strategic planning activities. From this perspective BITM has a much greater significance than a purely technical imperative as it encompasses an additional range of activities, for example, strategic change, global management, e-commerce, methodologies, knowledge management and organisational learning. This represents an added layer of complexity to research in BITM as the frameworks proposed commonly identify with concepts which in themselves are also not well defined. The challenge within the field of BITM therefore is to undertake valid theoretical and empirical analysis which offers practical insights into systems design and implementation that will complement *alternative* and *adaptive* organisational strategy research.

The range of chapters within this book includes many aspects of strategic, global, organisational and systems considerations. They have not been selected to represent the technological imperative notion of BITM alone. They are reproduced from research contributions to the overall eclectic field that has become BITM. BITM, therefore, may be interpreted as organisational management with an edge – *the edge of systems and technology*. The following sections within this introduction provide a brief overview of the main themes from the included chapters. This is to illustrate the significant contribution to the discipline which these international researchers demonstrate through the interdisciplinary nature of BITM and its position with the broader context of organisational analysis and management.

RESEARCH AND METHODOLOGIES

The adoption of methodologies for BITM design and implementation has its roots in approaches for organising the systems development process. Early considerations were given most extensively to highly centralised systems which offered significant formalisation of the procedures from a transparent focus on project management techniques. More recently analysts have identified more than 1000 brand named methodologies which differ superficially from each other.

Fitzgerald (Chapter 1) addresses the issue of systems development from the perspective of adaptability and flexibility within organisations experiencing an increasing turbulent environment. The thrust of the chapter is to acknowledge that BITM cannot be changed quickly and cheaply enough to met these demands. It includes the findings from a recent survey of 300 organisations involved in the systems development process. It focuses on a range of critical factors including the environment of the development, maintenance workloads, enhancement, types of change and causes of change. **Adams** (Chapter 2) recognises the multiplicity of tasks involved in the planning for systems development. He adopts an interesting methodological approach to the research which involves a sample of people from a variety of socio-economic backgrounds who provide a window into every day contemporary life. The findings from these future views are considered in relation to BITM planning. It is concluded that individuals make use of existing planning skills and as such managers need to be aware of planning profiles when allocating BITM planning tasks. Potential synergies from this analysis are exposed and appropriate training needs are therefore identified. **Butler and Fitzgerald** (Chapter 3) introduce another important perspective and contribution to the BITM methodology process. This is to consider the widely applied Critical Success Factor (CSF) approach and its impact on both researcher and practitioner BITM development. They revisit the complex area of interpretative analysis which attempts to understand a social actors ontological, epistemological and methodological world view. The chapter argues that many researchers have chosen to ignore the original CSF formulation which included these notions. As a consequence analysts have failed to identify with the implicit interpretative conception rooted within the original CSF concept. The findings of the chapter highlight some useful insights into the field of BITM which has relevance for praxis. **Russo and Stolterman** (Chapter 4) outline a slightly different, but equally important, perspective for methodologies in general. They challenge the assumptions behind these activities through research which considered both theory and practice. Evidence can be found which conflicts with these results but the argument is made that the assumptions promoted indicate that information systems methodologies are far more complex than they initially appear. This raises very important questions for the field where increasingly these activites must be much more visible to the stakeholders involved.

STRATEGIC AND GLOBAL MANAGEMENT

Extensive research has been conducted into the role of BITM and competitive advantage and a number of frameworks have been proposed to identify potentially strategic applications. Many additional findings have contradicted earlier reports on the ease at which BITM can lead to improved business performance and particularly the potential for a sustained advantage. However, less emphasis has been placed upon the process of modification and monitoring of BITM strategic planning despite evidence to show that it is one of the top five critical management issues facing business in the 1990s and expected to remain so beyond the millennium.

Wainwright (Chapter 5) provides a rigorous perspective on strategic information systems planning (SISP) through an exploration of change issues involving an IT department within a major manufacturing company. This ongoing research attempts to determine the nature and status of the various roles for IS and IT which could conceivably be augmented to support strategic decision making. He reports on some interesting reflections on the use of a variety of techniques for group IT team planning. He concludes that the internal profile and confidence of the IT department should be significantly raised to achieve organisational advantages obtained through participation in strategic discourse. **Nahar, Huda and Tepandi** (Chapter 6) offer a different and highly valid approach to BITM which includes contemporary technology in the context of small medium/manufacturing enterprises (SMEs). They suggest the notion of layers of stakeholders which includes global communication and collaboration between buyers, customers, enterprises and suppliers. The enabling features of electronic commerce are analysed in this respect where it is concluded that the adoption of these facilities significantly reduces the business risk to the parties involved. Their study concludes with a conceptual framework for electronic commerce which supports organisational strategies within SMEs. **Gottschalk** (Chapter 7) addresses the complex and commonly avoided issue of implementing strategic IS/IT. He proposes 10 content characteristics of formal IT planning as a basis for implementation predictors. The study involved a survey reporting 471 submissions from members of the Norwegian Computer Society which were analysed through multiple regression to test a range of hypotheses. The findings suggest that two predictors for implementation content were most significant as descriptions of responsibility for the implementation plan and user involvement during the process. **Hidding and Williams** (Chapter 8) report that the basis of competition in the so-called new economy is intellectual assets, including financial services, software, media, etc. They suggest that many managers are reluctant to propose strategies given this increasing complexity in modern business. In this view traditional strategy thinking is inappropriate leading to incorrect interpretations of rapidly changing events. It is argued that there is a need to advocate a 'sustainability analysis' in these circumstances in order to take maximum advantage of competitor intelligence.

KNOWLEDGE MANAGEMENT AND LEARNING ORGANISATIONS

The notion of knowledge management is receiving a great deal of critical reflection as we enter the new millennium. The challenge for organisations to harness what has been described as intellectual capital has led to a plethora of knowledge-based systems developments but also, and perhaps more crucially, has revealed the necessity to capture and disseminate tacit knowledge which suggests a more strategic, rather than merely systems, approach is a fundamental requirement for business success. Learning Organisations might be viewed as those who best capture and disseminate organisational knowledge while at the same time set about creating an organisational culture to support their knowledge management endeavours.

Dunn and Fretwell (Chapter 9) highlight the theme of knowledge management and its impact upon organisations. The focus of their contribution is the need for adaptability and learning which can partly be achieved through the information dissemination infrastructure enabled through IT. They report on a UK survey which demonstrates the critical need for attention to the information and knowledge domains within organisations in this respect. They conclude that despite the added value of IT knowledge management requires significant human intervention. **Snyder and Wilson** (Chapter 10) report on the use of 'knowledge harvesting' predominantly in the USA, that enables organisational experts to surface their tacit knowledge thereby making it explicit and available via a software solution as a core organisational asset. Harvesting knowledge in this way can provide accessibility and transference only when and to the extent that it is needed, that is, a 'just-in-time' systems support mechanism, placing recipients with the capacity for effective action in decision-making. **Papaioannou and Theodoulidis** (Chapter 11) advance the view that the incorporation of enterprise information systems must reflect three key areas of knowledge, enterprise, requirements and information systems knowledge. They report on how the development of a theoretical framework was useful in assisting in a project concerned with Hypermedia Environment for Requirements Engineering (HERE) as a method of integrating the key areas specified into a more consistant and manageable entity. Attractively, the framework is complementary to existing information systems practices. **Ciborra and Hanseth** (Chapter 12) note that IT infrastructures and Business Process Redesign (BPR) are claimed to have the potential to enable effective globilisation. However, they indicate the lack of both empirical evidence and theory to support this view. They report a study on the deployment of six IT infrastructures which identified a variety of factors which should be considered. They conclude that there is 'no one best way' solution as is commonly proposed in the literature and they offer an alternative repository of knowledge processes which are believed to explain the empirical findings.

INTERNET AND INTRANET COMMERCE

Although it is acknowledged that e-commerce cannot deliver a sustainable competitive advantage within its industry, present-day forms of e-commerce are changing the structure of industrial forces. What came to be called 'the product cycle' no longer exists, the art of reverse engineering along with the growth of multinational companies interested in employing their technologies wherever production costs are lowest, has led to new product technologies which flow around the world almost as fast as capital and natural resources. Proprietary new product technologies are not necessarily employed where they are invented nor by those who financed them. Firms are now therefore open to competition from a global business community, increasing the likelihood of new entrants and substitute products. By using e-commerce strategically, organisations have attempted to externally disturb the competitive forces at work in an industry and in so doing change the industry structure.

Burn (Chapter 13) considers the relationship between strategic alignment within so called virtual organisations. She challenges the notion that virtual organisation is a panacea for successful structure/strategy alignment which, in the context of BITM, is poorly understood. She proposes six different models of virtuality which are particularly useful within electronic markets. The study reports that virtuality can be significantly constrained by pre-existing linkages in the market place and the sustainability and intensity of linkages within a virtual environment. **Loebbecke** (Chapter 14) outlines the economic impact upon organisations of offering content on the World Wide Web (WWW). She suggests that many organisations involved in Internet trading are currently not sustaining an adequate profit. The study usefully discusses four ways in which organisations may achieve more substantive returns through having an Internet presence and trading on the WWW. She sets this analysis within the broad context of the 'economic value of information and communication technology', 'value creation via electronic commerce' and 'macroeconomic business impacts of Internet-based commerce'. The study includes a number of industry examples and concludes with three dimensions for further research. **Callaghan** (Chapter 15) reports the tremendous growth in the implementation of corporate Intranets which adopt Internet technology using internal IT networks. He reports on a study involving an in-depth case analysis within a large UK company, which has recently developed an Intranet, and evaluates it impact on future organisational activities. In this respect the Intranet is treated as just another IT system which may augment systems for competitive advantage, planning and benefits accrued. He systematically relates the findings from the case data to illustrations within the recent literature and concludes that Intranets are indeed a new 'breed' of IT system which deserve additional attention through their integration with complementary managerial research. **Sieber** (Chapter 16) suggests that we do not actually know very much about the reasons for on-line buying decisions. The chapter offers a unique insight into one specific context to inform upon our understanding of selling on the Internet. He reports a study of grocery shopping in Switzerland which documents the characteristics of consumer buying behaviour. A number of inferences are drawn from the conclusions of the research which advance our learning of Internet shopping and the trajectories of this change.

THE MILLENNIUM, ORGANISATIONAL IS AND 'HUMPTY DUMPTY'

Even on the verge of the millennium there are those whose belief is that the promoted catastrophes of large-scale systems failure have been over-hyped. What is factual is that many organisations have spent a great deal of time and money on ensuring millennium compliance and that for some, perhaps more progressive, the issue has been seen as an opportunity to re-design or re-place systems completely and in so doing improve their competitive position. While concentration has been principally focused on the so-called millennium bug there appear to be more generic lessons to be learned not only in future design but also for business continuity in the face of the next self-induced BITM crisis in the organisational arrangements for these systems.

Beynon-Davies *et al.* (Chapter 17) look at the year 2000 problem (Y2K) from a number of perspectives reminding us that the issue is much more than merely technical failure requiring a technical response. The panic that Y2K has aroused illustrates the pervasive nature in which IS/IT is now firmly embedded into the very fabric of modern organisations and they highlight preliminary evidence of the effect that Y2K is having on the relationship between the IS function and organisations, particularly in relation to IS strategy and planning, outsourcing and organisational IS development portfolio. (A short Postscript brings this chapter up to date.) **Hackney and Hancox** (Chapter 18) consider another important aspect of organisational IS arrangements in that of outsourcing. They report on a study which involved an empirical investigation of both the public and the private sectors in the UK. The aim of the research was to determine the usefulness of four conceptual frameworks to analyse IS outsourcing decisions in these contexts. The chapter outlines implications for policy and concludes with a conceptual synthesis for a better understanding of the practice and perception of IS outsourcing. **Light** (Chapter 19) examines the concept of BPR as it has evolved from one of a 'clean slate' radical performance gain to a situation which recognises the context and multidimensional strategies involved. He emphasises the critical role of BITM in this respect as organisations move through a process-oriented change. His research into successful BPR identifies with the view that there is a need to consider a range of contextual variables which are inherent within complex organisations. These changes are noted to represent a perpetuation in the value of BPR beyond its current notion as a management fad. **Stubbs, Griffiths and Tucker** (Chapter 20) provide a final and lighthearted view that information and communication technologies (ICT's) are increasingly being taken for granted. They note that only when the 'black boxes' disappoint us do we seek expert advice and that we are ignoring, through this natural defence, our willingness to embrace complexity. The chapter communicates the motivation for this book very well as it belies the fragile and vulnerable nature of adapting to our BITM future.

Part I
Research and Methodologies

1 Adaptability and Flexibility in ISD

Guy Fitzgerald

INTRODUCTION

This chapter addresses the issue of flexibility of IS. More flexible and adaptable systems are required to meet the rapidly changing demands of modern organisations operating in an increasingly turbulent environment. Organisations are beginning to find that their existing IS cannot be changed quickly or cheaply enough and that information systems are becoming a barrier to change. Some of the issues are discussed in the context of findings from various research studies including a recent survey of over 300 organisations developing IS in the UK. Discussion focuses on environment of development, maintenance workloads, enhancement, types of change, and causes of change. One of the areas of particular concern is the time and resources required to effectively and quickly adapt systems to respond to the increasing change that organisations are undergoing.

In the business context we see a more complex environment, increased competition, global challenges, and market shifts together with rapid technological developments (e.g. Toffler, 1990; Behrsin *et al.*, 1994) and the increasing importance of the Internet and electronic commerce. Change is endemic and the environment is increasingly turbulent. Change must be handled effectively and successful organisations are those that are seen to be able to deal with change and the opportunity it presents. Ciborra (1993) suggests that: 'Within a firm what seems to matter is the flexibility and adaptive capability in the face of environmental discontinuities'. Modern organisations seek to be responsive, adaptive, and flexible in their operations and their strategy.

However, even those organisations that embrace the challenge of change have found that it is not easy to achieve, not least because their IS and IT are anything but flexible and adaptive. Much of the literature of the early 1990s has been concerned with using IT to gain competitive advantage and to leverage business benefit. Ironically

13

managers are finding in practice that IT is often a barrier to change rather than an enabler of change. The problems of 'legacy systems' are well known and continue to be disruptive with the problems of the year 2000 just the latest legacy system variant. In addition organisations have found that the cycle of business change is often shorter than the cycle for IT/IS change which produces bottlenecks. In 1990 *The Economist* suggested that 'businessmen have discovered a disconcerting problem: markets change, but computer systems do not', and according to Allen and Boynton (1991) the challenge for businesses today is to break these rules of the past and structure IS to meet the variety of changing information requirements that businesses are now facing.

There are many reasons why it has proved so difficult to change information systems. Technology, people, management, infrastructures, and communication problems have all been blamed. In this chapter we seek to narrow the focus and examine the issue in the context of ISD, which is not to minimise the problems elsewhere, nor to say that other solutions are not appropriate. It is recognised that a combination of a variety of approaches may well be most effective. In the context of ISD various attempts to address this challenge have been made, and there are a variety of recent approaches claiming to embrace change and make systems more flexible. For example, RAD (Rapid Application Development), Object Oriented Analysis, Re-use, and Component-based development, and in the academic world the issues have also received some attention from, for example, Avison *et al.* (1995), Spoor and Boogaard (1993) and Gardner *et al.* (1995).

This chapter also attempts to shed some light on the issues and examines IS adaptability and flexibility using the findings of a recent study of ISD practice (Fitzgerald *et al.*, 1998). This study was based on a questionnaire sent to over 2000 individuals involved in managing and undertaking ISD in organisations in the UK. A response rate of around 17 per cent was achieved and the findings are based on a return of over 380 questionnaires.

DEVELOPMENT ENVIRONMENT

Before considering the detail of the adaptability and flexibility issues it may be of interest to consider the general development environment that was found in the surveyed organisations. The majority, 56 per cent, of the surveyed companies were in the smallest category of

100 employees or less, and just under three-quarters were below 500, with only 11 per cent in companies of 1000 to 5000 employees and another 11 per cent greater than 5000. This tends to indicate that a considerable amount of ISD in the UK is undertaken in relatively small companies. In the majority of these organisations, 61 per cent, the number of people working in ISD was less than 21 and only 8 per cent had over 200 people. If these figures seem low it should be noted that this is not those working in IT, or the IT Department as a whole, it is just those working in ISD, which suggests that much ISD is performed in relatively small groups. It also probably reflects the growing use of packages and outsourced development and the increasing concentration of ISD in a number of specialist organisations.

Table 1.1 shows on average the time spent on various activities that form the ISD process. The activities were further elaborated in the questionnaire so, for example programming specifically included use of Fourth Generation Languages (4GLs) and package modification/ integration. The results are interesting and reflect a continuing emphasis on programming, albeit with this wide interpretation, and a range of other activities none of which dominates. There is perhaps a surprising low emphasis on requirements determining activities, given the problems this area presents and one could also argue that testing activities appear low.

The questionnaire also sought information on what was characterised as a 'typical development project' (or where no typical project existed they were asked for information on their latest project). The

Table 1.1   Activities forming part of the systems development process (% of time spent)

Activities	%
Strategic planning	6
Feasibility	6
Project management	8
Requirements analysis	9
Systems analysis	8
Systems specification	9
Systems design	10
Programming	27
Testing	14
Implementation	8
Evaluation/Review	4

average duration was 10 months, involving 8 systems developers and 5 outside contractors/consultants, showing that many developments are of relatively short duration, although the range did vary from 3 months to 5 years. The balance between different types of development also suggests change. Thus, bespoke in-house development accounted, on average, for about 50 per cent of development, outsourced development was 10 per cent, straight use of commercial packages was 16 per cent, and use of commercial packages with some in-house modifications was 12 per cent. These figures would seem to indicate that bespoke in-house development is still significant but that packages and outsourcing are of increasing importance.

Within ISD, 57 per cent claim to be using a ISD methodology. Of these, only 11 per cent use a commercial development methodology, 30 per cent a commercial methodology adapted for in-house use, and 59 per cent a methodology which is claimed to be unique to the organisation, i.e. internally developed and not based on a commercial methodology. It would appear that despite the emphasis in the literature on commercial methodologies their influence is greater than their use, at least their unmodified use. Most organisations are using some kind of methodology, presumably for the discipline that it provides, but the large majority are using something developed or adapted to fit the needs of the developers and the organisation, which is perhaps a more thoughtful and sophisticated use pattern than the straightforward adoption of commercial methodologies. A somewhat similar conclusion was drawn from a study conducted in the Republic of Ireland (Fitzgerald, 1996).

Irrespective of the use of a methodology or not, Computer Assisted Software Engineering (CASE) tools did not feature very highly, with only 28 per cent usage. Of these, 83 per cent used a commercially available tool with 39 per cent indicating that it was mandated as compulsory by the organisation. Again, based on the literature relating to CASE tools, it might have been expected that usage would be higher. Perhaps the various problems relating to the use of CASE tools in practice is thought to outweigh the potential benefit (Avison and Fitzgerald, 1995).

IS MAINTENANCE

Turning now to the question of effort devoted to adapting and maintaining systems, which is at least a part of flexibility, it has long been recognised that the maintenance phase has consumed a disproportionate amount of time and resources (Boehm, 1976: Swanson and Beath, 1989). Figures for effort required for maintenance of a system in comparison to the original development have been quoted of around 70 per cent. This means that large amounts of effort have always been devoted to keeping systems going and making them relevant to the organisation. Clearly such a high figure does not just refer to corrective maintenance, in the sense of correcting errors in the implementation of the original specification, but includes adaptation and enhancement of the system to meet new and evolving requirements. In one sense this is admirable and reflects the notion that systems are typically not stable but are changing and evolving all the time. However, the problem is that such maintenance is usually slow and costly.

These figures are based on studies that were undertaken quite some time ago and clearly there have been major changes in technology over that time and significant changes in ISD context and practice. Findings from this recent study indicates that today a smaller proportion of effort is devoted to maintenance. Making adjustments for various differences in the exact questions asked on average systems development accounted for 56 per cent of total IS departmental effort and maintenance 44 per cent. This is not the very high levels previously found and it might suggest that the practice of ISD has improved, maybe as a result of better methods and techniques. Nevertheless it is a significant figure and an indication of the scale of resources still devoted to maintaining and enhancing IS.

To provide a more detail and give a greater understanding of the findings maintenance was broken down into three components; corrective, adaptive and perfective, as suggested by Leintz and Swanson (1980). Corrective maintenance was found to account for 28 per cent of the total, adaptive maintenance was 30 per cent and perfective maintenance 42 per cent. Corrective maintenance was thus found to be the smallest component whereas the other components (non-corrective) of maintenance, i.e. those dealing with enhancement and adapting the system to changing requirements, were over 70 per cent. So although the overall percentage effort devoted to maintenance and enhancement has declined, that devoted to enhancement is a large proportion of that total. It may be that systems are getting better at meeting the original requirements but that these systems are requiring more change.

ADAPTABILITY AND FLEXIBILITY

One of the relatively few approaches to directly addresses adaptability and flexibility in IS (Land, 1982) is termed Flexibility Analysis (FA) (Fitzgerald, 1988, 1990). This approach advocates the consideration of how requirements may change in the future, during the life of the system. It is based on the rejection of the notion that requirements are fixed and stable. It argues against the snapshot view of requirements that are determined at a fixed point in time and suggests that future needs and requirements are a legitimate consideration at the development stage. It does not argue that *all* potential future requirements should be accommodated but rather that they should be assessed and considered at the development stage of a system. FA can be a new and additional stage in the life-cycle that fits in the analysis process. In this stage relevant questions are asked about likely changes to IS requirements in the future. Potential future requirements are identified and the probability of that they actually occur is assessed. This information is then combined with an assessment of the difficulty of building into the system (proposed or existing) an accommodation of this future need. If the probability of change is high and it is easy to accommodate then it is probably worth doing, if the probability is low and it would be very difficult and costly to accommodate, then probably it is not worth doing. Cases in the middle of this spectrum would be carefully debated but the point is that not all potential change is addressed, only those that merit it. Clearly trying to accommodate every potential change would be far too costly and time consuming. Thus FA attempts to be selective and concentrate resources on those that are likely to be worthwhile.

As an example, and in a real case, of FA it was discovered that there was a high probability that an organisational change was in prospect within the organisation, and further, that the organisation had a history of such organisational change. An assessment of this information on a system under development was undertaken and it was discovered that there were considerable implications because the system developers had made various assumptions about the way the organisation worked, including stable reporting structures. Further investigation indicated that these assumptions could be removed and the system made more flexible to easily accommodate a wider range of organisational structures. This was relatively easy because it was identified when the system design was still chapter based. Had it been only a few weeks later it would have been much more difficult and costly because coding would have been under way. Nevertheless there was great reluctant by the developers to change the design to accommodate this potential future change. It was argued that it would delay the development and that anyway the change might never happen. In the end the changes were made to the design and characteristically, a few months later the predicted organisational change did happen. Whether the FA was a success or not, in this case, was a moot point because although the accommodation of the organisational change was extremely straightforward there were many other changes which had not been predicted which caused widespread rewriting of the system and it was argued that in this context the ease of changing only one thing was not very relevant. Nevertheless it provides an example of how FA can operate and the benefits that might accrue.

An additional benefit of FA is the discussion and debate that it generates, which can itself elucidate and reveal requirements. This often proves useful particularly as it should involve the views of the wider stakeholders, who are often not included in the traditional approach. In the above example the people involved with the development of the system had no idea that the organisational change was a possibility, it was only when a seniour manager outside of the immediate domain became involved that this emerged. As an aside, the history of organisational change in the organisation was also not known about by those involved with the development of the system. Possibly because although they typically had changes every 3 to 5 years most of the developers had only been in the organisation for 18 months to 3 years!

FA is not easy to undertake and involves a change in cultural attitudes towards development. As has been shown in the case above it is often feared that it takes too much extra time and that it will delay the implementation of the system. This is undoubtedly a real concern particularly with the focus of so much systems development on avoiding overruns and being within budget. However, this is often a false measure because 'on-time within budget', although highly desirable, does not reflect the larger picture. What is equally relevant is whether the system does what it is supposed to do, and continues to be relevant over its life span without incurring enormous costs. An argument against FA is sometimes made that says it is not possible to predict potential future changes. For example, Paul (1995, pp. 50.1) suggests that 'it is in the nature of modern business that the future is uncertain – if it is certain, then courses of action based on the certainty would be adopted that would change the future!' This criticism is made within the context of a wider critique of what Paul (1995) calls the fixed-point theorem. This is the notion that the specification of an IS is complete at some fixed point, while organisational life continues to adapt, change and evolve in response to changes in the environment. FA is totally in harmony with the need to reject notions of a fixed-point but it obviously is not based on the notion that examining potential changes is unlikely to be successful. Clearly the future cannot always be predicted, that is accepted. There is always the possibility that something crops up that has not, and perhaps could not have been, foreseen. FA does not capture all future change but it can capture some, some changes are predictable, or at least more likely than others. Indeed, as will be shown, it is not always necessary to capture a future that is unknown because often the potential change is already well known by some people in the organisation. It is just that the system developers do not know it, and often they do not want to know because it complicates their lives. If the development of packages is considered it is clear that the issue of flexibility is paramount. Indeed some package developers have told me that they spend at least 50 per cent of their effort just trying to make their products flexible for a range of potential future users that they do not know.

In a study of why IS needed to be changed Sutton and Fitzgerald investigated 20 systems and found that in the majority of cases the changes that had to be made to these systems were already known about (Sutton, 1988). It was found that in these organisations the majority of major changes were planned by the organisation over a considerable period of time and were not the result of sudden impulses. However, these changes often came as surprises to the systems developers and maintainers. For example, 45 per cent of the changes analysed were known about by the functional area concerned during the development of the IS, and a further 50 per cent were thought probably to have been known about by somebody in the organisation, although not by the developers. The implication being that a significant proportion of major changes to our IS are indeed potentially predictable (or perhaps revealable is a more accurate term). If this is true, it follows that some form of FA could (and should) be carried out during 'routine' systems development to try to discover what changes, currently known about by someone in an organisation, might need to be made to an IS in the future.

A further finding from this study (Sutton, 1998) suggests that IS appear to have a much longer life than is frequently assumed. The average life of these systems was closer to 20 years than 10, and the usual assumption made be systems developers is more like five years or less. This can clearly be seen by the evidence of the Y2K problem where system developers were clearly not taking a system life view of 20 years. Some have not even taken a 5 year view. The implication being that if systems last a lot longer than the developers and designers assume we need to devote even more effort to making them adaptable and flexible to accommodate the inevitable changes that will occur over this long life. Again the survey of Fitzgerald *et al.* (1998) sought to further explore this issue and information was sought on one specific recent example of a 'problem' system, i.e. one that had required substantial enhancement and/or re-development since its implementation. It was clear that such 'problem' systems still exist as 78 per cent of the organisations had one or more such systems and that the degree of change required to enhance these as a percentage of the effort required for the original development was severe at 126 per cent, i.e. over one and a quarter times the original effort. These systems would seem to have been ideal subjects for FA. Respondents were asked to identify the main causes of these systems to be changed and the results are shown in Table 1.2.

Factors associated with inadequate original development, i.e. corrective maintenance, are essentially just the first two in the list. The totals indicate that these are responsible for relatively little of the changes. The rest are causes that were not considered, or catered for, at the time of the original development. However, it is interesting to

Table 1.2   Main causes of changes (in specific systems)

Main causes of changes	%
Original specification not properly implemented	4
Original specification inadequate	11
Organisational changes	13
Personnel changes	3
Government/legal changes	9
External factors (e.g. banks, Inland Revenue, suppliers)	7
New business/strategic development	22
New policies (e.g. security review/financial cutbacks)	6
Technology (e.g. old hardware no longer maintainable)	18
Other	7
Total	100

note that although some of these are probably out of the control of the organisation (although still potentially predictable), such as technology, legal changes and external agencies, the majority are within the remit of the organisation. Indeed 43 per cent of respondents thought that the causes of changes in these 'problematic' systems were known about by someone in the organisation at the time of the original development. Most of these, 64 per cent, were known about by seniour managers and users rather than by professional systems developers, but they were known about within the organisation. Had they been predicted then potentially the necessary changes could have been catered for, at least to some extent, in the original development. These findings would seem to support the arguments for FA.

What kinds of changes might be required to make systems more flexible? It is difficult to be precise but the areas in which change had to be made to the 'problematic' systems in the survey are listed in Table 1.3.

This is clearly helpful in identifying the areas where effort needs to be made to enhance systems flexibility and indicates that the greatest benefit would be in relation to processes and logic. More attention to finding out how individual processes might change and making them easier to change is thus likely to be beneficial. Examples from outside the survey suggest that identifying the types of additional processing that might be required is beneficial. Even if the code for them is not provided, i.e. the potential change is not fully accommodated, what can be ensured is that this specific change is not hindered or restricted for the future. In the development of systems we typically have little idea of what changes can easily be accommodated and what cannot, until an investigation is actually made. This is why some things perceived as relatively minor changes in fact turn out to be major. Users

Table 1.3   Main areas requiring change

Main change areas	%
Data (e.g. new/amended fields in files or databases)	15
Processes (e.g. logic/code changes, new procedures)	24
Interfaces (e.g. user/systems interfaces)	18
New/upgraded packages	16
Other	27
Total	100

frequently complain of this problem. Using an analogy with architecture, it might be said that in systems we do not know which are the load bearing walls and which are internal partitions, i.e. some can be easily moved and others involve significant redesign and rebuilding work. In the area of data it is much easier to build in flexibility at source rather than adding it once a system has been developed. This might be extra fields, or space for larger volumes, or additional validation rules, or a look-up table of values, or something more sophisticated, such as currently redundant data collected for a future potential requirement. But whatever is required these findings would seem to suggest that FA should provide some benefit in the provision of more flexible systems.

CONCLUSION

The findings from this research and others indicate that ISD is still a somewhat problematic area despite the great attention devoted to improving techniques and methods. The effort devoted to maintenance and enhancement is still large and that the great hopes of recent approaches and tools such as methodologies, object-oriented techniques, and CASE, are not much seen in practice. The exact reasons for this are not obvious but what is clear is that there is still much that needs improving and that in the areas related to dealing with adaptability and change techniques such as FA are of potential benefit and are at least addressing important areas of concern.

References

ALLEN, B.R. and BOYNTON, A.C. (1991) 'Information architecture: in search of flexibility', *MIS Quarterly*, Dec, 435–45.
AVISON, D.E. and FITZGERALD, G. (1995) *Information Systems Development: Methodologies, Techniques and Tools*, London: McGraw-Hill.
AVISON, D.E., POWELL, P., KEEN, P., KLEIN, J.H. and WARD, S. (1995) 'Addressing the need for flexibility in information systems', *Journal of Management Systems*, 7(2), 43–60.
BEHRSIN, M., MASON, G. and SHARPE, T. (1994) *Reshaping IT for Business Flexibility*, London: McGraw-Hill.
BOEHM, B.W. (1976) 'Software engineering', *IEEE Transactions on Computing*, December, 1226–41.
CIBORRA, C.U. (1993) *Teams, Markets and Systems*, Cambridge: Cambridge University Press, 10.

The Economist (1990) 'How computers can choke companies', *The Economist*, 9 June, 65.

FITZGERALD, B. (1996) 'An investigation of the use of systems development methodologies in practice, in Coelho, Jelassi, Konig, Kremar, O'Callaghan and Saaksjarvi, *Proceedings of the 4th European Conference on Information Systems*, Ficha Technica, Lisbon, 2–4 July, 143–61.

FITZGERALD, G. (1988) 'Information systems development for changing environments: flexibility analysis', in Bullinger, H.J., Protonotarios, E.N., Bouwhuis, D. and Reim, F., *Proceedings of the First European Conference on Information Technology for Organisational Systems: Concepts for Increased Competitiveness*, Amsterdam: North-Holland/Elsevier, 587–93.

FITZGERALD, G. (1990) 'Achieving flexible information systems: the case for improved analysis', *Journal of Information Technology*, 5, 5–11.

FITZGERALD, G., PHILIPPIDES, A. and PROBERT, S. (1999) 'Information systems development maintenance and flexibility: preliminary findings from a UK survey', *International Journal of Information Management*, 19(4), 319–29.

GARDNER, L.A., PAUL, R. and PATEL, N.V. (1995) 'Moving beyond the fixed point theorem with tailorable information systems', in Doukidis, G., Galliers, B., Jelassi, T., Krcmar, H. and Land, F. (eds), *Proceedings of the 3rd European Conference on Information Systems*, Print Xpress, Athens, 183–92.

LAND, F.F. (1982) 'Adapting to changing user requirements', *Information and Management*, 5(2), 59–75.

LEINTZ, B.P. and SWANSON, E.B. (1980) *Software Maintenance Management*, Menlo Park, CA: Addison-Wesley.

PAUL, R. (1995) 'An O.R. view of systems development', in Lawrence, M. and Wilsdon, C. (eds), *Operational Research Tutorial Papers of the Operational Research Society*, Birmingham, 46–56.

SPOOR, E.R.K. and BOOGAARD, M. (1993) 'Information systems flexibility: a conceptual framework', *Serie Research Memoranda 1993–59*, Amsterdam: Vrije Universiteit.

SUTTON, J. (1988) 'Analysing the future requirements of computer systems,' MBA Project, Warwick University.

SWANSON, E.B. and BEATH, C.M. (1989) *Maintaining Information Systems in Organizations*, Chichester: John Wiley.

TOFFLER, A. (1990) *Powershift*, New York: Bantam Books.

2 Planning Activities: Lessons for Information Systems Development

Carl Adams

INTRODUCTION

ISD involves a variety of planning tasks, probably more so than other professions. The planning activity permutates throughout all stages of development, implementation, management and use. Given the key role that planning plays in ISD and use, this chapter examines whether the people involved in the development and use of IS are equipped to cope with the required planning tasks. To accomplish this, a survey is used to chart the planning profiles from a sample of the general population. The survey, conducted through the Mass-Observation Archive (MOA) at the University of Sussex, was not fully representative of the general population and contains age and gender biases. However, it does represent people from a wide selection of socio economic backgrounds and is likely to provide a good window into 'every day contemporary life'. The survey responses give an indication of what people usually plan for, how people plan and how long in the future people plan for. Further examination enables two different future-views, those of 'planners' and 'non-planners', to be generated. These future-views are considered with the planning needs for ISD management and use. People involved in planning tasks are likely to make use of existing planning skills gained in 'every day life'. As such managers need to be aware of planning profiles when allocation planning tasks and identifying training needs. Potential synergies and problems for effective ISD planning activities are discussed.

Developing IS involves many planning activities (Avison and Fitzgerald, 1988, p. 30). As Sprague and McNurlin (1993, p. 105) relate, 'Planning has always been an important task in Information Systems'. ISD involves a variety of planning tasks, probably more so than many other professions. As much as a third of development activity can be related to planning tasks (Brooks, 1982, p. 20) and permutates through

25

all the stages of a development. Some development methodologies can be considered as based around a set of prescribed planning activities, such as SSADM (Structured Systems Analysis and Design) (Downs *et al.*, 1988, p. 151), and a range of tools exist to help planning project developments (e.g. Lowery, 1992). From the perspective of the managers and users of the IT, planning also becomes an important skill as effective and efficient running of any IS requires considerable planning of resources and activities (Case and Smith, 1995, p. 268). At the strategic level, effective IS planning has become key for businesses to operate in today's technology based world (Ward *et al.*, 1990; Flynn 1992, p. 337; Laudon and Laudon, 1996, p. 292).

As can be seen, planning is a key issue for the development, management, introduction and use of IS and concerns users, managers, strategic managers as well as the ISD community. Given this reliance on planning tasks for IS, the question is raised 'how well equipped are developers, users and managers to cope with these planning tasks?'.

This chapter examines the planning profiles from a sample of the general population and compares them with planning tasks needed for ISD, management and use. The following research questions are addressed:

- *What are the planning profiles of the general public (i.e. the pool from which developers and other relevant people, will be selected)?*
- *Are there any synergies or mismatches with these profiles and the planning tasks required for ISD, implementation, management and use?*

Potential planning problems and synergies are not just relevant to ISD and use, but are also applicable to any major adventure in business and society where planning forms an integral part (Hall, 1980). The rest of this chapter is structured as follows. First, the rationale for the survey sample and the survey itself is described. The expected and actual responses are examined, then the responses are analysed to develop distinct planning profiles. These profiles are then examined in the light of planning tasks required for ISD and use, with potential synergies and barriers being identified.

RATIONALE

The focus on the planning profiles of a selection from the *general public* as apposed to concentrating on planning profiles of, say, just IS *developers*, deserves some discussion. First, there is a problem in identifying who are the developers since there are a whole set of job titles which constitute a 'developer' role, including Analyst, Systems Analyst, Designer, Software Engineer, Programmer, to name a few. One could concentrate on a specific category, say 'designer', however, there can be much overlap between these job descriptions, indeed a 'designer' at one organisation may well be performing a similar set of tasks to an 'analyst' at another; and 'designers' at two different organisations may well be performing substantially different sets of tasks. So the definition of a 'developer' can embrace a diversity of activities and job descriptions. In addition one would expect the user(s) to have some influence on the planning activities, it is their system, their set of requirements that have to be addressed. Further, the people involved and influencing an ISD are likely to constitute more than just the 'developer' and associated user(s) (Finlay, 1994, p. 190): Typically people separated from the development process, both geographically and functionally, are likely to have some influence. Also, the distinction between developer and user is becoming blurred. For instance in participative approaches (Mumford, 1983; Avison and Fitzgerald, 1988, p. 35) development activity involves considerable input from both users and developers. A further example is in Decision Support Systems (DSS) where the manager/user involvement in the development process is multifaceted:

> Management involvement in DSS is extensive in both breadth and depth. Management's role cuts across each of the areas of approval and administration, developer, operator and user.
>
> (Hogue, 1993, p. 54)

As such, researching planning activities affecting the development process would be limited if only developers were examined. The approach taken in this work is to explicitly research planning profiles from a 'selection of the general public' and apply those to the requirements of ISD, rather that consider 'developers' as isolated from the rest of society.

Further rationale for considering planning profiles from a sample of the general public is that developers themselves will be selected from the public pool. As such they will be bringing with them a whole set of skills and experiences related to planning activities. Johnson and Scholes (1993) use the analogy of a 'recipe' to describe how one deals with a situation similar to one previously encountered by reverting to the 'recipe' of how they dealt with that similar situation previously.

This concept was developed further with Boland and Greenberg (1988) who show that even when a situation is relatively new, people still need to draw upon analogies of previous familiar situations and experiences:

> The symbolic function has an important impact on our everyday life in organizations. In particular, the metaphors we draw upon to frame our analysis of organizational situations can radically affect the kind of analysis we will make. The more ambiguous a situation is the more important metaphors become for ordering the situation and making sense of our organisational experience.

The survey of a sample from the general public was conducted through the MOA at the University of Sussex. The survey, called a directive within the MOA, was sent out to a self-selecting panel of 460 people nationwide. The panel is not fully representative of the general population and contains age and gender biases (more females and weighted towards older people). However, the panel does represent people from a wide selection of socio economic backgrounds and is likely to provide a good window into 'every day contemporary life' (Sheridan, 1996).

The directive contained a set of three open questions on planning activities under a heading of 'The Future', these being:

1.   How far into the future do you usually plan?
2.   What things do you usually plan for?
3.   What does the 'millennium' mean to you?

The responses were 'free format' in that respondents could write as much (or little) as they wish and answer the questions however they wished. The responses were written on a variety of paper in a variety of writing styles; some were handwritten, some were typed, one or two even contained pictures. As such, a framework was used to categorise responses. This entailed using a table to record each response to identify what events and activities people usually plan for, how people plan and, how far in the future people plan for. The question on the millennium was included as a focus for considering a possible planning activity, the analysis of these responses are not covered in this chapter.

The survey was sent out as the third part of the Autumn directive in November 1997, the first two parts of the directive covering aspects of music and dance. The third part of a directive often results in relatively poor response rates, however, the actual response rate for this part of the directive was fairly good at 51 per cent overall (48 per cent for men and 54 per cent for women). The content was also relatively good consisting of a variety of responses ranging from just a few handwritten lines to over nine, typed, pages. The average length of response was a little over one and a half pages for both males and females (though it is difficult to make direct comparisons given the variability in handwriting etc.). The quality of response (relative to the research of planning) was also varied and was not always related to the length of the response: some responses spanning multiple pages contained interesting insights on 'life's activities' but little on planning, while other responses spanning half a page would contain succinct poignant planning information. The average ages of respondents was in the high 50s for females and near mid-60s for males (the panel contains a comparatively large number of retired people). The youngest male respondent was 17, the oldest 84. The youngest female respondent was 18, the oldest 86. There were over twice as many female than male responses (which roughly matches the panel gender distribution). As such the responses contain biases towards the older members of the population and the female gender. The age bias will be discussed latter in the chapter.

The MOA administer the distribution, collection and coding of the directives and associated responses. The confidentiality of each respondent is ensured by a coding system which enables researchers to identify the gender, occupation, town (or approximate location) and age of respondents without actually giving information which could uniquely identify a respondent. To further ensure confidentiality of respondents, access to the returned responses was limited to visits at the MOA. The confidentiality of respondents is a key issue for the MOA and goes some way to ensure free and frank responses.

EXPECTED RESPONSES

Before the survey was distributed some responses were expected, one such area being with gender. From a cognitive perspective the gender debate has a long history predating the introduction of intelligence tests in the early 1900s, and still provokes much controversy (Brannon, 1996, p. 87). For instance, the Wechsler intelligence test, though showing no difference in overall performance, shows differences between specific types of skills: women scored higher on the verbal sections, men performed better in action-orientated tasks. Later studies showed more complex relationships (*ibid.*, p. 91). Many of the gender-related differences are attributed to spacial awareness (Geary, 1996, p. 241), though again there are differing views on the effect and magnitude of any disparity in these abilities (Chipman, 1996; Dowker, 1996). In addition there are role differences (e.g. generally women are more likely to stay at home and look after children than men). It is clear that any gender-related differences are likely to be very complex involving many factors. (For a more full discussion of possible gender differences readers are referred to Brannon, 1996, and Geary, 1996.) Clearly, with such a weight of evidence it was expected to see some gender differences, however, given the debate over gender issues, the inconsistencies between different works and the interpretations of their results, it was not clear how any gender differences would manifest. Cognitive differences at the individual level were expected with some people been more oriented towards planning tasks than others and, that people will have different 'future views' (Waddington, 1977, p. 185). However, it was unclear what these different planning orientations would constitute and particularly how far into the future people plan for.

Age differences were also expected, given the 'common perception' that younger people are more 'rash' and spontaneous, while older people being more conservative and more inclined to plan. However, it was unclear how much this 'common perception' would actually hold true for planning activities. In addition, given the age bias of the panel, it was expected the issues more pertinent to older people (e.g. retirement related issues) would be more in evidence. Common planning items, such as holidays and retirement/pensions, were expected, though it was unclear what would constitute a full list of items planned for and it was unclear what the relative distribution of those items would be.

ANALYSIS OF RESPONSES

An initial list and analysis of cited planned items along with the overall relative occurrences of these items are displayed in the first two columns of Table 2.1. In addition, the third and fourth columns show the relative proportions of cited planning items for males and females respectively. Overall, females cited a slightly higher number

Table 2.1   Percentages of cited planning items

Cited items	% of total cited items	% of male cited items	% of female cited items
Holidays	24	21	25
Social events	15	11	16
Financial	11	15	10
Daily activities	8	7	8
Work related	6	6	6
Retirement	5	8	5
Home improvements	5	5	5
Death/wills	5	6	5
Christmas	5	4	5
Birthdays	3	3	3
Moving house	3	3	3
Gardening	3	4	2
Large items of expenditure	2	1	2
Anniversaries	2	1	2
Dentists/doctors	2	1	2
Others	1	3	1
Planning for a family	1	0	1
Total	100	100	100

of planning items per respondent (2.8 per response for females and 2.3 for males), which may indicate that females are involved in more planning activities than males. However, this sort of frequency data should be treated with caution as there may well be other influences which could account for any differences. For instance, other studies have shown that females may have a better affinity for writing than males (Brannon, 1996), so the female respondents may have recorded more items but may not actually plan for more items.

In addition, not all respondents cited items that they planned for, indeed some were adamant that they do not plan. The most frequent planning item cited for both males and females was 'holidays'. The second and third places were reversed for males and females: 'Social Activities' was the second most listed item for females and 'Financial' was third; whereas for males 'Financial' second and 'Social activities' third. In addition, females cited a higher proportion of 'Holidays' and 'Social activities'. It seems the females from this sample were more involved in organising and planning the holidays and social activities than the males.

An examination of 'how far into the future people plan' proves interesting. For 'Holidays', the most cited item, replies on how long into the future varied from just a few days or weeks to several years. However, a more typical representation is that people generally start to think about holidays 6 to 12 months in advance and book the holidays 3 to 9 months in advance. The Christmas and New Year period is a water shed time for some people, i.e. they can't start to think about holidays until Christmas is over. Relatively few people had longer than a 12 months future-view for holidays, and where this occurred it was usually a special holiday (e.g. 3-week visit to Australia). 'Holiday' was also an interesting item as several people wrote that the time-frame for planning holidays was effectively prescribed for them, e.g. they needed to book specific times off work within a holiday rota. People seem less able to deal with long-term plans. Even with 'planners' long term planning is a problem:

> I'm a fairly obsessive planner for the immediate future. I'm full of lists of things to do today, tomorrow, next week. But I rarely plan further ahead. (H2784, a 48-year-old aid worker in Oxford)

This did not seem to be age dependent, but the topic of planning was, e.g. older people were more focused on planning for retirement or burial arrangements. People generally planned in different ways for different activities. The closer to an event then the more detailed the planning became, as the following demonstrates:

> I plan into the future really on a few scales:
>
> 1. Very close planning of professional, social, leisure and domestic activities approx. a week ahead.
> 2. Slightly less close, but still fairly detailed planning of professional, social and leisure activities up to around a month ahead.
> 3. Broad outline planning of important professional and leisure activities for aprox. a year ahead.
> 4. Very vague long term plans like eventual retirement.
>
> The closer short and medium term plans are vital in my occupation, not choice but necessity. (C2256, male, 49, teacher from Birmingham)

The descriptions of respondents seemed to fall into that of 'planners' or 'non-planners', and people mostly classed themselves as one or the other. This seemed to be irrespective of age and gender. It was interesting to note that some people classed themselves as 'planners' but described fairly spontaneous activity. The reverse was also true with people classing themselves as non-planners yet describing some fairly detailed planning activities (albeit, in the short term). Though there may be proportionally slightly more females classing themselves as non-planners yet describing some fairly involved planning tasks. The concept of planner or non-planner is open to a certain amount of subjectivity.

Some examples of responses from the 'planners':

I am an inveterate planner and worrier so I am always planning ahead, be it one hour, twenty four hours or the next week or month. The older I get the more I try and plan for financial provision for the twilight years ahead and this is my main area of long term planning. I find it very difficult to relax and go with the flow, just letting things happen. (M1593, 51 year old male, technical person in the oil industry, based in London and Aberdeen)

I usually plan things for the future. I cannot live day to day. I need goals and things to look forward or strive towards. This has always been the case. (S2813, female, 29, Television Producer from Devon)

I try to plan as far into the future as I can, as I don't like uncertainty, and always prefer to know what is happening. (S221, 41 year old male, writer from Watford)

I like to know, at least provisionally, what I am going to be doing a couple of months ahead. I don't like surprises and I hate being insecure about what is going to happen in the future. (B2638, female, learning resource officer from Manchester)

Planning, if only working out what to get for the next meal, is a normal activity and I have always liked things in order. Thus planning is a personal thing: my late wife never planned, never filed anything away, yet she was in her own way organised and as a result, left far more than I will. (S2246, male retired teacher from Northants)

I enjoy planning and looking forward it's part of the enjoyment of the event, even if it never happens for some reason. (C2091, female retired. librarian from Eastbourne)

Some examples of responses from 'non-planners':

live for today. About the only planning I have consciously done is to put my delivery notes in the right order and find out where an unknown delivery point is. So I suppose the precise answer to the question is 24 hours. (R470, male, a retired driver from Basildon)

I dislike planning very far ahead for most things, more than a couple of months seem far too far ahead. (B1426, male, a school science technician from Bracknell)

I fear the Future. I find it impossible to plan for the future. It's impossible to plan I don't know what will happen. (D2664, female, recent graduate based in Bristol)

Look, I can just about get to the end of today remembering every thing I've got to do. Even tomorrow is 10 years away. I know I should think and plan ahead, and I have to for my jobs, but apart from that, just get me thro' today please. (A1706, female, artist from Shoreham by Sea)

I have never, but never, planned for the future as it is a fact that has sometimes caused me concern, but of cause I have also reached the age when nothing on earth can make me do what ever is sensible. I only live for today. (T2459, male, a retired railway clerk from Birkenhead)

I tend to not plan very far into the future, probably because I am a bit of a fatalist and expect any long-term plans to be upset. I feel sorry for people who have to plan their lives a long time ahead, it doesn't allow for much spontaneity in life does it? (C2053, female, 44 year old chartered librarian from Norwich)

I don't plan very far into the future and tend to let events take their own course, unlike my wife who likes to plan ahead and know what we're going to do from one week to the other. (G2134, retired civil servant from London)

A summary of the response for planners and non-planners is contained in Table 2.2.

The responses indicated that there was a full range of combinations of 'planners' and 'non-planners' within marriages and partnerships. Sometimes it seemed to be role filling activities within partnerships,

Table 2.2   Summary of planner/non-planner characteristics

	Planners	Non-planners
Male	Need to plan. Use lists and diaries. Don't like changes to plans and can be stressed when changes take place. Top four items planned for: Main holidays Financial Social events Retirement	Like spontaneity. Happy to 'go with the flow'. Difficult to consider things long-term. Can be stressed when confined to a prescribed plan.
Female	Need to plan. Use lists and diaries. Don't like changes to plans and can be stressed when changes take place. Top four items Planned for: Main holidays Social events Financial Daily activities	Like spontaneity. Happy to 'go with the flow'. Difficult to consider things long-term. Can be stressed when confined to a prescribed plan. More fatalistic expect longer-term plans to be unsuccessful.

where one of the partners (male or female) assumed the role of 'planner'. The mixed combinations, as shown in S2246 and G2134 responses, that opposite planning orientations can work together very well, but that it takes work and communication:

I think the crux of successful planning and seeing our schemes for the future come to fruition is communicating our dreams and hopes and fears to each other. (B1215, female, 44, shop supervisor from Plymouth)

There were a few cases of major events 'blinding-out' other events:

At present we are not planning far into the future as we are moving house in a month, and so most of our planning is on a short term scale. (D2123, female, bookshop manager from Isle of Man)

Planning activities and approaches to planning are affected by external events:

being long term unemployed I give little thought to the future and make no future plans. (K2721, male, former NHS administrator from Bognor Regis)

If you had set these questions two years ago, my answers would have been very different . . . the *word* farm at the top of the page is a clue. From being a confident producer of top quality food we are now still producers of top quality food but with no confidence in. (H1820, female, 42, farmer from Cornwall)

'Stress' is directly mentioned in some of the responses, particularly when external events are introduced outside of the respondents control. Stress was also raised when a mismatch between a planning activity and individual's planning orientation arose. For instance when a 'planner' unexpectedly had to change plans or when a 'non-planner' had to conform to and contribute to some prescriptive plan. Control issues came up in several places, notably when describing how people planned:

I find lists make me feel more secure. In an uncertain world I feel I've got a grip if my lists are up to date. It's far more important to me than getting the task done. (S2207, female, 45, writer from Brighton)

The most popular techniques to support planning activities were diaries (including calenders and wall charts) and lists (including mental lists and lists of lists). The most ardent of planner invariably used lists. The bias towards the older population gave some concerns before the survey was distributed. However, after analysing the responses, the older perspective proved useful as a guide to how people change their views on planning over time. Several older respondents reflected on how their planning activities changed.

ISD

This section examines some possible synergies and miss-matches between planning profiles and planning activities associated with ISD.

Possible synergies:

1. Match planning task to individuals. This would require identifying 'planners' and 'non-planners'. It may also involve getting the right mix of planners and non-planners involved in the task.
2. Use list and/or diary based techniques. These are what people are most likely to have used in previous planning experiences. Failing that, people will need to be *trained* in using other techniques.
3. Be up-front in that some plans, particularly long term plans, may not turnout as expected. There is an expectation, certainly from the non-planners, that long term plans will not work out.
4. Employ older people for planning tasks, particularly those who have experience of planning activities such as holidays, social activities, financial and every day life activities. There is a wealth of planning experience to be made use of.

CONCLUSION

Allocating a planning task to a 'non-planner' could be stressful to the individual. Excessive stress can be harmful and affect the individuals performance (Fletcher, 1991; Atkinson, 1994). The same applies to 'planners' in spontaneous situations. People need some control over the items they are planning. The study showed that lack of control over planning items lead to considerable stress for some people. The Planning Horizon (PH) for most people is one year, with many people having a PH considerably less than that. Given ISD involves task requiring a longer PH, then this is likely to be the cause of many potential problem. People, both developers and associated users may need training to develop longer PHs.

Other results include the existence of some gender differences in planing activities which are relevant to ISD, management and use: females may be more involved, and so more experienced in planning tasks. This may influence selection practice particularly favouring mature females returning to work.

References

ADAMS, C. (1996) 'Techniques to Deal with Uncertainty in Information Systems Development', Bit'96 conference, Manchester University.

ATKINSON, J. (1994) *Coping with Stress at Work*, London: Thorsons Publishing.

AVISON, D.E. and FITZGERALD, G. (1988) *Information Systems Development: Methodologies, Techniques and Tools*, Oxford: Blackwell Scientific.

BOLAND, R. and GREENBERG, R. (1988) 'Metaphorical structuring of organisational ambiguity', in Pondy, L., Boland, R. and Thomas, H. (eds), *Managing Ambiguity and Change*, Chichester: John Wiley and Sons, 17–36.

BRANNON, L. (1996) *Gender: Psychological Perspectives*, London: Allyn & Bacon.

BROOKS, F.B. (1982) *The Mythical Man-Month: Essays on Software Engineering*, London: Addison-Wesley.

CASE, T. and SMITH, L. (1995) *Managing Local Area Networks*, London: McGraw-Hill.

DOWNS, E., CLARE, P. and COE, I. (1988) *Structured Systems Analysis and Design Method, Application and Context*, London: Prentice-Hall.

CHIPMAN, P. (1996) 'Still far too sexy a topic', *Behavioral and Brain Sciences*, 19, 248–9.

DOWKER, A. (1996) 'How important is spacial ability to mathematics?', *Behavioral and Brain Sciences*, 19.

EPSTEIN, H. (1996) 'Omissions relevant to gender-linked mathematical abilities', *Behavioral and Brain Sciences*, 19.

FINLAY, P. (1994) *Introducing Resign Support Systems*, Oxford: NCC Blackwells.

FLETCHER, B. (1991) *Work, Stress, Disease and Life Expectancy*, Chichester: Wiley.

FLYNN, D. (1992) *Information Systems Requirements: Determination and Analysis*, London: McGraw-Hill.

GEARY, D. (1996) 'Sexual selection and sex differences in mathematical abilities', *Behavioral and Brain Sciences*, 19, 229–85.

HALL, P. (1980) *Great Planning Disasters*, London: Weidehfeld & Nicolson.

HOGUE, J. (1993) 'A framework for the examination of management involvement in Decision Support Systems', in Sprague, R. and Watson, H. (eds), *Decision Support Systems, Putting theory into practice*, 3rd edn, Englewood Cliffs: Prentice-Hall, 41–56.

JOHNSON, G. and SCHOLES, K. (1993) *Exploring Corporate Strategy*, Englewood Cliffs: Prentice-Hall.

LAUDON, K. and LAUDON, J. (1996) *Essentials of Management Information Systems*, Organisation and Technology, 2nd edn, Englewood Cliffs: Prentice-Hall.

LOWERY, G. (1992) *Managing Projects With Microsoft Project*, New York: Van Nostrand Reinhold.

MUMFORD, E. (1993) 'Designing human systems for new technology: the ETHICS method', Manchester Business School.

SHERIDAN, D. (1996) 'Damned anecdotes and dangerous confabulations' *Mass-Observation as Life History*, Falmer: University of Sussex Library.

SPRAGUE, R.H. and MCNURLIN, B.C. (1993) *Information Systems Management in Practice*, Englewood Cliffs: Prentice-Hall.

SPRAGUE, R. and WATSON, H. (1993) *Reversion Support Systems: Putting Theory into Practice*, 3rd edn, Englewood Cliffs: Prentice-Hall.
WADDINGTON, C.H. (1977) *Tools for Thought*, St Albans: Paladin.
WARD, J., GRIFFITHS, P. and WHITMORE, P. (1990) *Strategic Planning for Information Systems*, Chichester: Wiley.

3 New Light Through Old Windows: The Interpretive Foundations of the CSF Concept and Method

Tom Butler and Brian Fitzgerald

INTRODUCTION

CSF are those few things that must go well for an individual or an organisation to ensure success in a business undertaking: consequently, they represent those organisational, managerial, or individual activities that must be afforded particular and continuous attention so as to achieve the level of performance necessary to achieve desired goals. Since John Rockart first introduced the concept in 1979, this simple concept has been applied in a variety of forms, by both practitioners and researchers, within the IS field. In recent years, however, the concept has fallen into disuse among the IS research community; indeed, a *vox pop* of IS academics revealed that the concept was considered 'old hat' as a research approach. There are many possible reasons for this. One explanation may be that it is, in essence, an interpretive rather than a functionalist/rationalist approach for research and praxis, as such, it would be fundamentally incompatible with the ontological perspectives of many researcher's within the field. However, given that it was originally adopted for research purposes by adherents of the dominant functionalist paradigm within the IS field (see Burrell and Morgan, 1979, for an appreciation of this paradigmatic classification), it was only a matter of time before its basic ontological, epistemological and methodological foundations were altered. The objective of this chapter is to illustrate that, although Rockart did not express it as such, the CSF approach is clearly interpretive in its foundations, and therefore needs to be applied within the appropriate paradigm. The ontological, epistemological and

40

methodological principles of the constructivist philosophy of phenomenological hermeneutics provides a suitable vehicle for this exercise. The following section provides an overview of the concept. Next, an overview of the paradigmatic origins of the concept is discussed. In the fourth section a phenomenological and hermeneutic analysis of social behaviour is presented, this prepares the reader for the interpretive analysis of the original CSF approach in the main section, which follows. Finally, the chapter's conclusions are offered.

THE CSF CONCEPT

The use of a CSF approach for IS planning was developed at MIT's Sloan School of Management. Subsequently, Rockart (1979) employed the method to determine the key information needs of top executives. However, the writings of Aristotle provide some indication of the origins of the CSF concept, for example, in describing the foundations of human action Aristotle states that:

> Now the cause of action (the efficient, not the final cause) is choice, and the cause of choice is desire and reasoning directed to some end.[1]

Aristotle thus describes the teleological nature of human action and in so doing he illustrates that social actors choose particular means to achieve desired ends. A more recent antecedent of the concept may be found in the writings of Baron Von Clausewitz.[2] Von Clausewitz held that the more competent and successful military commanders focused their available resources on the few battles of significance, whereas, the less competent commanders dispersed their forces throughout the entire battle front: he termed this the principle of 'concentration of forces'.

The genesis of the CSF approach in a managerial context, that incorporates a role for information system, was first delineated by Daniel (1961; p. 111) who argued that an IS should focus on small group of '*success factors*', the 'key jobs must be done exceedingly well for a company to be successful.' Other seminal contributions are to be found in the writings of Anthony *et al.* (1972) who reported that CSFs were different across organisations, and also between managers within individual organisations; Zani (1970) illustrated that key success variables (e.g. CSFs) might identify the most important elements of a firm's success and, thereby, help specify priorities for ISD; finally, King and Cleland (1975) argued that critical decision areas[3] had a major role to play in information requirements analysis and in the design of IS. The work of these researchers prompted academics in the IS field to investigate the informational role of CSFs (Mooradian, 1976; Rockart, 1979). This research found a home in MIT and culminated in Rockart's seminal chapter on the subject in 1979.

The CSF approach, as conceived by Rockart (1979), is essentially an IS planning methodology for top level management. Rockart (*ibid.*, p. 217) defines critical success factors as:

> The limited number of areas in which results, if they are satisfactory, will ensure successful competitive performance for the organisation. They are the few key areas where 'things must go right' for the business to flourish. If the results in these areas are not adequate, the organisations efforts for the period will be less than desired.

Within the context of IS planning, the CSF method attempts to make explicit these areas, and their associated information needs, such that IS appropriate to these requirements can be planned and developed. Bullen and Rockart (1986) later extended the application of the CSF concept to other managerial levels within an organisation. Again, focusing on the organisational IS planning process, they suggest that the CSFs of managers at multiple levels within an organisation be obtained so as to arrive at a 'collective' set for the entire organisation. This 'collective' set is also aggregated to arrive at what Rockart (1979) terms a 'generic' set. Information resources and activities are then targeted at enabling the enterprise to realize these 'collective' and 'generic' CSFs.

Since the original application of the CSF concept and method for defining the information needs of business executives (Rockart, 1979), the CSF approach has been applied by both practitioners and researchers in a number of areas. Bryers and Blume (1994, p. 53) report that 'both academics and practitioners have accepted the top-down CSF approach as an appropriate planning methodology'. Slevin *et al.* (1991) indicate that most of the literature on CSFs focuses on the planning utility of CSFs and/or the integrative result of tying the IS function more directly into specific performance measures for the overall organisation. However, Rockart (1982) was one of the first to use the concept for research purposes in a study of the roles of IS objectives.

A CSF study by Butler and Fitzgerald (1998) indicated that of 25 research papers published in major journals in the IS field since 1979, and in which the CSF concept was employed, 5 were theoretical analyses, 7 survey-based field studies, 3 interview-based field studies, and 10 case studies only one of these studies could have been described as being interpretive (Nandhakumar, 1996). Lederer and Seith, 1988) report that many of the more 'popular' SISP methodologies, e.g. Business Systems Planning and Information Engineering (Martin, 1986), use the CSF approach, and, given the wide spread use of these methodologies, it would seem that practitioners have more exposure to the CSF concept and method than researchers. This may be explained, in part, by fact that practitioners are drawn to methods that are functionalist in orientation, and which bestow a certain rationality on their activities (Rowlinson, 1997). That may be so, but, as this chapter argues, there is reason to believe that the CSF concept and its associated method represents something more primordial than the simple and superficial reductionist cause/effect formula found in the research and praxis. The following section lays the foundation for this chapter's main thesis namely. that the application of the CSF method is a hermeneutic exercise and that the concept itself is congruent with a phenomenological ontology.

FUNCTIONALIST OR INTERPRETIVIST? FOUNDATIONS OF THE CSF CONCEPT

Without entering to an extended debate on the issue, it is reasonable to argue that much of the research and praxis within the IS field, as indeed in the social sciences in general, falls into what Burrell and Morgan (1979) have terms the functionalist paradigm. This paradigm has a predominantly positivist orientation which Hirschheim and Klein (1989) point out is chiefly concerned with providing explanations of the status quo and which assumes that social actors are rational in their choice of both means and ends (cf. Coyne, 1995). Burrell and Morgan (1979) provide insights into the incommensurable and incompatible nature of different paradigms, and this applies especially to the two discussed herein, functionalism and interpretivism. However, Hirschheim and Klein (1989, p. 1213) are of the opinion that

that 'the mixing of paradigmatic influences leads to interesting and creative solutions [in praxis]'. Whether the same could be said of research remains a moot point. As described above, in a recent review of research in the area, only one out of 25 studies that employed the CSF concept was interpretivist, the remainder have tended to operate from predominantly positivist research foundations, including those which were case study-based. The reason for this may be that to be accepted as rigorous research within the IS field, studies must conform to the tenets of the dominant paradigm (see Hirschheim and Klein, 1989; Orlikowski and Baroudi, 1991; Walsham, 1995). However, if more researchers are prepared to take the step toward mixing the so-called paradigmatic influences perhaps creative solutions will result, as Hirschheim and Klein (1989) indicate, hence, the present research endeavour (cf. Rowlinson, 1997).

The acceptance of the CSF approach into the chiefly positivist functionalist disciplinary matrix of the IS field is indicated by comments made by Davis (1979, 1980) in his evaluation of the concept. Davis draws on theories in cognitive psychology and organisational behaviour/economics to underline perceived weaknesses in the method. While there is a certain merit in these theoretical perspectives they have been the subject of criticism for their exclusively positivist orientation (see, for example, Bruner, 1990, and Fransman, 1998). There have been those within the IS field who have voiced similar reservations; Winograd and Flores (1986), Boland (1987), Boland and Tenkasi (1995), and Introna (1997), for example, have been particularly trenchant in their rejection of the type of rationalist approach normally associated with the application of the CSF concept. While on a more general level there has been much debate and comment on these issues throughout the field (for example, Mumford *et al.*, 1985; and Hirschheim and Klein, 1989). These critiques inform the present endeavour and Table 3.1, for example, indicates certain assumptions evident in the CSF literature are testament to its rationalist orientation. Such perspectives are very much in evidence in Rockart's (1979) original paper on the topic, and in his quoted conceptual antecedents. Certainly, if one considers his seminal paper in isolation, there would be very little indication to suggest that the CSF method was, at base, interpretive in its orientation. However, in a later research working paper, Bullen and Rockart (1986) describe the concept and method in some detail and it is from this that the first mention of terms like 'world view' and 'understanding' emerge. Rockart (1982) makes this explicit in a research context by arguing

Table 3.1   Rationalist orientation evident in extant perspectives on the CSF concept

Perspective	Description	Adapted from
CSFs and managerial roles	Making decisions is what managers do. Decisions are oriented towards objectives. Decisions need and define facts. Information consists of facts, (e) CSFs are the activities associated with decision making. Managers need information to support these activities.	Introna (1997)
Rationalistic application of the CSF method	Rationalism: characterizes a phenomenon in terms of identifiable objects with well defined properties; posits a search for general rules that apply to phenomena in terms of these objects and properties, and; applies these rules logically to the phenomenon of concern and draws conclusions about what should be done.	Winograd and Flores (1986)

that the CSF method must capture a social actor's 'world view'. These terms are far removed from those in use within the rationalist tradition where 'facts' are elicited in order to provide 'causal explanations'; hence, it is clear that the language and techniques used by Bullen and Rockart are more in tune with those of interpretivist paradigm than its functionalist alternative. That said, in order to understand fully the objective of this chapter, and to make clear its central arguments, a phenomenological and hermeneutic analysis of being is required in order to help delineate the interpretive dimensions of the CSF concept and method.

A PHENOMENOLOGICAL AND HERMENEUTIC ANALYSIS OF SOCIAL BEHAVIOUR

This section draws on the constructivist philosophies of Martin Heidegger and Hans Georg Gadamer in order to provide a phenomenological analysis of social action. In so doing it adheres to a recent trend in the IS field begun at the Manchester Colloquium (see Mumford *et al.*, 1985), where Boland (1985) was, perhaps the first to introduce phenomenology and hermeneutics to the discipline. On from this Winograd and Flores (1986) made a significant contribution, and more recently Lee (1993, 1994), Westrup (1994), Myers (1995, 1997), Coyne (1995), Introna, (1997) and Butler (1998), among others, have continued this trend. The objective here is, therefore, to set the stage for the forthcoming interpretive appreciation of Rockarts's CSF concept and method.

To begin, Heidegger (1976) argues that social actors are 'thrown' into their 'life-world'; as such, their existence has, from the outset, been 'tuned' or 'situated' to be a specific existence with other actors, within, for the purposes of this analysis, a specific organisation and cultural tradition. As historical and temporal beings, social actors possess a tradition-bound 'lived experience' that provides the contexts for their understanding; but because of the 'thrownness' of their existence, Heidegger maintains that social actors will, from the outset, possess an understanding of their 'life-world'. Without this understanding, actors would not be in a position to realise the 'possibilities' presented to them in their everyday existence. In a related vein, Gadamer (1975; p. 269) argues that actors possess a particular 'horizon' of understanding; this is simply 'the range of vision that includes everything that can be seen from a particular vantage point'. In the normal course of events, all phenomena within this horizon of understanding possess the ontological status of being 'ready-to-hand'; that is, they will possess a degree of familiarity that effectively sees them dissolved into an actor's daily existence. They will not, therefore, be the object of reflection and interpretation by social actors. It is only when there is trouble, or a problem to be solved, that is, when a 'breakdown' in understanding occurs, that a phenomenon becomes the object of interpretation. Its ontological status is now that of something which Heidegger refers to as being 'present-at-hand'. The interpretation of phenomena that are 'present-at-hand' is informed by an actor's horizon of understanding. This provides an actor with the Heideggerian 'preunderstanding' of the phenomenon and, also, informs the actor's Gadamerian 'prejudice' toward it. It is an actor's 'lived experience' that contributes to the formation of a 'prejudice' and 'preunderstanding' of a phenomenon. In Gadamerian terms, a prejudice is simply an initial judgement levelled at a new or little understood phenomenon, as such, it may be true or false, accurate or inaccurate. In any event, 'critical reasoning' is required to distinguish between legitimate and illegitimate prejudices and to verify the accuracy of the actor's 'foreconception'.

Heidegger uses the concept of 'care' to illustrate that social actors will be concerned about their existence and the phenomena that constitute it; they will also be involved in looking after the entities that are of import to them. In this involvement in their 'life-world' actors may, or may not be 'resolute'; by this is meant that they will possess a determination to realise the 'possibilities' they are confronted in their daily round. The whole notion of 'resoluteness' gives rise to the concept of purposeful action and, accordingly, in Being and Time, Heidegger (1976, p. 73) argues that 'essentially the person exists only in the performance of intentional acts . . . that are bound together by the unity of meaning'. Hence, a social actor's everyday existence is, for Heidegger, teleological in its constitution. The 'life-world' of actors is specified in language that consists of terms like 'in-order-to', 'for-the-sake-of', 'for-which' and 'by-means-of'. The social world is therefore constituted by a web or network of relations that are generated by social actors' objectives and goals: these serve to help actors formulate and realise the possibilities presented to them in the course of their everyday existence. Again, it is clear from Heidegger that these possibilities give rise to new horizons of understanding, and, accordingly, involve the occurrence of a 'breakdown' in respect of related phenomena that can only be repaired through the act of interpretation.

Because understanding and interpretation always relate to some phenomenon or other, there is a requirement to posit the basic structures of such phenomena. Gadamer (1975), for example, points out that the 'whole' that is a phenomenon is comprised of the 'parts' or 'details' that constitute it. There is, as Gadamer illustrates, a formal relationship between these 'parts' (component phenomenon), the 'whole' (as constituted by its component phenomena), and what he terms the 'subjective reflex' that an actor adopts toward the phenomenon – that is, an intuitive anticipation governed by the Heideggerian 'fore-conception' of the 'whole' and its subsequent articulation in the 'parts'. Gadamer goes on to stress that the means of apprehending this relationship possesses a circular structure, the 'circle of understanding'. However, the understanding attained in 'working out' this relationship, that is in negotiating the 'circle', is not in any way perfect; rather, a temporally-based understanding is realised. This understanding results from the fusion of horizons (e.g. 'world views') of both interpreter and interpreted.

The 'fusion of horizons' that results from negotiating the 'circle of understanding' is accomplished through the structure of a question within the context of a dialectic that: (a) is suitably reductionist in that it allows actors to probe beneath the surface of social phenomena by employing an analytical dialectic, this involves the Aristotelian method of division or repeated logical analysis of genera into species or, in hermeneutic terms, of deconstructing the 'whole' into its component 'parts' (Ricoeur, 1981); (b) is Socratic and takes the form of question and answer (Gadamer, 1975); and (c) is Hegelian in it involves an interpretive synthesis of expectation or preunderstanding with 'objective' observations in order to make sense of a phenomenon and thus attain an understanding of it (Tarnas, 1991; cf. Butler, 1998).

Gadamer (1975) places particular emphasis on the role of language in all understanding; it is through the medium of language, for example, that the dialectic is effected. Social phenomena are described and explicated through the use of language, and in its most natural context, language is employed in the form of a narrative, be it written or spoken. As the constructivist cultural psychologist Jerome Bruner (1990) has illustrated, human dialogue typically gives rise to a narration of experiences. The structure of the narrative usually involves the following components; an actor, a scene (e.g. the backdrop of an organisation, an industry and cultural tradition), an action (aimed at achieving some goal or end), an instrument (the means employed to achieve the end) and some form of trouble (a 'breakdown' to be repaired or understanding to be appropriated). Thus as Heidegger (1976) and Ricoeur (1981) argue, social action may be interpreted as if it were a text. This description accords well with the foregoing phenomenological analysis of the Being of social actors. The next section attempts to apply these concepts in a critical manner to the critical success factor concept and method as articulated by John Rockart.

TOWARDS AN INTERPRETIVE APPRECIATION OF THE CSF CONCEPT

Although Rockart (1979) speaks at length about industry and organisational CSFs, it is clear the source of CSFs lies with the individual actor in organisations. Indeed Bullen and Rockart's (1986) detailed method underlines this, so this provides our point of departure.

To begin, the phenomenon that is an individual's existence is expressed through the actor's horizon of understanding or 'world view'. According to Rockart (1979) and Bullen and Rockart (1986) it is the primary task of a CSF analyst or researcher to apprehend and understand an actor's 'world view'. Bullen and Rockart indicate that each individual's *lived experience* is shaped by social forces that emanate from the industry, the organisation itself, its sub-units, and chiefly the actor's immediate business environment. Although the emphasis in Rockart's original application of the CSF method is in identifying phenomena which can be captured and described quantitatively by formal information systems, the concept and method does not rule out the identification of phenomena that are informal or which can be described in a 'soft, qualitative manner' and which emanate from an actor's immediate business environment, this point is made explicit by Bullen and Rockart (1986). From a phenomeno-logical perspective, the every day existence of organisational actors is constituted by formal and informal phenomena that are 'ready-to-hand', that is, they blend into the actor's day-to-day existence. For example, in regularly performing business activities such as drawing up an end of period report, actors draw on their practical experience in an unreflective manner. However, the first time that an actor is presented with the goal of generating such a report he will experience a 'breakdown' in his understanding of that particular phenomenon. 'In-order-to' attain this goal of report generation, the actor is presented with several possibilities; these possibilities help him to identify and perform particular activities and also obtain certain information that will help draft the report.

To achieve his goal the actor must be resolute and be purposeful, all this is indicative of the intentional nature of social action described previously; however, as shall be seen, purposive behaviour does not necessarily presuppose or involve either full or bounded rationality nor does it mean that the ends arrived at will accord with those chosen. Although some of the activities involved in creating such a report may be well known to the actor, and thus be 'ready-to-hand', the totality that is report creation and especially those related activities that do not form part of the actor's practical repertoire will, in Heideggerian terms, be the subject of some reflection, and, hence, be 'present-at-hand'. So too will activities which will be of a mutable nature and perhaps, also, those which may be dependent on other actors inputs etc. and, thereby, are beyond the immediate control of the report generator, hence, because of these factors, desired ends (Rockart's goals and objectives) will be indeterminate.

These latter activities will be open to 'breakdown' on an ongoing basis. However, after a period of time, report generation-related activities, including those that are volatile or outside of the actor's locus of control, will become routine and the phenomena with blend into background of the actor's daily round, the phenomenon of report creation and its related activities (component phenomena) will now become 'ready-to-hand', or in Rockart's terminology they will become 'implicit' CSFs. That said, actors would always be conscious of the possibility of breakdown in certain activities and the concomitant failure to attain desired goals, hence, Bullen and Rockart's insistence that CSFs or critical managerial activities should receive constant and careful attention because of the likely occurrence of problems (the phenomenological concepts of 'care', 'resoluteness', 'breakdowns' and 'present-at-hand', for example, could easily be substituted here for many of the terms Rockart employs.

A CSF analyst wishing to determine the important activities that an actor performs in drafting an end of period report will first have to acquire a preunderstanding of the phenomena that constitute the interviewee's social world. Hence Rockart's insistence on the analyst having to fully understand the industry, organisation and business environment etc. Then, at the interview proper, she will have the interviewee reflect on his goals and subsequently identify and articulate what he considers to be the chief activities or, alternatively put, the CSFs for the attainment of these goals. This will entail a dialectic process of question and answer between the analyst and interviewee, the aim of which will be reductionist in that the phenomenon of goal attainment (ends) will be analysed to determine component phenomena (means to chosen ends) in the form of CSFs. The interviewee will tend to narrate his experience in terms of the organisation or business environment, his actions, the instruments of action and the 'trouble' at the source of his actions etc. The latter three provide both analyst and interviewee with the raw material of their interpretations. A set of 'candidate' CSFs will result and these will be interpreted in a circular manner within the context of the relationships that exist between 'whole' and 'part' until the horizons of interviewer and interviewee have 'fused' and the 'parts' or component phenomena that are interpreted as being critical to the success of the actor's goals are clearly identified and understood.

As Rockart rightly observes, the CSFs of individuals in an organisation will differ because of the 'lived' or 'practical' experience of each individual will not be the same. Each will have different experiences within their industry, organisation, sub-unit or business environment. These CSFs, as component phenomena, help actors know and understand the related phenomena of interest. In the same way, by aggregating the CSFs of actors within an organisation, Rockart's objective is to know and understand those phenomena that help it achieve success in its business activities. The only problem here is that the further away the CSFs are from the context and process that gives meaning to these phenomena, the more likely it is that they will lose their relevance. In comparing the conceptual themes evident in Rockart's functionalist theory of CSFs and the interpretivist perspective presented herein, there are striking similarities between both perspectives as presented. These leads one to conclude that what Rockart and others at MIT arrived at in their CSF concept was closer to phenomenological and hermeneutic conceptual thought, in that they 'rediscovered', albeit implicitly, the fact that social action is teleological and hermeneutic in its essence, and that the act of interpretation is central to the all understanding by social actors, than the functionalist perspective which they apparently operated from. This was no bad thing in itself as the concept has been employed fruitfully by practitioners who have little desire or need to inquire into its philosophical foundations. The same, however, cannot be said of the academic research community where such issues are of import, and where it is vital for the process and product of research that such matters be investigated and understood.

DISCUSSION AND CONCLUSIONS

This chapter has revisited the CSF concept as Rockart originally proposed it, and has illustrated the concept's relevance for research and praxis from an interpretive perspective. A comprehensive delineation of the concept's ontological, epistemological, and methodological foundations was provided. This was effected by drawing on aspects of Heidegger's (1976) phenomenological project and Hans Georg Gadamer's (1975) treatise on hermeneutics in order to conduct a phenomenological analysis of the CSF concept and method. What this chapter has illustrated is that in a CSF analysis social actors are being asked to identify phenomena that have acquired the status of being 'ready-to-hand', that is, phenomena that are not presently, perhaps, the object of reflection by social actors, but were either once 'present-at-hand' or very likely to be so in the future, that is, phenomena that are subject to a 'breakdown' in understanding which causes the actor to reflect upon them in order to understand them and, perhaps, then take some form of action. From an interpretive perspective, this is the central aim of the CSF method. As with Rockart's original conception, here CSFs are the prerequisites or activities that lead toward goal attainment, however, as indicated, they constitute only a selection from the range of phenomena that act as means to achieve desired ends. Hence, in a CSF interview an actor may describe many phenomena/activities that are so-called 'candidate' CSFs; however, through the hermeneutic process of interpretation by both interviewer and interviewee a mutual horizon of understanding is arrived at in which those phenomena which were, or have the potential to be, problematic are uncovered, these are Rockart's CSFs. Viewed from a phenomenological perspective they are component phenomena ('parts') of the phenomenon of interest (the hermeneutic 'whole').

In conclusion, this chapter has attempted to take seriously the point made by Hirschheim and Klein (1989) that a creative mixing of paradigmatic influences can be constructive. What has resulted from the present phenomenological and hermeneutic analysis of the CSF concept is that one of the IS field's most established concepts can now be viewed in a new light, one which illuminates its utility as an interpretive research approach, and which illustrates its empirical fidelity with the reality of organisational life. The findings of this study thereby contribute to the cumulative body of research on the CSF concept and method by highlighting its utility as a fruitful interpretive approach for research in the IS field.

Notes

1. In Aristotle's *Nicomachean Ethics* (1962, Book VI, ii, p. 329) trans H. Rackham; Rackham indicates that Aristotelian choice refers to a 'choice of means, not of ends'.
2. Cited in Rockart (1979).
3. It is evident from the King and Cleland's (1975) research chapter that critical decision areas are basically synonymous with CSFs.

References

ANTHONY, R.N., DEARDEN, J. and VANCIL, F. (1972) *Management Control Systems*, Homewood, IL: Irwin.
ARISTOTLE (1962) *The Nicomachean Ethics*, English trans H. Rackham, London: Heinemann.

BOLAND, R.J. (1985) 'Phenomenology: a preferred approach to research in information systems; in Mumford, E., Hirschheim, R., Fitzgerald, G. and Wood-Harper, T. (eds), *Research Methods in Information Systems*, Amsterdam: Elsevier Science North-Holland, 193–201.

BOLAND, R.J. (1987) 'The in-formation of information systems', in Boland, R.J. and Hirschheim, R.A. (eds), *Critical Issues in Information Systems Research*, Chichester, John Wiley, 362–79.

BOLAND, R.J. and TENKASI, R.V. (1995) 'Perspective making and perspective taking in communities of knowing', *Organization Science*, 6(4), 350–72.

BRUNER, J. (1990) *Acts of Meaning*, Cambridge, MA: Harvard University Press.

BRYERS, C.R. and BLUME, D. (1994) 'Tying critical success factors to systems development; A contingent analysis', *Information & Management*, 26, 51–61.

BULLEN, C.V. and ROCKART, J.R. (1986) 'A primer on critical success factors', in Rockart, J.F. and Bullen, C.V. (eds), *The Rise of Managerial Computing: The Best of the Center for Information Systems Research*, Sloan School of Management, Massachusetts Institute of Technology, 383–423.

BURRELL, G. and MORGAN, G. (1979) *Sociological Paradigms and Organisational Analysis*, London: Heinemann.

BUTLER, T. (1998) 'Towards a hermeneutic method for interpretive research in information systems', *Journal of Information Technology*, Special Issue on Qualitative Research, December.

BUTLER, T. and FITZGERALD, B. (1998) 'A review and application of the critical success factors concept for research on the information systems development process', *Executive Systems Research Centre Working Paper*, 09/98, University College Cork.

COYNE, R.M. (1995) 'Designing information technology in the postmodern age: from method to metaphor', Cambridge, MA: MIT Press.

DANIEL, D.R. (1961) 'Management information crisis', *Harvard Business Review*, September–October, 111.

DAVIS, G.B. (1979) 'An opinion . . . Comments on the critical success factors method', *MIS Quarterly*, 3(3), 57–8.

DAVIS, G.B. (1980) 'Letter to the editor', *MIS Quarterly*, 4(2), 69–70.

DEGROSS, J.I., BOSTAUM, R.P. and ROBEY, D. (eds) (1993) *Proceedings of the Fourteenth International Conference on Information Systems*, Orlando, Florida.

FRANSMAN, M. (1998) 'Information, knowledge, vision, and theories of the firm', in Dosi, G., Teece, D.J. and Chytry, J. (eds), *Technology, Organisation, and Competitiveness: Perspectives on Industrial and Corporate Change*, New York: Oxford University Press, 147–92.

GADAMER, H.G. (1975) *Truth and Method*, New York: The Seabury Press.

HEIDEGGER, M. (1976) *Being and Time*, New York: Harper & Row.

HIRSCHHEIM, R. and KLEIN, H.K. (1989) 'Four paradigms of information systems development', *Communications of the ACM*, 32(10), 1199–1216.

INTRONA, L.D. (1997) *Management, Information and Power: A Narrative for the Involved Manager*, London: Macmillan.

KING, W.R. and CLELAND, D.I. (1975) 'Manager–analyst teamwork in MIS', *Business Horizons*, 14(2), 59–68.

LEDERER, A.L. and SEITH, V. (1988) 'The implementation of strategic information systems planning methodologies', *MIS Quarterly*, 12(3), 444–61.

LEE, A.S. (1993) 'Electronic mail as a medium for rich communication: an empirical investigation using hermeneutic interpretation', in DeGross, J.I., Bostaum, R.P. and Robey, D. (eds), *Proceedings of the Fourteenth International Conference on Information Systems*, Orlando, Florida, 13–21.

LEE, A.S. (1994) 'The hermeneutic circle as a source of emergent richness in the managerial use of electronic mail', *Proceedings of the Fifteenth International Conference on Information Systems*, Vancouver, BC, 129–40.

MARTIN, J. (1986) *Information Engineering, Volume 2: Strategies and Analysis*, Savant.

MOORADIAN, G.G. (1977) 'The key variables in planning and control in medical group practices', unpublished master's thesis, Sloan School of Management, MIT.

MUMFORD, E., HIRSCHHEIM, R., FITZGERALD, G. and WOOD-HARPER, T. (eds) (1985) *Research Methods in Information Systems*, Amsterdam: Elsevier Science/North-Holland, 219–36.

MYERS, M.D. (1995) 'Dialectical hermeneutics: a theoretical framework for the implementation of information systems', *Information Systems Journal*, 5, 51–70.

MYERS, M.D. (1997) 'Qualitative research in information systems', *MIS Quarterly*, 21(2), 221–42.

NANDHAKUMAR, J. (1996) 'Design for success? Critical success factors in executive information systems development', *European Journal of Information Systems*, 5, 62–72.

ORLIKOWSKI, W.J. and BAROUDI, J.J. (1991) 'Studying information technology in organisations: research approaches and assumptions', *Information Systems Research*, 2(1), 1–28.

RICOEUR, P. (1981) 'The model of the text: meaningful action considered as a text', in Thompson (ed.), *Hermeneutics and the Human Sciences*, Cambridge: Cambridge University Press, 197–221.

ROCKART, J.F. (1979) 'Chief executives define their own data needs', *Harvard Business Review*, 57(2), 81–93.

ROWLINSON, M. (1997) *Organisations and Institutions*, London: Macmillan.

SLEVIN, D.P., STIEMAN, P.A. and BOONE, L.W. (1991) 'Critical success factor analysis for information systems performance measurement and enhancement', *Information & Management*, 21, 161–74.

TARNAS, R. (1991) *The Passion of the Western Mind*, London: Penguin.

WALSHAM, G. (1995) 'Interpretative case studies in IS research: nature and method', *European Journal of Information Systems*, 4(2), 74–81.

WESTRUP, C. (1994) 'Practical understanding: hermeneutics and teaching the management of information systems development using a case study', *Accounting, Management and Information Technology*, 4(1), 39–58.

WINOGRAD, T. and FLORES, F. (1986) *Understanding Computers and Cognition: A New Foundation for Design*, Norwood, NJ: Ablex Publishing Corporation.

ZANI, W.M. (1970) 'Blueprint for MIS', *Harvard Business Review*, November–December, 97.

4 Identifying Assumptions Underlying ISM

Nancy Russo and Erik Stolterman

INTRODUCTION

By examining research and other writing about ISM and by observing methodology use in practice, it is possible to identify several assumptions made by researchers, educators, and practitioners. These assumptions are: (1) methodologies have a positive impact on the process and product of IS design; (2) design practice is considered to be a basically irrational process; (3) knowledge about good design practice exists; (4) this design knowledge can be communicated to practicing designers; and, (5) the behaviour of design practitioners can be changed. This chapter discusses the impact of these assumptions, and their converses, on research and practice in IS design.

An ISM is generally considered to be a systematic approach to computer information system design and development consisting of a set of guidelines, activities, techniques and tools, based on a particular philosophy of ISD and understanding of the target system (Wynekoop and Russo, 1995). ISM are promoted as a means of improving the management and control of the system design and development process by specifying and standardising the activities to be performed and the documentation to be produced. Although there are a wide variety of development methodologies available, research indicates that they are not universally accepted. Use tends to be inconsistent, and methodologies are frequently adapted to fit particular situations (Stolterman, 1992; Fitzgerald, 1994; Russo et al., 1995; Hardy et al., 1995).

There are a number of possible explanations for this less than complete acceptance of methodologies. Changes in organisations' development environments, due to the popularity of client-server architectures, distributed systems, and graphical user interfaces, and changes in the technologies themselves may be changing both the process and product of ISD. Methodologies' linear, technical focus and failure to recognize context, contingencies, creativity, and intui-

56

tion may limit their usefulness (Fitzgerald, 1994). It appears that there is a misfit not only between existing methodologies and the needs of developers (Stolterman and Russo, 1997) but also between methodology research and practice (Wynekoop and Russo, 1997). Only a small percentage of research on ISM has employed in-depth studies of the actual process of system design and development. The bias towards conceptual/normative studies and one-shot surveys has limited the knowledge of what is actually happening in IS practice. We will never be able to understand practice if we look only at 'conscious expressions and manifestations', we also have to look for the 'basic assumptions representing theories in practical use' (Dahlbom and Mathiassen, 1993).

This chapter will examine several assumptions that have been identified in the existing literature and practice regarding ISM. The set of assumptions was developed as a result of the authors' experiences in studying the practice of IS design and in exploring the related literature. Whereas we would not claim that these assumptions should be viewed as scientific results, we nevertheless believe that they can serve as intellectual tools in our on-going attempts to study the role of ISM. Newman (1989) illustrated ways in which beliefs shape practice in ISD. Accordingly, if these assumptions are not explicitly identified and analyzed by IS researchers, we believe that there is a risk that research and practice will continue to face the same problems of 'misfit' over and over again. When studying assumptions we need to focus on thoughts and ideas that we normally find both natural and unquestionable. Important assumptions might often be invisible to us, not so much because they are difficult to see, but because they are generally accepted as fact, rather than as just one interpretation of a contextual situation.

By uncovering these assumptions, and reflecting upon their impact on ISM research and practice, we can gain a better understanding of what we are trying to do as methodology researchers to influence the practice of design. There is a close relationship between what we as researchers consider to be our goals and the underlying assumptions governing our thinking and behaviour. By examining our assumptions we may open up for discussion the question of *why* we do research. For example, we may see our role as helping organisations to improve systems design in terms of efficiency, economy, or productivity, or we may work towards providing better tools or a better work environments for the IS professional, or we may focus on the benefits for the ultimate system user, in terms of better systems, or on the benefit for society as a whole through the impact on the economy, the environment, work conditions, or democracy. In the following section we will present and discuss some of the underlying assumptions of ISM, and identify examples of these assumptions. These examples are derived from existing ISM literature as well as our own experiences as IS researchers. Following this we will challenge each assumption and then discuss the implications for ISM research.

ASSUMPTIONS ABOUT ISM

There are many implicit assumptions regarding ISM research, development, and use. We have chosen to focus on some of those we believe to be fundamental, but seldom recognized or acknowledged. It should be made clear that we do not mean to imply that all ISM researchers and users follow this set of assumptions; in fact, evidence can be found that some have explicitly chosen to challenge these assumptions. However, this set of assumptions is believed to represent a large portion of ISM research over the past several decades.

Some of these assumption may appear very ordinary and commonsense, particularly the first one we present. But we do believe that it is exactly the commonality of the assumptions that make them 'dangerous' and very seldom analysed. To identify our most basic assumptions enables us to challenge the thoughts and ideas that we believe to be obvious and self-explanatory.

A discussion of each assumption and its impact on ISM research and practice follows.

1   Methodologies have a positive impact on information system design

The fact that IS researchers and practitioners continue to develop and promote new methods indicates that there is some underlying assumption that methodologies add value to the development process and/or product. Evidence of the belief in the positive impact of ISM is also found in what researchers and practitioners say about methodology use. The belief in the good of methodologies is widely held. Introductory systems analysis and design texts typically present methodological systems development as a necessary approach to reach good design. Organisations continue to buy and create methodologies. Designers and managers generally believe that ISMs improve communication and standardisation in the development process (Russo *et al.*, 1995), conditions that often *a priori* are thought to be a prerequisite to a qualitative design process.

It is often implied that failing to use the 'correct' methodology will result in projects that are overdue and over budget and ultimately in bad systems. Chatzoglou and Macaulay (1996) write that: 'the problem of not using a methodological approach during the development process is well known' (p. 209) and 'the importance of employing a methodological approach during the system development process is widely documented' (p. 214). (It should be noted, however, that they refer almost exclusively to methodology texts to support these statements.) The benefits of methodologies are often described as similar to the benefits of scientific research methods, as in 'The software engineering design process encourages good design through the application of fundamental design principles, systematic methodology, and thorough review' (Pressman, 1987, p. 192). This 'pro-methodology bias' is reflected in many methodology studies, which ask practitioners 'which methodology do you use' rather than 'when do you use the methodology, and when do you work around it?'.

This focus on 'using' the methodology in the complete sense may contribute both to the identified misfit between the proposed benefits of methodologies and the lower-than-expected levels of usage reported in surveys. By assuming that methodologies are basically good, we may neglect to investigate and differentiate between the circumstances under which they are beneficial and those in which they are not.

2 The practice of system design is basically irrational

The assumption of an irrational practice is a necessary condition for the development of new methodologies. If present practice were not considered to be irrational in some way (ineffective, slow, leading to poor quality, etc.), then there would be no motivation to make it more rational. That is, if design practice were already considered to be rational, then there would be no need for new methodologies. To be rational can in this context be defined as, to act in a way that, to an observer, makes sense both according to means and ends. If the practice of system design is rational, then we would expect to see predictable, positive outcomes from methodology use, based on a reasonable process. However, this isn't always the case.

We see examples of the suspected irrationality of design practice in methodology writings and research. Robey and Markus (1984) state that ISD can be viewed as not only a rationally motivated process but also as a political ritual. Parnas and Clements (1986) advocate 'faking' rationality when using methodologies. This is done by producing all the documentation required by the methodology, even though the diagrams, etc. are not used in the design process. The benefit of this is that the system designers get to work the way they want to work (unhindered by methodology) and yet produce the required documentation. So, even if system design is basically thought to be irrational we can pretend it is rational. In these examples design practice is basically understood as (inevitably) irrational, and therefore a suitable goal for methodology researchers.

In an analysis of engineering and software engineering standards of practice, Shapiro (1997) writes, 'The design process in any area of technological practice is often just as potentially variable as the ultimate outcome of that process, the artifact it produces' (p. 286). As we know that a great variability exists in the IS produced, it would then follow that the development processes could be just as variable. A similar conclusion can be reached by studying practice as it is carried out, as for instance in 'In many organisations a mild form of anarchy reigns. Some people develop an orderly and efficient approach to software development by trial and error, but many others develop bad habits that result in poor software quality and maintainability' (Pressman, 1987, p. 15). But the most convincing arguments for existence of an irrational practice is to most people all the problems experienced with projects not done on time and within the allocated budget and not reaching the desired result. It is easy to interpret these problems as signs of irrational actions. And if the definition of rationality is to perform without those problems, then practice is irrational. If we hold this assumption to be true, then it makes good sense to create new methods with the aim to solve some of the experienced problems, i.e, to make practice rational. As we will show later on, this assumption may not be the best possible way to interpret present practice.

3   People can identify and make explicit their understanding of good design practices

The third belief about design practice that we have found is that it is possible to have or to come up with knowledge about what constitutes good design practice. If this was not believed there would be no point in constructing new methodologies. Evidence of this comes from normative, prescriptive statements describing how design *should* be done, as well as from descriptions of successful development projects. Examples of this can be found in systems analysis and design texts (e.g. Wetherbe and Vitalari's *Best Practices* text, 1994), and in papers and books about development. All these rest on the assumption that the authors have the ability both to *recognise* and *make explicit* 'good practice'. There are, though, differences in the beliefs on how 'good practice' can be recognised and, even more importantly, made explicit. Some advocate the transformation of good practice into formal methods, while others advocate more descriptive or even narrative approaches.

Everyone who designs and develops a new methodology must believe that they have the skill to identify and make explicit 'good practice'. In one study, all system designers stated that they had the skill to know what to do in a specific situation, they knew good practice (Stolterman, 1992). What distinguished them from developers of methods was that they could not easily make their good design practice explicit. To a practitioner it is enough to recognise good design practices, but a developer of methods also has to be able to make these practices explicit.

4 It is possible to communicate design knowledge to practising designers

The third belief is about communication. There is no reason to formulate knowledge about good design practice if it is not believed that it is possible to communicate this knowledge to those who do not have the same knowledge. According to this belief important knowledge cannot be 'tacit knowledge'. It must be possible to externalise and communicate this knowledge. This assumption is present in almost all fields of professional work. Education is built on this assumption, even if there are very different opinions on the relative difficulty to communicate 'knowledge' and 'ability'. If design practice is thought to be based on *knowledge* it seems to be reasonable to assume that it is possible to transfer that knowledge. If design practice is considered to be an *ability*, the difficulty of communicating good practice becomes more apparent. This was found in a small study where students in computer science were compared with students in IS. Computer science students were more willing to see design practice as based on knowledge and therefore easier to transfer, while information systems students saw practice as based on personal abilities, and therefore more difficult to transfer (Andersson *et al.*, 1997).

This assumption is obviously very fundamental and common, based on the existence of courses in systems analysis and design and conferences, seminars, and books on design methodologies, all of which have as their purpose to 'deliver' design knowledge to those who need it.

5   It is possible to change the way practicing designers view the design process

The last belief is perhaps the most important. Every method is in some way meant to change the behaviour or thinking of the designer; therefore the designer's rationality and view of the process must be seen as something that *can* be changed.

This assumption implies that through communicating information in the form of methodologies and design practices, we can affect the way designers think and act in regards to the design process. This is closely related to the previous assumption, but goes a little further. If this assumption were not true, there would be no reason for the existence of methodologies. But because we do see a constant stream of new methods, books describing these methods, automated tools embodying these methods, and classes teaching these methods and tools, it appears that researchers and practitioners do believe that the thinking and behaviour of designers can be changed. There are numerous examples of explicit descriptions of this belief. 'The value of the methods and tools, and their conglomerates, methodologies, is that they embody practices and cognitive frames that can be taught, shared, and refined over continued trials' (Hirschheim *et al.*, 1996, p. 25). 'Successful introduction of OO technology needs both good education for every developer and managers who know what they are doing. OO has succeeded spectacularly with individual developers and small skilled teams' (Martin, 1993, p. 45).

These examples show the strong belief in the possibility to change the behaviour of designers by education, i.e. by changing their way of acting in a rational way.

SUMMARISING THE ASSUMPTIONS

If these assumptions are present then the task of developing design methodologies becomes a both possible and worthwhile task. Based on these assumptions, methodologies become the most promising way to enhance efficiency and quality in IS design. But we have seen, in our research and in other studies, many forms of 'misfit' between the methods presented by researchers and those used in practice. It is not unusual to see developers not willing to use a methodology or situations not suitable for a specific methodology. If we hold the assumptions true our response to these misfits will probably be to design a new methodology or to redesign the present ones. It is seldom that these basic assumptions are challenged.

In the following section we will review what it means if we challenge these assumptions.

CHALLENGING THESE ASSUMPTIONS

It has been said that the opposite of a great truth is also true. Obviously, the assumptions described above are extreme positions. We can also learn something by examining the inverse of each assumption. Our goal is not to 'prove' that an assumption is right or wrong, but instead to focus our attention on hidden beliefs that might influence our work. Through this dual-sided examination of assumptions, we can gain a more complete picture of real-world complexities.

1 Methodologies are *not* beneficial for the design process

The meaning of this inversed assumption can, for instance, imply that methods impose unwanted restrictions on the design process (cf Checkland and Scholes, 1990). Introna (1996), Baskerville *et al.* (1992), and Coyne (1995) challenge the overall belief in methods. Baskerville *et al.* (1992) suggest that the entire concept of methodological development is obsolete in today's organisations. In their view, methodologies are a burden and constraint to the development process. It is suggested that in a rapidly changing organisational environment, adherence to methodologies limits the ability to respond to these changes, and results in inappropriate or even failed systems.

However, these attempts to challenge the basic purpose of methods are still not having a great impact. Textbooks still present ISMs as if they cannot be questioned. And the goal of much ISM research still seems to be to add yet another method to the vast number already present.

2   The practice of system design is basically *rational*

There are ways to explain and understand design practice as it is conducted, with all its problems, still as rational. This is done by radically changing our understanding of what it means to be rational and of what characterises good practice. Two of the strongest proponents for this view are Schön (1987) and Suchman (1987). To Schön design practice cannot be understood based on 'technical rationality'; it is instead a rationality characterised by artistry and situatedness. Suchman also uses the idea of situatedness and contextual dependence. Both these views shape a new understanding of design rationality where 'rationality anticipates action before the fact and reconstructs it afterwards' (Suchman, 1987, p. 53). The process of system design, particularly when integrating separate IS, has been defined as 'fitting together a complex jigsaw puzzle, without an understanding of the overall jigsaw picture' (Finkelstein, 1992, p. 8).

This might help us understand problems (such as the 'misfits' identified earlier) that occur when attempts are made to apply scientific, engineering principles to the design and development of IS. When this is done a universal rationality is forced on a design practice based on a situated rationality, often with unsuccessful results (Stolterman and Russo, 1997). Design practice can, according to Schön and Suchman, be understood as basically rational, but the meaning of being rational has to be re-evaluated. Practice can be approached based on a new understanding of what it means to be rational, which takes greater account of contextual realities.

3   People cannot make explicit their understanding of good design practices

Designers are not always able to explain why they do what they do. It may be that whereas designers can say after the fact that a particular project was good or bad (successful or unsuccessful), they may not be able to isolate the effect of a particular design practice on the outcome. There are so many situational and contextual factors that influence the outcome of the development process that it may be difficult if not impossible to identify which design practices led to which outcomes.

In a study of system designers it was shown that most of them could not present a coherent view or even basic concepts describing good design quality in systems design (Stolterman, 1992). This may be explained by research focused on the concept of 'tacit knowledge' (Polanyi, 1973). Tacit knowledge is defined as a kind of knowledge used in practice. It is a knowledge that cannot easily be made explicit by the practitioners themselves (or any one else). It is a situated and context dependent skill (Suchman, 1987). The concept of 'flow' has also been developed to frame the kind of experience a practitioner has when he/she is carrying out a task in the best possible way, in a way that creates 'flow' (Csikszentmihalyi, 1990). Flow is a state of action typical of the professional practitioner when he/she experiences a balance between challenge and pressure. In this state, or after the fact, the practitioner has difficulty in reconstructing the logic and rationality behind the process (Csikszentmihalyi, 1990).

There exists a lot of research pointing to the fact that some aspects related to skill performance are not possible to frame and make explicit. This is a fact that cannot be dealt with by further research advocating more and more detailed description (or prescription) of practice. Instead these findings show that we have to find new and different ways to approach the core of a designer's skill. There are ways we can help a designer without trying to remove the real core of design, which is that it has to be based on situational considerations and on judgement.

4 It is *not* possible to communicate design knowledge to practicing designers

The inability to communicate good design knowledge or principles could be due to designers' distrust of academia because they feel researchers do not understand the reality of current design practice. It also may be due to the lack of communication in general between academia and practice. A great majority of IS research is not published in journals typically read by practising system designers. There is little overlap between professional and academic conferences. Maybe it is not possible, both depending on intrinsic properties of design practice and also on political reasons, to communicate good design practice from academic researchers to practitioners.

An example of this can be illustrated by a study of methodology use. This study found that 83 per cent of the projects developed by academics use a methodology; 70 per cent of the projects developed by software houses or consultants use methodologies, but only 34 per cent of the projects developed in industry use methodologies (Chatzoglou and Macaulay, 1996). The acceptance of academically developed methods is low and the general rate of transfer of research results to practice is slow (Bubenko, 1986). It appears that whereas researchers and consultants are willing to use their own methodologies, they have not been particularly successful in spreading these methodologies outside their own institutions.

Continued development of new methodologies is not likely to change this outcome. Instead, a new paradigm of greater cooperation between research and practice is required to develop methodologies which are accepted by practicing designers.

5   It is *not* possible to change the way practising designers view the design process

In a study of 20 practising designers, the designers strongly believed that skill can only be gained through experience, not through education or methodologies (Stolterman, 1992). DeMarco and Lister (1989) found that even when a methodology use is rigidly enforced, there is a discrepancy in design style. This would seem to imply that methodologies cannot be 'inflicted' on designers (Fitzgerald, 1994). It can be argued that the prevailing habits and traditions within a profession and also the surrounding cultural climate makes it almost impossible to, in any radical way, change the individual designers conceptions and 'theories' of their own skills and competence (Schön, 1987). To make such an impact, to really change practice, may not only demand knowledge on what constitutes good practice and communication skills, it may also demand true rhetoric skills. The present professional skill is often at the core of the identity of a profession. To change this core is therefore challenging to their identity and professional authority (Schön, 1987).

If it is true that methodologies cannot be used to change the behaviour of designers, then there is no need to have methodologies at all. Developing new methodologies will have no influence on the design process. Following this scenario, there is no reason to study design processes, because even if we are able to learn more about 'good' design practices, we won't be able to change other designers' behaviours to incorporate these practices.

SUMMARISING THE CHALLENGES TO THE ASSUMPTIONS

As shown in this section, evidence can be found and arguments can be raised which conflict with the initial list of assumptions. This apparent conflict is not surprising. Little, some would say nothing, about system design is absolute. Instead, this contradiction tells us that our assumptions about ISMs are more complex than they appeared at the outset. We believe that by challenging these assumption we are faced with a much more complex question, how can we as IS researchers contribute in the best way to present practice, and what should be our purpose?

CONCLUSION

In the previous discussion we have not tried to show the assumptions to be basically wrong or right. What we have done, initially, is to make them visible, and through the analysis of the assumptions, added some complexity to the issues. By focusing on the extreme positions of the assumptions, we can see more clearly the reality that is somewhere in between. We do see some benefits to be gained from ISMs. If we did not, then there would be no point in continuing to study ISM development and use. This does not mean that we expect there to be a universal ISM that is applicable in all situations. However, methodologies can be viewed as 'way stations' between the universal and the particular in regard to system design. Methodologies can embody the good standards of practice identified through research (cf. Shapiro, 1997).

Some irrationality must exist in the design process, at least in the sense that rationality becomes so complex that it defies every attempt to be fully prescribed or even described. If not, then one methodology could be applied to all situations, the same way every time, with the same outcome. But this seems impossible to achieve in practice. Instead, methodologies are ignored, adapted, or used on a piecemeal basis. This might explain why problems arise when the goal of a methodology is to standardise or control the process. By having standardisation and control as a goal, a price is paid in terms of flexibility and creativity. ISMs are more likely to be used if they support the creative activity of a designer by allowing designers the freedom and flexibility to shape their own rational views of the design process and by acknowledging the uniqueness of every design situation. To be able to develop methodologies that will have a desired influence on the design process requires an understanding of the nature of the design process and its practice in its full complexity and richness.

It is possible to communicate good design practices, but there are a number of obstacles to overcome. Although descriptions of methodology use in practice would be useful, few are found in IS scholarly journals. Practice descriptions rarely make it through the review process, both for lack of *a priori* intention to do research and for the bias towards discussing only successful practices (Avison and Fitzgerald, 1991; Wynekoop and Russo, 1997). It is possible to change designers' behaviour. Some change happens naturally as designers gain experience. The problem is how to convince designers that they can learn from the experiences of others. How can we get the knowledge we gain from research into practising designers' learning experience? Methodologies should 'leverage the wisdom' of the designer, allowing both individual ability and past experience to shape the situated use of the methodology (Fitzgerald, 1994, p. 700).

Designers do believe that they can identify good practice (Stolterman, 1992). Perhaps what is needed is a better language for articulating different aspects of information systems design. Practitioners have the experience, they have practised their skills, they have been challenged in their understanding of rationality, but they usually do not have time to reflect and interpret their experiences. ISM research should therefore as one of its goals try to create concepts and theories that can help practitioners to reframe their own experience and to make progress in their understanding. From this perspective, ISM research will not be a provider of ready-made methods or guidelines; instead the purpose will be *learning*. Therefore, research should focus on creating conceptual tools that will allow practitioners to reflect, analyse and develop their skills and competence.

This redirected focus relates to the purpose and approaches taken in the research and development of ISMs. ISM research can be viewed as a means of translating research findings into practice (i.e. design based on scientific truths). Or, ISM research can be viewed as a way of formulating existing good practices into a universal language and then transferring that into new practices. We believe the latter way is the only possible option if we are to avoid repeating the mistakes of the past. Following this path, then, requires that ISM research focus more on *existing practice*. We need to redefine the role of ISM research to recognise and take advantage of the specific competencies of researchers, not as deliverers of new normative structures to practice, but as skilled commentators and critics of prevailing practice. Whereas practitioners are primarily concerned with 'getting the job done', researchers may have the time and opportunity to reflect upon practice in a way not possible for practitioners. By examining practice from a disinterested perspective, researchers can give new interpretations of practice, make assumptions visible, and criticise ineffective practices and traditions when technology, organisations and society are changing. Researchers have the advantage of being able to look at the big picture because they are able to integrate the experiences of many system designers in many different environments. To be able to do this, ISM research must focus on in-depth studies of practice, create rich descriptions of practice, and come up with interpretations and analysis of this practice if we are to move the field ahead.

References

ANDERSSON, P., KARLSSON, U.K. and LARSSON, P. (1997) 'Does educational background affect how students consider a designers personal qualities?', Student report in the course design theory, Department of Informatics, Umeå University, Sweden.

AVISON, D.E. and FITZGERALD, G. (1991) 'Editorial', *Journal of Information Systems*, 1(4), 221–2.

BASKERVILLE, R., TRAVIS, J. and TRUEX, D. (1992) 'Systems without method: the impact of new technologies on information systems development projects', in Kendall, K.E., Lyytinen, K. and DeGross, J.I. (eds), *The Impact of Computer Supported Technologies on Information Systems Development*, Amsterdam: North-Holland, 241–70.

BUBENKO, J.A. Jr. (1986) 'Information system methodologies: a research view', in Olle, T.W., Sol, H.G. and Verrijn-Stuart, A.A. (eds), *Information Systems Design Methodologies: Improving the Practice*, Amsterdam: North-Holland.

CHATZOGLOU, P.D. and MACAULAY, L.A. (1996) 'Requirements capture and IS methodologies', *Information Systems Journal*, 6(2), 209–25.

CHECKLAND, P. and SCHOLES, J. (1990) *Soft Systems Methodology in Action*, Chichester: John Wiley.

COYNE, R. (1995) *Designing Information Technology in the Postmodern Age*, Cambridge, MA: MIT Press.

CSIKSZENTMIHALYI, M. (1990) *Flow, The Psychology of Optimal Experience*, New York: Harper Perennial.

DAHLBOM, B. and MATHIASSEN, L. (1993) *Computers in Context: The Philosophy and Practice of Systems Design*, Cambridge: NCC Blackwells.

DEMARCO, T. and LISTER, T. (1989) 'Software development: state of the art v. state of the practice', *Proceedings of the 11th International Conference on Software Engineering*, 271–5.

FINKELSTEIN, C. (1992) *Information Engineering: Strategic Systems Development*, Sydney: Addison-Wesley.

FITZGERALD, B. (1994) 'Systems development dilemma: whether to adopt formalised systems development methodologies or not?', *Proceedings of the Second European Conference on Information Systems*, Baets, W.R.J., Nijenrode University Press, 691–706.

FITZGERALD, B. (1997) 'A tale of two roles: the use of systems development methodologies in practice', *Proceedings of the British Computer Society's Annual Conference on Information System Methodologies*, Autumn.

HARDY, C.J., THOMPSON, J.B. and EDWARDS, H.M. (1995) 'The use, limitations and customization of structured systems development methods in the United Kingdom', *Information and Software Technology*, 37(9), 467–77.

HIRSCHHEIM, R., KLEIN, H.K. and LYYTINEN, K. (1996) 'Exploring the intellectual structures of information systems development: a social action theoretical, analysis', *Accounting, Management & Information Technology*, 6(1–2), 1–64.

INTRONA, L. (1996) 'Notes on ateleological information systems development', *Information Technology & People*, 9(4).

MARTIN, J. (1993) *Principles of Object-Oriented Analysis and Design*, Englewood Cliffs: Prentice-Hall.

MCGUIRE, W.J. (1973) 'The yin and yang of progress in social psychology: seven koan', *Journal of Personality and Social Psychology*, 26(3), 446–56.

NEWMAN, M. (1989) 'Some fallacies in information systems development,' *International Journal of Information Management*, 9, 127–43.

PARNAS, D. and CLEMENTS, P. (1986) 'A rational design process: how and why to fake it', *IEEE Transactions on Software Engineering*, February, 251–7.

POLANYI, M. (1973) *Personal Knowledge*, London: Routledge & Kegan Paul.

PRESSMAN, R.S. (1987) *Software Engineering: A Practitioner's Approach*, New York: McGraw-Hill.

ROBEY, D. and MARKUS, M.L. (1984) 'Rituals in information systems design', *MIS Quarterly*, March, 5–15.

RUSSO, N.L., WYNEKOOP, J.L. and WALZ, D. (1995) 'The use and adaptation of system development methodologies', *Proceedings of the Information Resources Management Association International Conference*, May.

SCHÖN, D. (1987) *Educating the Reflective Practitioner*, San Francisco: Jossey-Bass.

SHAPIRO, S. (1997) 'Degrees of freedom: the interaction of standards of practice and engineering judgment', *Science, Technology, & Human Values*, 22(3), 286–316.

STOLTERMAN, E. (1992) 'How system designers think about design and methods: some reflections based on an interview study', *Scandinavian Journal of Information Systems*, 4(1), 137–50.

STOLTERMAN, E. and RUSSO, N.L. (1997) 'The paradox of information systems methods: public and private rationality', *Proceedings of the British Computer Society's Annual Conference on Information System Methodologies*, Autumn.

SUCHMAN, L. (1987) *Plans and Situated Actions: The Problems of Human–Machine Communication*, Cambridge: Cambridge University Press.

WETHERBE, J.C. and VITALARI, N.P. (1994) *Systems Analysis and Design: Best Practices*, St Paul/Minneapolis: West Publishing.

WYNEKOOP, J.L. and RUSSO, N.L. (1995) 'System development methodologies', *Journal of Information Technology*, Summer, 65–73.

WYNEKOOP, J.L. and RUSSO, N.L. (1997) 'Studying system development methodologies: an examination of research methods', *Information Systems Journal*, 7(1), 47–65.

Part II

Strategic and Global Management

5 Experiences of SISP: Evoking Change within an IT Department

David Wainwright

INTRODUCTION

This chapter explores change management issues affecting participants involved in a SISP process. The field study is based on the early phases of an SISP exercise conducted in a major engineering company, named Engco in order to maintain confidentiality. The work is focused on the process of raising SISP awareness. This involves repositioning an IT department (one primarily concerned with the provision of a resilient network technology infrastructure), enabling it to take a more pro-active and balanced Information Systems (IS) role, (concerned with developing IS applications prioritised to business needs) ready to cope with the increased pressures of adopting a higher internal organisational and strategic profile. These pressures now seem to be prevalent amongst industry, the alignment of IT and business objectives remaining a top management concern over seven consecutive years of the Price Waterhouse IT Review (Price Waterhouse, 1995–6). Two typical quotes from this report (from the section 'managing the IT infrastructure') succinctly identifies the problems related to the IT/business/top management culture gap:

Mentioned by 35%, and not the biggest issue, but surely the biggest disappointment, is the non-recognition, by top management, of the importance of the IT infrastructure. Just when we thought IT was finding its place as one of the key, long term, strategies to get right, the reflection of that strategy, which manifests itself far more in the infrastructure than in any transient application, seems to pass unnoticed.

Top management has little concept of the complexity of the IT infrastructure, and gives little support in enforcing its standards.

It is this question of how to tackle the problem of raising the profile of the IT department to enable the participants to engage in strategic discourse that might provide some answers towards more effective business/IT alignment. A proposition therefore is that raising the confidence and profile of an IT department to engage in strategic discourse will result in more effective alignment of business and IT objectives.

The chapter is structured as follows. Firstly, a brief review of some of the key SISP literature, looking at both prescriptive advice and some critical discourse, is discussed. Secondly, an exploration of some of the key issues arising out of a consultancy exercise conducted over a period of three years is outlined in order to identify significant milestones where IT engages with the business in a process of strategic alignment. Finally, a comparison of these issues is made with advice distilled from current SISP literature which concludes that greater effort should be addressed in terms of raising the internal confidence of IT departments as they can be disadvantaged by a lack of expertise in engaging in strategic discourse.

SISP

Prescriptive design school

In recent years there has been an encouraging trend towards higher quality academic and practitioner publications and advice relating to SISP. A contingency theme related to the SISP discipline is now beginning to emerge leading to the concept of an SISP toolkit. These toolkits detail various models, tools and techniques derived from over a decade of work and research in the area of strategic information systems planning. This emanated originally from work on strategic information systems from the USA, ranging from Porter and Millar (1985) in the 1980s on competitive forces through to Rockart *et al.* (1996) in the 1990s on IT organisation. These lessons were interpreted and applied to the European context as typified by the work of Earl (1989, 1995) on IT strategy; Galliers (1994) who identified key strategic issues and growth models as a diagnostic aid to strategic IS planning and a range of key authors, Willcocks *et al.* (1997) on managing the IT and IS function. Comprehensive and excellent texts (Earl, 1989; Remenyi, 1991; Peppard, 1993; Ward and Griffiths, 1996; Robson, 1997) are extremely useful sources of information about SISP planning and implementation. Currie (1995) emphasises that rationality permeates the work on IT strategy formulation whereby managers are advised to impose a framework under the auspices of senior executives, the strategists. She identifies these frameworks as being goal-oriented; a linear process carried out in logical steps typically based on the rational assumptions that decision-makers:

- can evaluate all the relevant information
- can select the most appropriate course of action
- can formulate a strategy
- are able to implement the strategy
- can improve performance
- can enhance competitive position.

The rational approach has spawned much published research with an ever expanding range of frameworks, techniques and methods to facilitate the rational IT planning process. In all of this managers are seen as carriers of rationality and initiative; management is a technical process which operates in the common good and processes become almost matters of procedure. Any problems encountered are dealt with by expanding the remit of the strategy to subsume and 'solve' those problems, so that the IT strategy process has become broader and broader over time.

As such this might be seen to represent the prescriptive and contingency schools of SISP derived from many years of observation of real world SISP exercises led by consultants, academics or both. Despite this range of SISP advice, which is available to both academics and consultants alike, attempts at creating a culture shift towards business and strategically literate IT professionals (managers), exemplified by the era of the 'hybrid manager' (Earl and Skyme, 1992), is still very problematic. There is still a reinforcement of the power held by those who are articulate in the art of traditional business strategic discourse, dominated by the languages of accounting, market analysis and strategic planning. Even IT managers who now possess the requisite MBA qualification are still regarded as illegitimate relatives to the traditional business functional senior managers of marketing, finance or human resource management, etc. The opportunity to engage in, and contribute to, business strategic discourse is by definition limited for the average IT manager. They certainly hold referent power as IT experts but little legitimate power as business experts.

Applying SISP

There is certainly no lack of planning frameworks, portfolio tools, bullet point advice lists and prescriptions and conceptual models, readily available for use by IS/IT professionals to facilitate SISP processes. It is still a far from simple task, however, to put these concepts, ideas, frameworks and tools into practice especially when faced with organisational cultures that regard IT purely as a technical support operation and not as an essential strategic function. Practical advice, lessons and theories on the implementation of SISP (most work is related to planning, that is, the 'what' as opposed to the 'how') are still scarce, much of it contained within the personal experiences of senior staff in major IT consultancy companies. It is not in the interest of such companies to transfer this knowledge and skills into client organisations but more to reinforce the status quo, wrap a mystique around strategic discourse and create a culture of dependency for repeat business.

These observations are supported to an extent by an emerging field of critical discourse of strategic planning and SISP itself.

The critical strategy school

Many academics now question the nature of strategic discourse (Knights and Morgan, 1991; Thomas and Wainwright, 1994), strategic planning generally (Mintzberg, 1994) and of SISP itself (Galliers, 1991; Peppard *et al.*, 1996; Knights *et al.*, 1997). These critiques are based on the argument that strategic planning is not altogether a rational approach but very dependent on power, cultural, behavioural, emergent and serendipitous factors. There is a requirement therefore that SISP, in order to be successful, has to be a dynamic and flexible learning process that can adapt to emergent strategy development. This is in direct contrast to the present emphasis on prescriptive frameworks for IT strategy, planning and implementation. Many business alignment models (Venkatraman, 1993) also state that IT must be aligned with the business with a requirement that business managers must drive the process top-down. Again in contrast, research has shown that most strategic applications of IT have occurred 'bottom up' as opposed to being rationally aligned and planned. Finally, IT is increasingly seen as not providing competitive advantage in its own right but is more of a commodity which, if applied effectively, can enhance business competitiveness. The onus is therefore on the ability of the internal IS/IT experts to leverage the IT within a company; the IT professional is therefore the source of the competitive advantage. This emphasis is reflected in the work by Prahalad and Hamel (1990) who developed the notion of core competencies. This is where the real sources of advantage are to be found in management's ability to consolidate corporate wide technologies and production skills into competencies that empower businesses to adapt quickly to changing opportunities. Technological opportunities emerge through an incremental process of trial, error and learning in knowledge building and strategic positioning.

If the role of the internal IS/IT expert and/or manager is so crucial there seem to be few rich and in-depth organisational research findings to provide advice and solutions for many of the identified weaknesses of the IT department's perceived role within strategic planning and SISP. Many prescriptive models of the organisation of the IS/IT function exist (Ward and Griffiths, 1996; Willcocks *et al.*, 1997). The same authors point to many research studies which demonstrates that the selection of the most suitable organisational structure with its attendant roles, responsibilities, functional orientation and reporting relationships is dependent on many contextual factors. These include the critical role of IT within the business, the degree of centralisation or decentralisation and the maturity/stage of evolution of the IT function (and conversely the IT literacy of the business community) within the company. It seems therefore that many of the problems associated with effective SISP, coping with the IT and business culture gap, enabling business and IT strategic alignment are centred on the qualities and competencies of the IT staff themselves. These comprise internal strategic planning expertise, the perceived image of them by other business managers and also the inherent confidence of the IT staff. These factors, when combined, may be a limiting factor on the degree of contribution by the IT department to business and IT strategy discourse.

CASE STUDY

Introduction of SISP at Engco

Engco is a major engineering company which manufactures sophisticated and technically innovative highly engineered products. The market is globally extremely competitive and the company increasingly needs closer alignment of its business and IT strategy in order to have more effective engineering, project management, product data management, production management, quality and management IS. The systems problems are compounded by a requirement to rationalise and move towards an integrated IT infrastructure over three geographically dispersed manufacturing sites. A legacy of a past heavy engineering culture combined with a traditional centralised IT function had conspired to leave the company with a large business and IT culture gap. The IT department was managed by four IT co-ordinators across three sites. There was a current vacancy for an IT manager with no senior business manager to report to. At this time the IT co-ordinators lacked confidence and the opportunity to engage management at a senior level, even though they were certainly educated in the skills of management (two with MBA and one more in the process of study).

This problem was recognised as hindering progress by the IT co-ordinators themselves and a recent major re-organisation was used as a catalyst to promote IT more proactively within the business. This was to be achieved by conducting an SISP exercise for the first time. Prior to this, IT strategy had been implicit, reactive to functional departmental needs, and concentrated on technically focused policies for common network infrastructures, systems security and reliability. A limited budget; the low strategic profile of IT and a degree of cynicism concerning major consultancies (resulting from a recent and very expensive failed business process re-engineering project) resulted in a common desire by the IT co-ordinators to conduct the SISP exercise themselves. This was to be guided by an informed but not too prescriptive academic facilitator acting in an independent consultancy role. The first stage of this process involved a two day off-site meeting (held in December 1996) for the IT team with the facilitator (alone in a haunted castle!). Participants were primed beforehand with selected references and material providing an overview of the SISP process. They were also then supplied with and briefed on a selected toolkit of portfolio techniques such as awareness, positioning, opportunity frameworks, CSF analysis, etc.

The objective of the overview and description of the 'toolkit' of SISP techniques was to:

- raise awareness of the objectives of a rigorous SISP process
- identify appropriate techniques and tools that could facilitate/ enhance SISP

- provide the opportunity for a 'first cut' attempt to apply them to the Engco situation
- to apply the CSF technique to each application area presented.

Individual presentations by the IT team participants (on their own project responsibilities and functional areas) and preliminary CSF analyses dominated the initial 2-day session. Key issues to emerge from the first review meeting were subsequently identified, written up and circulated, prior to a phased series of follow up sessions as the input to focus on a more detailed review of the current IT infrastructure and the IS applications portfolio.

Over the next few months a series of half-day and one-day workshops was held resulting in a more thorough review of the internal IT infrastructure and data architectures. At each session, more material was provided by the participants themselves, utilising techniques and tools borrowed from the SISP toolkit such as; awareness, positioning, opportunity frameworks, process diagrams, data architecture models, etc. The facilitator from academia provided advice and support for the application of the SISP tools and techniques and provided examples of how they might be applied. This information was reinforced by two members of the IT team taking part in an IT visit to another major heavy engineering contractor as a learning and benchmarking exercise to compare their IT strategy. Over this period of time the confidence of the IT team started to grow together with a greater involvement and contribution to producing outputs for the SISP process. Confidence was still not up to a level, however, whereby, the team felt ready to present their plans to senior management or interact more strongly with the business area applications managers. Key outcomes for this stage were:

- the engendering of a common team approach to SISP with full ownership by all team members;
- the promotion of a culture shift for the team from a reactive IT department to a pro-active IS integrated business and manufacturing unit;
- the compilation and synthesis of available documentation, analyses and notes from review presentations by team members creating the skeleton of the IT strategy documentation.

It was agreed that the next phase was more dependent on greater interaction of the IT department with the business and manufacturing managers. The team therefore focused on alignment of IT and business objectives, whilst consolidating on their technical analyses. A milestone was achieved within this phase when models of the Engco IT data and systems architectures mapped to business objectives were presented to senior management in an intensive one-day workshop in April 1997. The model of strategic alignment was then critically discussed, modified and verified against the senior manager's strategic view of the business. This point marked the meeting of IT and business cultures, acceptance of IT's role to conduct a valid SISP process and acceptance that IT could make a valid contribution to strategic discourse within the business. The senior manager concerned (Director of Quality) was formally given overall responsibility for IT and the IT co-ordinator who had championed the SISP process was promoted to Divisional IT manager. These events signified a new era of top management commitment to pursue a new and aligned IT and IS strategy. This resulted in the final drafting of an IT strategy document which was presented to the Engco senior executive team and formally approved in the winter of 1997.

Discussion

At Engco a formal SISP initiation event was planned to adopt 'modern' state of the art planning techniques and methods in order to apply them to the Engco IS applications portfolio and IT infrastructure. This was a formal announcement to the business (due to the unusually high expense of offsite team building meetings in Castles that were usually only the domain of senior management) legitimising a process of IT team building. This resulted in the development of core skills and the first opportunity to formally discuss both business and IT strategic issues. A deliberate decision was also made by the IT co-ordinator championing the event to use an external academic facilitator and not one of the large IT consultancy companies (perhaps influenced by his learning from an MBA programme).

The rationale was concerned with embedding the learning about the SISP process into the IS team itself as opposed to outsourcing the creation of a plan to external consultants. An educational and facilitative approach was adopted whereby the plan was developed in a phased but continuous mode and driven by the IT co-ordinators using their own core skills and knowledge. The academic facilitator provided guidance on tools and techniques with advice relating to their appropriate application in the Engco context. The important point is that the actual process of SISP planning had to be learnt and embedded within Engco itself. It was becoming increasingly apparent that information and knowledge management was a major strategic concern for the company and therefore SISP would become a core competence. The innovative nature of the products and production processes create an equal demand for innovation and flexibility within the IS and business planning teams. It was important therefore not to outsource such a critical source of corporate knowledge, as this was an important attribute of the products themselves. One might ask however, what is wrong about outsourcing SISP to the major consultancies? Except it is perhaps an argument of expenditure and when and how much to pass over ownership and control. This may have reinforced the dominance of both the internal and external business experts over the IT team itself and hindered any organisational learning and prevented the opportunity to contribute to strategic discourse within the business.

An awareness of each of the key components of a SISP process was raised. It was noticed that most of the material presented only represented one component of SISP (IT strategy as opposed to IS and IM strategies) and that the IT department was evolving the plan in a 'bottom-up' fashion reactive to current business and manufacturing problems. A 'top-down' organisational, business unit and manufacturing strategic dimension was missing and needed to be incorporated along with many other dimensions comprising: analyses of the internal/external IS/IT environments, review of the current IS applications portfolio and formulation of IS and management of change strategies.

CONCLUSIONS

The results to date point to some interesting reflections on the use of different SISP techniques and tools. Techniques and tools were only useful when applied contingent on the stage of learning of participants in the SISP process. For example, it might have seemed logical to use business portfolio and competitive strategy analysis techniques fairly early on, in a top-down process, to define a prioritised applications portfolio. However, this was not possible during the first year as the IT team did not possess the requisite expertise and knowledge of the business unit strategic imperatives. These techniques only became useful after a series of workshops on IT/business alignment culminating in a meeting with senior management to verify the business imperatives. The CSF approach was useful to focus priorities but of limited use overall, due to a lack of knowledge of business unit goals (even amongst business unit managers themselves). Simple models of business, internal customer and technical drivers were more easily understood and used to define objectives and tactics for the IT strategy. Similarly, basic pyramid models comprising IT network architecture, operating systems, data management, IS applications and business goals were more easily assimilated by the IT team. This points to a learning curve which is initially fairly technically focused but which later acts as the foundation for the application of the same techniques in a more business focused manner.

IT professionals need to be slowly extricated from their immediate technical, problem based and legacy dominated mindsets. A process of learning must take place, coupled with periods of experimentation and reflection, whilst adhering to goals of team building and the continued technical support of the IT infrastructure. Such an approach can engender a culture shift within the IT function into a broader based IS unit focused on business and IT alignment. This is coupled with a matching shift of perceptions within the business of the changing and more business focused nature of the IT department and their new pro-active role. There is an emerging recognition that the business and IT culture gap is still at the root of many of the problems of successful SISP and attempts for business and IT alignment. Doubts exist over hybridisation programmes with some authors stressing the need to review strategies for redressing the culture gap (Rourke and Elliott, 1996; Bashein and Markus, 1997). The early findings of this project to date indicate that current blind adherence to prescriptive IS/IT planning, driven by external management consultants, may exacerbate the current problems of aligning IT and business strategy. A way forward could be to research the effects of applying SISP methodologies in a critically aware fashion. This would involve analysing the amount, content and pace of learning, together with identifying suitable mechanisms for change, that would be required by IT and business teams in order to undertake successful SISP implementation.

Finally, in order to create a critical awareness of how the SISP process really operates, with all its attendant complexity in terms of power and organisational politics, the participants in the SISP process must be involved in a learning process. They must be educated and trained to compete in an environment dominated by more traditional functional area managers articulate in strategic discourse. The IT and business culture gap may then be reduced by creating a more level playing field with more equal participation, particularly from the IT professionals.

References

BASHEIN, B.J. and MARKUS, M.L. (1997) 'A credibility equation for the IT specialists', *Sloan Management Review*, Summer, 38(4), 35–44.

CURRIE, W. (1995) *Management Strategy for IT: an International Perspective*, London: Financial Times, Pitman Publishing.

EARL, M. (1989) *Management Strategies for Information Technology*, Englewood Cliffs: Prentice-Hall.

EARL, M.J. (1995) 'Integrating IS and the organisation: a framework of organisational fit', *Centre for Research in Information Management Working Paper Series*, London Business School.

EARL, M.J. and SKYME, D.J. (1992) 'Hybrid managers: what do we know about them?', *Journal of Information Systems*, 2(2), 169–87.

GALLIERS, R.D. (1991) 'Strategic information systems planning, myths, reality and guidelines for successful implementation', *European Journal of Information Systems*, 1(1), 55–64.

KNIGHTS, D. and MORGAN, G. (1991) 'Corporate strategy, organizations and subjectivity: a critique', *Organization Studies*, 12(9), 251–73.

KNIGHTS, D., NOBLE, F. and WILMOTT, H. (1997) 'We should be total slaves to the business: aligning information technology and strategy-issues and evidence', in Bloomfield, B.P., Coombs, R., Knights, D. and Littler, D. (eds) *Information Technology and Organizations, Strategies, Networks and Integration*, Oxford: Oxford University Press, 12–35.

MINTZBERG, H. (1994) *The Rise and Fall of Strategic Planning*, Englewood Cliffs: Prentice-Hall.

PEPPARD, J. (1993) *IT Strategy for Business*, London: Pitman.

PEPPARD, J., DHILLON, G. and HACKNEY, R. (1996) 'Emergent strategies, strategic renewal and serendipity in business strategy creation: the challenge for IS/IT planning', *Proceedings of the 6th Annual Conference BIT'96, Business Information Systems – Uncertain Futures*, November.

PORTER, M.E. and MILLAR, V.E. (1985) 'How information gives you competitive advantage', *Harvard Business Review*, July/August, 4, 149–60.

PRAHALAD, C.K. and HAMEL, G. (1990) 'The core competencies of the corporation', *Harvard Business Review*, May–June, 79–91.

PRICE WATERHOUSE (1995–6) *Information Technology Review*, London: Price Waterhouse Publications.

REMENYI, D.S.J. (1991) *Introducing Strategic Information Systems Planning*, Cambridge: NCC Blackwell.

ROBSON, W. (1997) *Strategic Management & Information Systems*, London: Pitman.

ROCKART, J.F., EARL, M.J. and ROSS, J.W. (1996) 'Eight imperatives for the new IT organisation', *Sloan Management Review*, Autumn, 43–55.

ROURKE, G. and ELLIOTT, G. (1996) 'Strategic management of the culture gap', *Proceedings of the 6th Annual Conference BIT'96: Business Information Systems – Uncertain Futures*, November.

THOMAS, P. and WAINWRIGHT, D. (1994) 'Gaining the benefits of integrated manufacturing technology: just who benefits and how?', *International Journal of Production Economics*, 34(3), 371–81.

VENKATRAMAN, N. (1993) 'Continuous strategic alignment: exploiting information technology capabilities for competitive success', *European Management Journal*, 11(2), 139–48.

WARD, J. and GRIFFITHS, P. (1996) *Strategic Planning for Information Systems*, Chichester: John Wiley.

WILLCOCKS, L., FEENEY, D. and ISLEI, G. (1997) *Managing IT as a Strategic Resource*, New York: McGraw-Hill.

6 Global Electronic Commerce Process: Business to Business

Nazmun Nahar, Najmul Huda and
Jaak Tepandi

INTRODUCTION

The integration of new communication and information technologies (CITs) with SMEs' existing IS provides the information technology infrastructure for global electronic commerce (GEC). These can be used to create competitive advantages for enterprises by facilitating worldwide communication and collaboration among buyers, potential customers, enterprises, partners and suppliers. By utilising CITs, SMEs are able to reduce the problems and risks related to technology and/or business and to provide effective assistance in the GEC process. This study introduces a new GEC methodology, which can systematically guide enterprises to globalise and facilitate rapid access to foreign markets. This study presents the results of research work, which examined how SMEs can gain competitive advantages through GEC. This study presents a conceptual framework of the GEC process (business-to-business) for SMEs. This framework can assist SMEs in identifying GEC opportunities and strategies. It is proposed that SMEs can communicate, collaborate and co-operate with customers, suppliers and partners through networking systems. They can achieve unique benefits in their GEC efforts as well as create competitive advantages in an intensely competitive and extremely turbulent global environment. This study also presents frameworks for problem and risk reduction.

Today's business environment has become global and competitive (Palvia, 1997; Tersine and Harvey, 1998). Due to the liberalisation of trade and the impact of new communication means, improved logistics services and electronic banking systems and other factors, there has been a clear increase in global competition (Nahar, 1998b, 1998d).

As a result, SMEs are already facing competition in their domestic markets and will face more intense competition in the future. SMEs should expand into the global market place in order to survive and enable long-term growth.

New communication and information technologies (CITs) can eliminate or at least diminish the barriers of distance, geography and time. Enterprises are benefiting from using the Internet technology in their internal operations (Intranet; Hills, 1997; Nahar, 1998b), in communicating with their partners and customers (Extranet, Baker, 1997; Nahar, 1998a, 1998c, 1998d) and in their worldwide open activities (Internet; Hoffman and Thomas, 1996; Quelch and Klein, 1996; Vassos, 1996; Hamill and Gregory, 1997; Nahar and Savolainen, 1997; Nahar, 1998b, 1998c; Kannan *et al.*, 1998). Huge number of enterprises and people from around the world are already connected to the Internet and the number is increasing rapidly. This explosive growth phenomenon of the Internet, in addition to the emerging capacities of electronic commerce are increasing opportunities for GEC, i.e. conducting exports or imports on a worldwide basis utilising new CITs).

GEC can revolutionise the way enterprises do international business. SMEs can obtain large benefits through innovative uses of the CITs in their GEC efforts. GEC can also provide various benefits to customers, suppliers, and even to countries. Electronic commerce is helping some enterprises to run businesses more effectively and efficiently. There is tremendous potential for GEC, yet there is no effective framework currently existing for the successful execution of the GEC (business-to-business) process. Due to this lack of framework many SMEs have not been able to understand and obtain competitive advantages (competitive advantage refers to the case where the enterprise's product and/or service has a greater added value than that of the competitors) from their GEC efforts. Problems and risks preventing the flourish of GEC include a lack of GEC process model, merchant/customer trust, privacy, network robustness, reliability, speed, intellectual property protection, etc. To date, only a limited number of large companies, such as Cisco Systems Inc., Amazon.com and Dell Computers are making profits from their GEC efforts.

The main research problem of this study has been identified as: How can new CITs facilitate GEC (business-to-business) effectively and efficiently for SMEs and overcome problems and reduce the risks? This study began with a literature review and subsequent investigation of Internet resources and databases. The study then conducted in-depth interviews of SMEs (e.g. Michael Richter Ltd, Pronet Inc., etc.). Through analysis, the study identified the tasks in GEC, identified CITs (e.g. e-mail, electronic data interchange, electronic funds transfer, Internet, Extranet, etc.) relevant for GEC and developed a model for the GEC process utilising new CITs. It also identified the problems and risks and suggested solutions for reducing the problems and risks. Global reach of the Internet and Extranet, Intranet and resources of conventional information technology systems have been synergistically integrated. These can provide the IT infrastructure for GEC. The Web, in addition to other CITs can be used to bring together suppliers, employees, partners and customers on a worldwide basis.

Our model and ideas are tested in practice by an enterprise (e.g. Akisumi Ltd. in Finland) and this enterprise has achieved different benefits (see Section 2.2). Finally, the results of literature review, interviews and testing were collected together, analyzed and conclusions were drawn. This study presents a conceptual framework of the GEC process for SMEs and argues that SMEs can communicate, collaborate and co-operate with customers, suppliers and partners through networking systems thereby gaining competitive advantages. This chapter is made up of five major sections. The introduction is first described. The next section develops a model for the GEC process in the context of SMEs. The advantages of this model are also described in this section. We then develop the frameworks that present the problems and risks associated with GEC. Remedies for reducing these problems and risks are also suggested in this section. The next section exhibits the recommendations for successful GEC, and the final section conclusions are drawn and implications of the research are discussed.

MODEL FOR THE GEC PROCESS

This study contends that to make GEC effective and efficient it should be considered as a series of collaborative processes. Global collaboration among enterprise's employees, suppliers, partners, customers and different activities of the GEC process can be conceptualised as a framework. Twelve interlinked and overlapping activities have been identified (see Figure 6.1) and described briefly below. Chronological order and the number of activities may vary in some cases, for example, some digital products and/or services can be delivered

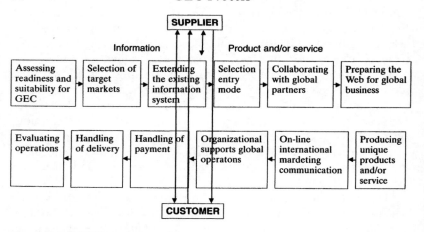

Figure 6.1   GEC process model

through the Internet, consequently shipping arrangement are not required. Through the GEC process, the supplier interacts with the customer, information flows in both directions, money is paid to the supplier and the product and/or service is sold/transferred to the customer. In this section, new CITs (e.g. Internet, Intranet, Extranet, etc.) have been integrated with SMEs' existing traditional information systems.

The new CITs can be integrated and implemented in two or more stages and therefore become cheaper for the enterprises as well as easier to implement. In the first stage, the enterprise could integrate and systematically utilise CIT tools and network services. The first stage can be implemented within 4 months. The enterprise should train the marketer to utilise the model effectively and efficiently as well as to make some adjustments according to the scope of the enterprise and the particular market to be promoted.

ASSESSING READINESS AND SUITABILITY FOR GEC

This activity includes the analysis of an enterprise's strengths and weaknesses and the determination of the extent to which they facilitate or hinder its competitiveness in the target markets. The analysis may cover several areas depending on the enterprise, its products and target markets as can be seen in Table 6.1 (Nahar, 1998b).

Table 6.1 Possible areas to be covered in assessing readiness for the GEC

A Product attributes	B On-line marketing capacity
• meeting customer needs/or segments • modification needs • packaging • stage of the product life cycle	• IT infrastructure and IT skills of the employees • willingness and ability to promote • familiarity of the enterprise brand name • ability to price competitively and contribute to overall profitability • adaptability and flexibility of logistics
C Production capacity and technical competencies	D Adequacy of resources
• plant capacity • technical skills of employees	• ability to finance international business • motivated human resources
E Managerial capacity	F Others
• qualifications of management, familiarity with international business • knowledge of foreign languages • flexible attitude, creativity, dynamism, commitment to international business • willingness to train and acquire needed skills	• willingness to do the needed R&D as well as the market research • ability to co-ordinate the international business activities and handle problems

Using modern CITs, SMEs can collect internal and external data in a planned way, process and analyse this data and thereby identify their strengths and weaknesses.

SELECTION OF TARGET MARKETS

International market research is important. It helps in the selection of potential markets and launching of a successful GEC. The following factors should be analyzed in selecting the markets: potential size of the market; potential market share/sales for the enterprise products and/or services; major characteristics of potential competitors; economic, political and social environments; IT and other technoogical developments; response characteristics of the market in terms of the marketing mix, i.e. product, price, promotion and distribution; international logistics requirements necessary to serve the market; the resource requirements to serve the market; and suitability of the market in relation to the enterprise's goals and competitive advantages.

The enterprise has several options for international market research. It can buy cost-effective international market research services from specialised companies (e.g. Vivamus, http://www.vivamus.comand Nielsenmedia, http://www.nielsenmedia.com/). Alternatively, the enterprise can send an e-mail message to a specialised mailing list in order to locate and contact an international market researcher. This expert can provide customised international market research services cost effectively. The enterprise can also do its own research utilising databases of DIALOG (http://www.dialog.com), LEXIS-NEXIX (http://www.lexis-nexis.com), Stat-usa (http://www.Stat-usa.gov/) or Strategis Canada (http://strategis.ic.gc.ca). The Michigan State University (http://ciber.bus.msu.edu/busres.htm) has extensive WWW resources relevant to the international marketing research.

EXTENDING THE EXISTING IS

In order to launch GEC, SME should extend its IT infrastructure. This extension of IT infrastructure can be divided into several stages. At the first stage, cheaper and easier to use CITs can be utilized. Using the tasks/functions identified in the GEC process review, CITs requirements can be developed. For each identified requirement, cheaper, easier to implement, easier to use and reliable performing solutions should be identified. Selected CITs may include: the Internet, Intranet, Extranet, Electronic Data Interchange (EDI), database, push technology, Web, teleconferencing, video conferencing, and autoresponders; they can vary slightly depending on the products and/or services to be marketed. Planning and budgeting for implementation should be done next and implementation should be managed. Also potential mistakes, problems and risks should be identified and counter measures should be taken.

EDI systems require extensive diffusion into the enterprise's own internal and external organisational systems in order to get strong benefits. Initial investments for acquiring Internet enabled EDI is often less expensive and therefore affordable for SME's. Internet-enabled EDI is easier to integrate with an enterprise's existing information systems. It allows the transfer of documents to all information systems. It also allows trade with companies that have implemented EDI, as well as those that have not. It enables better interaction between organisations, enhances responsiveness, streamlines business processes, increases productivity, and improves competitiveness. Internet EDI has become more reliable and is quite inexpensive. It can help in reaching new customers, suppliers, markets, and can speed messaging, and movement into global electronic commerce. Using EDI over the Net has become easier due to the advent of a variety of applications (e.g. Netscape's CommerceXpert). In addition, several VANs are offering EDI over the Internet on a limited scale, with plans to provide on a larger scale.

Training should be provided to supplier's employees in order to use the GEC process model. The enterprise should get its Internet connection from a cost-efficient reliable Internet service provider, who provides professional helpdesk service for long hours, keeps the network systems working smoothly 24 hours per day, and is able to solve problems very quickly and flexibly.

SELECTING ENTRY MODE

In conventional international marketing practice, SMEs start exporting through domestic middlemen, foreign representatives or directly to customers. All of these methods are very time consuming and slow; prices of the products increase due to high marketing expenses and the middlemen's commission. In addition, it is very difficult to get enough information regarding customers, competitors and markets. Through WWW, SMEs can offer their products and/or services directly to buyers. They can also collect important information about customers. WWW diminishes the importance of middlemen, decreases marketing expenses and facilitates GEC. As a result, customers get lower-priced products and/or services and SMEs make higher profits.

COLLABORATING WITH GLOBAL PARTNERS

GEC is a series of collaborative processes. It requires collaboration among the enterprise's employees, suppliers, partners, customers and others. They must work synergistically in order to achieve their goals in the turbulent global environment. Web-based Groupware enables SMEs to establish worldwide Groupware environments and collaborate effectively with all their partners around the world. Web based Groupware is inexpensive, more quickly developed and more easily managed than other systems.

Various video conferencing systems provide video conferencing facility over the Internet on a worldwide basis. It allows the sharing of ideas among people across nations or continents. This offers enterprises the capacity to demonstrate products and services to overseas customers and press. It can be used for sales negotiations, problem-solving, business and project meetings, executive and corporate communication, expert consultation and so on. Video conferencing can save time and the expenses of overseas travelling. It should be noted that the quality of video conferencing over the Internet is not yet ideal due to limited bandwidth, but this problem will disappear when more appropriate CITs will be developed.

PREPARING THE WEB FOR GLOBAL BUSINESS

An SME can simultaneously reach people around the world at minimum costs through its multilingual Web pages. Customers from important markets such as Germany, Japan, France, China and Brazil are more willing to visit Web sites in their own language and get information in their local language (Nahar and Savolainen, 1998). The language content and visual component(s) should be developed with consideration of the cultures of the target markets. Automatic translator software can translate the inquiries into English, and a quick reply can be given. The automatic translation is less thorough than a translation by a professional translator, but nonetheless it can serve the purpose. Companies (e.g. Cisco Systems Inc., Dell Computers, Michael Richter Ltd.) are maintaining multilingual Web sites. The detailed Web page(s) can be in English with information about the enterprise, the people, products, risk-free buying, order form and different options of ordering, feedback form, the e-mail and postal address, telephone and fax numbers of the enterprise. The information should be accurate and comprehensive and the site must be kept current. The site must be quick to download, information should be easy to locate and the site may include databased search features. The Web site hosting service provider should possess advanced Internet technology and capabilities and should provide highly effective and efficient customer support. The Web page information should be integrated into the marketing strategy and overall business strategy of the enterprise.

PRODUCING UNIQUE PRODUCTS AND/OR SERVICES

Relational databases can be connected to an enterprise's Web site. The enterprise can then obtain the capacity to collect customer data. This allows the enterprise to produce unique products or services with the collaboration of suppliers. The enterprise can use the WWW to link its suppliers to the enterprise inventory system, and subsequently link this information to the enterprise's customer ordering process. This results at the enterprise's supply chain where inventory levels are automatically fitted to demand. The enterprise improves customer intelligence, as well as relations with suppliers, avoids problems of excessive or shortage of inventory, eliminates paperwork and increases productivity.

ON-LINE INTERNATIONAL MARKETING COMMUNICATION

There are several effective and low cost CIT tools and network services are available for an SME to communicate with the potential customers around the world and facilitate GEC successfully. One effective on-line marketing communication approach is to combine several of these tools and to use them innovatively and systematically in the on-line international marketing communication process.

1. There are several strategies to attract customers to non-English web pages: (a) registering the site to various local engines and indexes will direct the potential customer (inquirer) to non-English Web pages; (b) exchanging links with local relevant web pages of the industry, topic or concept. This will point people to the SME's web site; and (c) press releases of important issues or great incidents to local media can increase the interest among prospective customers and so encourage their visits to the web pages.

2. Sponsoring popular e-zines and digests, posting to trade mailing lists and posting buy/sell offers to trade sites of WWW, expose the

enterprise's offer to buyers all over the world. Publishing articles in e-zines will make the enterprise known as a specialist.

3. The inclusion of a signature file with posting to mailing list and newsgroups or to articles can draw attention to enterprise Web site and autoresponders.

4. Autoresponders can be utilised to respond 24 hours per day to inquiries with information in the languages of targeted countries. They are very useful and inexpensive.

5. Teleconferencing and video conferencing over the Internet are useful for making sales negotiations, for post sales communications, etc.

More detailed discussions of on-line international promotion can be found in (Nahar, 1998d and Nahar *et al.*, 1998).

ORGANISATIONAL SUPPORTS TO GLOBAL OPERATIONS

Organisations should achieve the capability to develop GEC strategies and be flexible enough to effectively and efficiently serve foreign markets and operations. Management must assign appropriate responsibility to appropriate persons, as the foreign markets typically require a number of distinct operational activities. GEC-trained and internationally experienced persons are required for documentation, international payment and international shipment. The organisational structure should be adapted at the various stages of globalisation. The SMEs can establish networked organisations (i.e. CIT-enabled geographically distributed organisation) and utilise international business-trained and internationally experienced teleworkers at a low cost.

HANDLING OF PAYMENT

The enterprise should use such payment mechanisms which are familiar in the target country (e.g. in the US credit card payments are quite normal, but this is not the case in Germany). The customer can provide credit card numbers by e-mail through a secure form on the supplying firm's web site. Credit cards are not suitable for the payment of large sums of money. Thomas Cook (http://www.thomascook.com) offers a customised on-line transfer procedure for an international transaction. The enterprise has also other options for international payment arrangements, such as wire transfer, CAD (cash against documents) or L/C (letter of credit). L/C may not suitable for the payment of services and digital products.

HANDLING OF DELIVERY

The products can be delivered to a foreign location by ship, air or multi-modal methods. If the enterprise sends goods by ship or multi-modal methods it can arrange reservations through the Web (e.g. Msas, (http://www.msas.com/). In the case of urgent delivery, it can use an express delivery service through the Web (e.g. FedEx, (http://FedEx.com). It can use Web sites (e.g. Forwarders) (http://forwarders.com) to request a freight quote on its shipment; it can confirm the shipment through the Web and arrange the international shipment. It is also possible to track the shipments via the Web. Software and services do not require shipment arrangements when they are delivered through the Web.

EVALUATING OPERATIONS

The enterprise should monitor the outcome of operations to ensure that the expected results are being achieved. Databases can provide necessary information for monitoring the results. The enterprise should monitor the changes in external environmental factors. Digital agents can constantly scan relevant information, collect and bring them to the mailbox of the enterprise. The enterprise should remain in control of the international marketing situation through the adaptation of its strategies and tactics. It should identify various problems which may occur in international markets as well as their causes and the means to solve them.

ADVANTAGES OF THE GEC PROCESS MODEL

The GEC process model has a large effect on an enterprise's GEC performance. It can provide different benefits to SMEs. The implementation and utilisation of the GEC model by an enterprise (Akisumi Ltd.) has provided the following benefits.

1. The model helps in conceptualising the GEC process in order to identify the action sequence and relationships between actions.
2. Information of a customer's inquiry is transmitted very quickly to the enterprise, partners, and suppliers; they can unitedly develop the solution through collaboration. The above process reduces the duration from customer inquiry until product delivery.
3. The GEC process increases the enterprise's order processing capacity.
4. The customer gets quick and customised service which improves customer pre-and post-sales service.
5. The customer gets cost efficient reliable service which may improve customer relations and satisfaction, and may increase loyalty.
6. The GEC process reduces international marketing and order processing expenses.
7. The GEC process shortens time, which in turn saves money and makes the enterprise cost efficient.
8. Customer knowledge is improved through collaboration with the customers. Through web and other CITs market data are collected which improve market intelligence.
9. The GEC process can help enterprises to win more customers and increase market share and makes them highly cost competitive.
10. The GEC process decreases expenses and increases profits.

By providing the above unique benefits, the GEC process model can create competitive advantages for SMEs. The model can be useful for large enterprises as well.

PROBLEMS AND RISKS REDUCTION

GEC can be complex and risky because of several negative, influential factors. Such factors include: a lack of GEC process model, merchant/customer trust, privacy, network robustness and so on. Even when the best CITs are used, if problems and risks are not identified beforehand, and precautions not taken, these problems and risks can cause high damage to GEC. Therefore, SMEs must take actions to avoid unnecessary jeopardy. Our empirical study identifies several factors creating obstacles to the flourish of GEC. In this chapter, we briefly describe the major factors and suggest some solutions in order to overcome these problems and risks. The problems and risks and their remedies are exhibited in Table 6.2 and Table 6.3.

The enterprise must research problems and risk-related issues at the inception stage of its GEC endeavour. It should identify potential problems and risks and determine the probabilities of occurrence as well as their impact. It must make plans to reduce the problems and risks. Most serious problems and risks should be monitored at least once a week.

RECOMMENDATIONS FOR SUCCESSFUL GEC

The empirical findings show that in order to become successful in GEC and gain competitive advantages in a competitive global environment, SMEs should:

1. Effectively perform international market research and identify market opportunities. SMEs should also do on-going international market research, as the present global business environment has become highly complex, with rapid and unexpected changes occurring often.
2. Focus intensely on customers and their needs, increase customer intelligence, improve customer satisfaction and loyalty. SMEs should develop and effectively utilise databases.
3. Offer value added, cost competitive, culturally compatible, unique products and services.
4. Focus on effective and intensive on-line international marketing communication.
5. Concentrate on developing brand name credibility.
6. Develop a Web site which is user friendly in locating the required information, rich in contents, and culturally friendly.
7. Offer risk free buying with easy ordering and several options for payment.
8. Arrange fast order fulfillment and speedy delivery.
9. Identify problems and risks in the inception stage of the GEC process and make plans to reduce the problems and risks.
10. Use the most productive CITs and upgrade continuously.
11. Adapt strategies and tactics according to changes of environment.

Table 6.2 Problems and remedies for reducing the problems

A Enterprise-related problems	A Remedies for enterprise-related problems
1. GEC is complex for many SMEs due to the lack of an effective GEC process model. SMEs lack the know-how to organise business activities that can be successful in the global electronic business environment.	1. The GEC model prioritises different activities and their processes. An SME can select one or few activities for learning. The enterprise can then check whether it has achieved the desired objectives. If it has not achieved the objectives, the enterprise should restart. When it achieves the objectives, the enterprise can proceed to the next activity. Thus an SME can proceed step by step.
2. SMEs are failing to effectively present and distinguish their Web pages from the existing millions.	2. SMEs can register their Web pages to overseas search engines and indexes. In addition, the use of electronic promotional tools, for example, software agents, mailing lists, electronic magazines and publishing the home page address in traditional media will create awareness of the product and/or service among customers.
3. Merchant/customer trust is difficult to achieve in the electronic environment as there is an absence of eye contact (Clarke, 1997).	3. Employees of SMEs can participate in specialised news groups and mailing lists. They can provide professional advice for the inquiries of others. These employees can add the signature file of the enterprise while posting their e-mail advice. The enterprise should also publish articles in e-zines and e-journals. These will establish the enterprise as an expert of a particular industry in the electronic environment. The enterprise should register itself with various organisations, for example with World Trade Centre, Dun and Bradstreet, etc.
4. The intellectual property protection mechanism is very weak in the electronic environment (Kosiur, 1997; Minoli and Minoli, 1997; OECD, 1997).	4. Putting copyright on digital products and services, patenting digital process, adding a copyright notice to every Web site page, using technology that prevents Web pages from being copied easily, and locking and distributing very valuable material by using Adobe Acrobat (PDF) security features, showing contents or demo version and after receiving payment the whole product will be delivered, recording information related to downloading by using agent software, adding a section to Web sites on how to become an

Table 6.2 Cont.

authorised representative for company products and services, including information on how people can use material legitimately and according to company rules, can improve intellectual property protection in the electronic environment. Through scanning the cyberspace by agent software, companies sometimes can find out where stolen digital materials have been used. Then they take the print out of the materials and the source code. They inform the Internet Service Providers (ISP) about the infringements and contact the Webmaster of the site where the stolen materials have been using. Companies ask the person to be either a company representative, or take a licence of the product or service and remove the material from illegal use. If the Webmaster does not obey, the ISP disconnects his Internet connection, which is very harmful for any Internet user.

5. Lack of electronic commerce skills within the enterprise.

5. SMEs can train themselves to utilise Internet resources. (There are abundant training resources in the Internet). They can get help from experts located in other parts of the world. SMEs can gain access to low cost consulting services of various international marketing organisations through Internet. In addition, they can post their inquires to various mailing lists and get replies within short periods.

6. Technology is changing extremely fast; employees can not keep pace with the speed of change.

6. The enterprise can recruit top talents and arrange continuous training to acquire new technologies, can collaborate with researchers, universities, R&D organisations and companies through CITs, in order to remain technologically competitive.

B Cultural related problems

1. Difficulties in communication due to different languages.

B Remedies for cultural related problems

1. There are bilingual remote workers, translation companies and translation software. These provide several options for SMEs to overcome language barriers.

Table 6.3   Risks and remedies for reducing the risks

A	Customer related risks	A	Remedies for customer related risks
1.	Customer protection law for GEC is not established (OECD, 1997).	1.	While buying over the Internet, customers should check the various aspects (e.g. approval of international standard organisation, reputation of the brand name) of the enterprise.
2.	There is a high chance of misuse of sensitive customer information which can cause damage to privacy (Kosiur, 1997; Minoli, Minoli, 1997; and Soko, 1995).	2.	Customers should provide personal information only to reliable and credible enterprises. Normally these enterprises are very sensitive to their image, they do not want to destroy their image through causing damage to the customer's privacy.
3.	Customers do not have confidence in the safety and soundness of electronic payment systems (Loshin and Murphy, 1995; Minoli, Minoli, 1997; and Soko, 1995).	3.	The enterprise can use software and other security technologies such as SSL, payment systems such as First Virtual and CyberCash, and digital currencies such as eCash and Smart Cards (Loshin and Loshin, 1995) for EC from reliable companies which ensure that the advanced secured electronic transaction technology is being used in protecting the credit card transactions on the Web.
B	**Technical related risks**	**B**	**Remedies for technical related risks**
1.	The Internet may not be fully secure for information storage nor for information transmission (Minoli and Minoli, 1997; Loshin and Murphy, 1995).	1.	For the Internet security, several options are available including address filtering, access lists, firewalls, encryption, emergency disconnection and so on (Vargo and Hunt, 1996).
2.	Computer viruses easily infect the information systems of the enterprise through the Internet.	2.	Installing and continuous upgrading computer virus protection software, instructing employees strictly about the installation of their own private software and keeping back up files can reduce the risk of computer viruses.
3.	The Internet's performance may not be consistent and is not fully reliable (Kosiur, 1997; Vassos, 1996).	3.	Highly professional network service providers can eliminate the majority of reliability problems.
4.	The Internet can not carry a high communication load (Vassos, 1996).	4.	The use of ISDN line, cable modem, satellite technology, and new technologies (Northern Telecom and NORWEB Communications technology) allow data to be transferred over electricity power lines into homes at speeds of over one megabit per second, up to ten times faster than ISDN. Transmission of compressed files can also reduce the problems related to communicating over the Internet.

This list is not exhaustive. Managers should identify the difficulties and problems and their causes in order to rectify the situation. They will then be in the position to propose new solutions.

CONCLUSION

The business environment has become global, intensely competitive, complex and turbulent. Companies are facing competition in their domestic markets. Therefore, the study of competitive advantages of companies through GEC is important. Due to the advancement of CITs in recent days, faster, cheaper and easier to use CITs are available. Considering these factors, it has become important to study how companies can utilise new CITs, manage risks and execute GEC successfully. This study began with a literature review of printed and digitised resources (databases of journals, Internet resources, etc.). In-depth interviews with companies, practitioners and researchers were then conducted.

This study introduces a new GEC methodology, which can systematically guide companies to globalise and facilitate rapid access to foreign markets. The aims of this study have been to develop a GEC process model, and frameworks for problem and risk reduction. First, a conceptual model of the GEC process was conceived and developed. The GEC process model consists of 12 inter-linked and overlapping activities or phases. The chronological order and number of activities may vary in some cases. Secondly, problem and risk reduction frameworks were developed through identifying potential problems and risks that can create negative impacts on GEC. Solutions for reducing the problems and risks are suggested. The GEC process model has been tested in practice. The test(s) proved that the process model offers the following unique advantages. By utilising the model and frameworks, companies can identify these problem and risk factors and plan effectively for managing them. GEC can be executed in a controlled way, which avoids problems and risks. The model provides other benefits such as shortened time between customer inquiry and product delivery. The model facilitates worldwide collaboration; increases cost efficiency, improves market intelligence, improves pre- and post-sales service, increases customer satisfaction, increases customer loyalty, increases market share, reduces problems and risks, and creates a competitive advantage. The GEC process model is, therefore, effective and efficient.

Some implications can be offered to governments. Governments are providing conventional export training to companies in an effort to start and/or increase exports, a time consuming, complex and costly operation. Governments can train companies to utilise the GEC model and frameworks as an alternative to conventional export training. The research delivers a GEC process model, which can be used as a basis for further research in the field of GEC. Future empirical and conceptual research will be helpful in further refining the model. GEC has the ability to uncover new and critically important areas of research, as it offers numerous benefits and utilises global computer networking.

In-depth research is necessary, however, to discover how more advanced CITs could improve the following:

- Global market intelligence
- Collaboration among global partners
- GEC project management in global environment

References

BAKER, H.R. (1997) *EXTRANETS: Complete Guide to Business to Business Electronic Commerce*, New York: McGraw-Hill.

CLARKE, R. (1997) 'Promises and threats in electronic commerce', <http://www.anu.edu.au/people/Roger.Clarke/EC/Quantum.html>.

HAMILL, J. and GREGORY, K. (1997) 'Internet marketing in the internationalization of UK SMEs', *Journal of Marketing Management*, 13, 9–28.

HILLS, M. (1997) *Intranet Business Strategies*, New York: John Wiley.

HOFFMAN, D.L. and THOMAS, P.N. (1996) 'Marketing in hypermedia computer-mediated environments: conceptual foundations', *Journal of Marketing*, 60, 50–68.

KANNAN, P.K., CHANG, A.M. and WHINSTON, A.B. (1998) 'Marketing information on the I-ways', *Communications of the ACM*, 41, 35–43.

KOSIUR, D. (1997) *Understanding Electronic Commerce*, Washington, DC: Microsoft Press.

LOSHIN, P. and MURPHY, P. (1995) *Electronic Commerce: On-line Ordering and Digital Money*, Charles River Media, Massachusetts.

MINOLI, D. and MINOLI, E. (1997) 'Web Commerce Handbook', *McGraw-Hill Series on Computer Communication, Computing*, New York: McGraw-Hill.

NAHAR, N. and SAVOLAINEN, V. (1997) 'Information and communication technologies for global productivity increase', *Proceedings of the 19th Information Systems' Architecture and Technology (ISAT '97)*, October, Wroclaw, 220–30.

NAHAR, N. (1998a) 'Globalization of small and medium-sized enterprises through the management of IT-enabled technology transfer projects', *Proceedings of the 14th World Congress on Project Management*, 2, June, Ljubljana, 583–91.

NAHAR, N. (1998b) 'IT-enabled effective and efficient international technology transfer for SMEs', *Proceedings of the Evolution and Challenges in System Development*, September, Bled, 85–98.

NAHAR, N. (1998c) 'Risks assessment of IT-enabled international technology transfer: case of globalization of SMEs', *Proceedings of the Fifth World Conference on Human Choice and Computers on Computers and Networks in the Age of Globalization*, August, Geneva, 407–18.

NAHAR, N. (1998d) 'IT-enabled international promotion of technology transfer for high-tech enterprises', *Proceedings of the UIC/AMA Research Symposium on Marketing and Entrepreneurship*, August Boston.

NAHAR, N., HUDA, N. and TEPANDI, J. (1998) 'Globalization of enterprises through electronic promotion', *Proceedings of the Global–Local Interplay in the Baltic Sea Region Conference*, October, Pärnu. 1–10.

OECD (1997) *Electronic Commerce, Opportunities and Challenges for Government*, Parss: OECD.

PALVIA, P. (1997) 'Developing a model of the global and strategic impact of information technology', *Information and Management Journal*, 32(5), 229–44.

QUELCH, J.A. and KLEIN, L.R. (1996) 'The Internet and international marketing', *Sloan Management Review*, 38, 60–75.

SOKO, P.K. (1995) *From EDI to Electronic Commerce: A Business Initiative*, New York: McGraw-Hill.

TERSINE, R. and HARVEY, M. (1998) 'Global customization of markets has arrived!', *European Management Journal*, 16(1), 79–90.

VARGO, J. and HUNT, R. (1996) *Telecommunications in Business: Strategy and Application*, Chicago: Irwin.

VASSOS, T. (1996) *Strategic Internet Marketing*, Indiana: Macmillan Computer Publishing.

7 Content Characteristics of Formal IT Strategy as Implementation Predictors

Petter Gottschalk

INTRODUCTION

The need for improved implementation of IT strategy has been emphasised in both empirical and prescriptive research studies. In this study, 10 content characteristics of formal IT plans were identified from the research literature as potential implementation predictors. A survey was conducted in Norway to investigate the link between plan and implementation. The analysis of 190 surveyed companies with strategic IT plans revealed a significant relationship between content characteristics of the plan and the extent of plan implementation. Two implementation predictors proved significant in the testing of hypotheses: description of responsibility for the implementation and description of user involvement during the implementation.

The need for improved implementation of IT strategy has been emphasised in both empirical (Lederer and Seith, 1988, 1992; Earl, 1993; Lederer and Mendelow, 1993; Premkumar and King, 1994) and prescriptive studies (Galliers, 1994; Lederer and Salmela, 1996; Lederer and Seith, 1996). These studies show that implementation is important for four reasons. Firstly, the failure to carry out the strategic IT plan can cause lost opportunities, duplicated efforts, incompatible systems, and wasted resources (Lederer and Salmela, 1996). Secondly, the extent to which strategic IT planning meets its objectives is determined by implementation (Earl, 1993; Lederer and Seith, 1996). Further, the lack of implementation leaves firms dissatisfied with and reluctant to continue their strategic IT planning (Lederer and Seith, 1988, 1992; Premkumar and King, 1994; Galliers, 1994). Finally, the lack of implementation creates problems establishing and maintaining priorities in future strategic IT planning (Lederer and Mendelow, 1993).

Lederer and Salmela (1996) have developed a theory of SISP which contributes to helping researchers study SISP and present their findings in an organised and meaningful manner. This chapter adds to the body of empirical implementation research by evaluating the plan implementation link suggested by Lederer and Salmela (1996). The research question is presented in the next section, followed by the literature review, research model and research method. Finally, research results are provided and key study findings are discussed.

RESEARCH QUESTION

The theory developed by Lederer and Salmela (1996) consists of an input-process-output model, seven constructs, six causal relationships and six hypotheses. The input–process–output model provides the initial bases for the theory. The seven constructs are (i) the external environment, (ii) the internal environment, (iii) planning resources, (iv) the planning process, (v) the strategic information systems plan, (vi) the implementation of the strategic information systems plan, and (vii) the alignment of the strategic information systems plan with the organisation's business plan. The seven constructs exhibit causal relationships among each other demonstrated by hypotheses. For this research on the implementation of strategic IT plans, the most important relationship in the theory is the effect of the plan on its implementation.

The plan implementation link inspired the following research question: 'What content characteristics of formal IT strategy predict the extent of plan implementation?'. IT strategy is defined as a plan comprised of projects for application of information technology to assist an organisation in realising its goals. The plan also comprises a gestalt view representing philosophy, attitudes, intentions, and ambitions associated with future IT use in the organisation. The term plan refers to a written document following Mintzberg's (1994) suggestion that when the word planning is used, the understanding should be that of formal planning. In this research, terms such as strategic information systems plan (Lederer and Seith, 1996) and information technology strategy (Galliers, 1993) are treated as synonymous. Two observations formed the basis for the specific research question:

1. Organisations engage in strategic IT planning. Kearney (1990), Galliers (1994) and Finnegan *et al.* (1997) found that 75 per cent, 76 per cent and 80 per cent respectively of those surveyed had a strategic IT plan. However, as discussed later in this chapter, the survey in this research was conducted in Norway where the organisations are smaller than those in previous studies, leading to a potential expectation that there would be a lower percentage of organisations with a formal IT strategy. Similarly, an Australian survey found the proportion claiming to undertake strategic IT planning ranged from 58 per cent in large organisations to 29 per cent in medium-sized organisations and 19 per cent in small organisations (Falconer and Hodgett, 1997).

2. Strategic IT plans are not implemented very extensively. Lederer and Sethi (1988) found that only 24 per cent of the projects in the strategic IT plans surveyed had been initiated more than two years into the implementation horizon. In a study of four Norwegian organisations, approximately 42 per cent of the projects in the formal IT strategy had been implemented after five years (Gottschalk, 1995). Ward and Griffiths (1996, p. 97) found that 'despite a belief in its importance, in the past decade many organisations have developed perfectly sound IS strategies that have been left to gather dust, or have been implemented in a half-hearted manner'. Taylor (1997, p. 336), too, found that 'all too often strategies remain "on the page" and are not implemented'.

Content characteristics of formal IT strategy as implementation predictors is an important research topic for two main reasons. First, there is a lack of empirical research, and where it exists, implementation is included as only one of several issues (Lederer and Salmela, 1996; Lederer and Sethi, 1996). Secondly, the strategic IT plan is one of the main concerns of IS/IT managers today (Watson *et al.*, 1997). In a survey conducted by Stephens *et al.* (1995), 80 per cent of the chief information officers (CIOs) reported that they had responsibility for IT strategy. The documentation process is, however, challenging for CIOs both because it is a time consuming effort to write the IT strategy (Gottschalk, 1995), and because the plan contents chosen by the CIO may influence the extent of plan implementation (Lederer and Salmela, 1996). Despite the existence of literature suggesting that a formal IT strategy is neither a true template of an organisation's

IT strategy process nor a reflection of its IT actions (e.g. Mintzberg, 1994), many organisations seem to concentrate on and struggle with their formal IT strategy implementation (Lederer and Seith, 1996). Their struggle is the concern of this chapter.

RESEARCH LITERATURE ON IMPLEMENTATION PREDICTORS

Though there exists an extensive range of literature on strategic information technology planning (e.g. Lederer and Mendelow, 1993; Raghunathan and Raghunathan, 1994) and on IT implementation (e.g. Alavi and Joachimsthaier, 1992; Gill, 1996), specific literature on plan implementation has been relatively sparse. While the literature on strategic information technology planning treats implementation only as one of many phases, the literature on information technology implementation lacks the Gestalt perspective which is needed when plan implementation is to be studied. Furthermore, much of the reviewed research literature consists mainly of theory (e.g. Joshi, 1991), often lacking empirical evidence. For the testing of the plan implementation link in the theory of strategic information systems planning suggested by Lederer and Salmela (1996), it was nevertheless possible to identify existing literature as listed in Table 7.1. The thirty-five organisational practices derived from the six research studies analysed constitute a comprehensive list of practices for the implementation of IT strategy.

In this research, the 35 organisational practices were reduced to a set of ten predictors (Gottschalk, 1998) as listed in Table 7.2.

The term implementation is given a variety of meanings in the literature (Montealegre, 1994). Nutt (1986) defines implementation as a procedure directed by a manager to install planned change in an organisation, whereas Klein and Sorra (1996) sees it as the process of gaining targeted organisational members' appropriate and committed use of an innovation. In Table 7.3, the reviewed research literature on implementation is listed according to their particular definition of implementation. The first references in Table 7.3 represent definitions where implementation is completed at an early stage, while those that follow represent definitions where implementation is completed at a later stage. The numbers may, therefore, represent a scale of stages at which authors place their definition of implementation. Some authors

Table 7.1   Organisational practices influencing IT strategy implementation

---

Earl (1993): Implementation Problems
E1	Resources were not made available
E2	Management was hesitant
E3	Technological constraints arose
E4	Organisational resistance emerged

Galliers (1994): Implementation Barriers
G1	Difficulty of recruiting
G2	Nature of business
G3	Measuring benefits
G4	User education resources
G5	Existing IT investments
G6	Political conflicts
G7	Middle management attitudes
G8	Senior management attitudes
G9	Telecommunications issues
G10	Technology lagging behind needs
G11	Doubts about benefits

Lederer and Salmela (1996): Effect of Plan on Implementation
S1	Contents of the plan
S2	Relevance of proposed projects in the plan to organisational goals
S3	Sections of the plan
S4	Clarity and analysis of presentation of the plan

Lederer and Seith (1992): Implementation Problems
L1	Difficult to secure top management commitment
L2	Final planning output documentation not very useful
L3	Planning methodology fails to consider implementation
L4	Implementing the projects requires more analysis
L5	Planning methodology requires too much top management involvement
L6	Output of planning is not in accordance with management expectations

Seith (1996): Prescriptions for SISP
X1	Prepare migration plan
X2	Identify actions to adopt plan
X3	Identify resources for new tools
X4	Avoid/dampen resistance
X5	Specify actions for architecture
X6	Identify bases of resistance

Premkumar and King (1994): Implementation Mechanisms
P1	Monitoring system to review implementation and provide feedback
P2	Resource mobilisation for implementation
P3	User involvement in implementation
P4	Top management monitoring of implementation

Table 7.2   Implementation predictors derived from organisational practices

Practices		Predictors	Measurement
E1	Resources were not made available	Resources	Multiple item scale by Lee (1995)
G1	Difficulty of recruiting		
P2	Resource mobilisation for implementation		
X3	Identify resources for new tools		
G4	User education resources	Users	Multiple item scale by Chan (1992)
P3	User involvement in implementation		
G5	Existing IT investments	Analysis	Multiple item scale by Segars (1994)
L3	Planning methodology fails to consider implementation		
L4	Implementing the projects requires more analysis		
X5	Specify actions for architecture		
Teo (1994), Salmela (1996)		Environment	Multiple item scale by Segars (1994)
E4	Organisational resistance emerged	Resistance	Multiple item scale by Lee (1995)
G6	Political conflicts		
X4	Avoid/dampen resistance		
X6	Identify bases of resistance		
E3	Technological constraints arose	Technology	Lederer and Seith, 1992; Items from Teo, 1994; Byrd et al., 1995; Salmela, 1996
G9	Telecommuncations issues		
G10	Technology lagging behind needs		
G2	Nature of business	Relevance	Lederer and Seith, 1992; Teo, 1994; Segars, 1994; Chan and Huff, 1994; Hann and Weber, 1996
G3	Measuring benefits		
G11	Doubts about benefits		
S2	Relevance of proposed projects in the plan to organisational goals		
L6	Output of planning is not in accordance with management expectations		

Table 7.2   Continued

Practices		Predictors	Measurement
P1	Monitoring system to review implementation and provide feedback	Responsibiliy	Gottschalk, 1995; Olsen, 1995; Ward et al., 1996
X1	Prepare migration plan		
X2	Identify actions to adopt plan		
E2	Management was hesitant	Manage	Jarvenpaa and Ives, 1991; Segars, 1994; Premkumar and King, 1994; Lee, 1995
G7	Middle management attitudes		
G8	Senior management attitudes		
L1	Difficult to secure top management commitment		
L5	Planning methodology requires too much top management involvement		
P4	Top management monitoring of implementation		
S1	Contents of the plan	Presentation	Lederer and Salmela, 1996; Hussey, 1996
S3	Sections of the plan		
S4	Clarity and analysis of presentation of the plan		
L2	Final planning output documentation not very useful		

find implementation to be completed when change is occurring, while others find it continues until intended benefits have been realised.

The purpose for using the stages in Table 7.3 is not to defend a certain rank order of the authors along the axis of implementation completion, but rather to indicate that the authors have different opinions about when implementation is considered completed. The dimensions of IT strategy implementation may be summarised as illustrated in Table 7.4. The purpose of Table 7.4 is to develop alternative measures of IT strategy implementation.

In Table 7.4, there are two dimensions of IT strategy implementation: the time dimension and the level detail dimension. The time dimension is the implementation stage derived from Table 7.3, where

Table 7.3   Stages of Implementation Completion

Stage	Implementation completed when:	Reference
1	System is installed	Lucas (1981)
2	System is put to use	Brancheau *et al.* (1989)
3	Programs are adopted	Baier *et al.* (1986)
4	Organisation acts on new priorities	Floyd and Wooldridge (1992)
5	Changes are installed	Nutt (1986, 1995)
6	Not abandoned or expensively overhauled	Markus (1983)
7	Adoption has occurred	Lucas, Walton and Ginzberg (1988)
8	Innovation is adopted and used	Leonard-Barton and Deschamps (1988)
9	Systems are installed and used	Srinivasan and Davis (1987)
10	Change is accepted	Baronas and Louis (1988)
11	Systems are accepted	Ginzberg (1981)
12	Innovation is accepted and used	Alavi and Henderson (1981)
13	Systems are accepted and used	Bradley and Hauser (1995)
14	Control rests with users	Alter and Ginzberg (1978)
15	Change process completed	Joshi (1991)
16	Committed use occurs	Klein and Sorra (1996)
17	Post-application phase is consolidated	Rhodes and Wield (1985)
18	Satisfaction with system is achieved	Griffith and Northcraft (1996)
19	Intended benefits are realised	Alavi and Joachimsthaier (1992)

Table 7.4   Dimensions of IT Strategy Implementation

Time Level	Installed (Earl, 1993)	Completed (Lederer and Salmela, 1996)	Benefits (Premkumar and King, 1994)
Plan		3	4
Project	2	1	
System			

the two extreme stages of implemented are 'installed' and 'benefits', while the middle stage is 'completed'. Benefits may be considered as the effect of the changes; that is, the difference between the current and proposed way work is done (Ward *et al.*, 1996). The detail dimension refers to the implementation content which may be the whole plan, one or more projects in the plan, or one or more systems in one project. Implementation content thus refers to a plan consisting of one or several projects (Falconer and Hodgett, 1997), and a project consisting of one or several systems. The term project is defined as the means by which the organisation's technological, organisational, and external assets are mobilised and transformed (Williams, 1992, p. 36): 'Projects, or initiatives as termed in this study, then, are the vehicles through which an organization's competitive and technology strategies are operationalized into organizational outputs'. For, according to Gupta and Raghunathan (1989, p. 786), 'the ultimate success of systems planning depends on the success of the individual projects covered by the plan'. Both the time dimension and the detail dimension may certainly be challenged. The detail dimension, for example, may in an organisation be such that a large system is broken down into several projects, and a project may itself consist of several phases or stages. The main purpose of Table 7.4, however, is to develop a definition and measures of implementation suitable for this research. As such, IT strategy implementation is here defined as the process of completing the projects for application of information technology to assist an organisation in realising its goals. As such, the column 'completed' is essential for this research.

Implementation is measured in four different ways in this research based on the two dimensions of time and detail discussed above. The first plan implementation measurement (1 in Table 7.4) is concerned with completion of projects in the plan which were to be completed to date. The second plan implementation measurement (2 in Table 7.4) is concerned with completion of projects in the plan which are expected to be completed, or at least installed, by the end of the implementation horizon. The third implementation measurement (3) measures completion of the whole plan in a gestalt perspective, while the fourth IT strategy implementation measurement (4) is concerned with improved organisational performance from plan implementation. According to Ward and Griffiths (1996, p. 102), the impact of an IT strategy implementation is not instantaneous; 'it may, in fact take some time, two or more years, between embarking on strategic IS/IT planning for the first time and demonstrating any consequent impact on business practices and results'. The operationalisation of these alternative implementation constructs is listed in Table 7.5.

Ten predictor constructs were listed in Table 7.2, while four alternative implementation constructs were listed in Table 7.5. To

Table 7.5   Four Potential Implementation Constructs

Construct	Measurement of construct
1 Implementation rate to date (Lederer and Seith, 1988)	Divide projects actually implemented to date by projects scheduled to be implemented to date
2 Implementation rate to end (Lederer and Seith, 1988)	Divide projects actually implemented to date by projects in the IT strategy and divide by per cent of expired time horizon
3 Implementation extent (Coolbaugh, 1993; Ginzberg, 1981; Salmela, 1996; Ward *et al.*, 1996; Williams, 1992)	*IT strategy has been implemented as planned* IT strategy implementation has been completed on time IT strategy implementation has been completed within budget IT strategy implementation has been completed as expected IT strategy implementation has achieved the desired results Deviations from the IT strategy have occurred during implementation You are satisfied with the IT strategy implementation
4 Contribution to organisational performance (Scale adopted from Teo, 1994, p. 121, Alpha = 0.87; one item added from Segars, 1994, p. 154)	*Contribute to improved organisational performance* Contribute to increased Return on Investment (ROI) Contribute to increased market share of products/services Contribute to improved internal efficiency of operations Contribute to increased annual sales revenue Contribute to increased customer satisfaction Contribute to alignment of IT with business needs

organise the research according to the theory of Lederer and Salmela (1996), a causal relationship between predictor constructs and implementation constructs is proposed in the research model as illustrated in Figure 7.1. For each of the ten predictors, one hypothesis was formulated stating that the greater the extent of description of the content characteristic, the greater the extent of plan implementation.

Information Plan (IP):		Plan Implementation
Resources needed for the implementation		**(PI):**
User involvement during the implementation		Implementation rate to
Analysis of the organisation		date
Anticipated changes in the external		Implementation rate to
environment		end
Solutions to potential resistance during the		Implementation extent
implementation		Contribution to
Information technology to be implemented		performance
Project's relevance to the business plan		
Responsibility for the implementation		
Management support for the implementation		
Presentation of implementation issues		

Figure 7.1   Research results

RESEARCH RESULTS

Data was collected through a survey. The CIO or person with CIO responsibilities was chosen as the informant for each organisation, following prior research such as Earl (1993), Stephens *et al.* (1995), Sabherwal and King (1995), and Teo and King (1997). Of 1108 mailed questionnaires, 471 (43 per cent) were returned. 190 subjects (40 per cent) confirmed that they had a written IT strategy and provided information on its content characteristics. Ten content characteristics of formal information technology strategy were measured in the questionnaire through 62 items as listed in Table 7.6.

The Cronbach alpha for all multiple item scales were between 0.73 and 0.93 as listed in table 6. Alphas greater than 0.70 are considered evidence of reliability (Bagozzi, 1996).

Alternative implementation constructs were developed in Table 7.5. The implementation extent scale was the most suitable measure for IT strategy implementation based on decision criteria such as statistical, methodological and theoretical considerations including the gestalt perspective. On a scale from 1 (very little extent) to 5 (very great extent), the CIOs reported an average implementation extent of 3.3.

The hypothesis testing was carried out using multiple regression analysis (Hair *et al.*, 1998). All observations with missing values were excluded, reducing the sample from 190 to 151 valid cases. Table 7.7 lists the results of multiple regression analysis between the 10 independent variables and the dependent variable implementation.

The full multiple regression equation with all ten independent variables explains 19 per cent of the variation in implementation,

Table 7.6   Items for Measurement of Implementation Predictor Constructs

Construct	Measurement of construct	Alpha
Resources needed for the implementation Lee (1995), alpha = 0.68	Financial resources needed for implementation Technical abilities needed for implementation Human resources needed for implementation Project team time needed for implementation External consultants needed for implementation (new) A 'project champion' needed for the implementation (new)	0.87
User involvement during implementation Chan (1992), alpha = 0.82	Degree of systems-related training received by information systems users Users' understanding of systems' functional and technical features Users' participation in systems projects Users' involvement in the operation of information systems Participation in the ongoing development of information systems Users' support for the implementation (new)	0.86
Analyses of the organisation Segars (1994), alpha = 0.86	Information needs of organisational sub-units How the organisation actually operates A 'blueprint' which structures organisational processes Changing organisational procedures New ideas to reengineer business processes through IT Dispersion of data and applications throughout the firm Organisation of the IT function (new)	0.87
Anticipated changes in the external environment Segars (1994), alpha = 0.82	Anticipated changes in competitors' behaviour Anticipated changes in suppliers' behaviour Anticipated changes in customers' behaviour Anticipated changes in information technology Anticipated changes in government regulations (new) Anticipated changes in the economy (new)	0.83
Solutions to potential resistance during the implementation Lee (1995), alpha = 0.64	Solutions to resistance caused by job security Solutions to resistance caused by change in position Solutions to potential resistance caused by new skills requirements Solutions to potential resistance caused by scepticism of results Solutions to potential resistance caused by a unit's interests Solutions to potential resistance caused by our customers	0.93

Table 7.6   Continued

Construct	Measurement of construct	Alpha
IT to be implemented New scale	Hardware to be implemented Communications technology to be implemented Databases to be implemented Applications software to be implemented Operating systems to be implemented A data architecture for the organisation	0.89
Projects' relevance to the business plan New scale	Projects in accordance with the expectations of management Organisational goals for the projects Benefits of the projects to the organisation Projects that contribute to new business opportunities Competitive advantage from IT Strategic applications of IT	0.88
Responsibility for the implementation New scale	Responsibility for the implementation on time Responsibility for the implementation within budget Responsibility for the implementation with intended benefits Responsibility for the stepwise implementation of large projects Responsibility for the implementation of high priority projects Responsibility for short-term benefits from initial projects Personnel rewards from successful implementation	0.91
Management support for the implementation New scale	Management expectations of the implementation Management participation in the implementation Management monitoring of the implementation Management knowledge about the implementation Management time needed for the implementation Management enthusiasm for the implementation	0.93
Clear presentation of implementation issues New scale	Evaluation of progress clearly Change management clearly A list of projects clearly A schedule for the implementation clearly Alignment of IT strategy with business strategy clearly	0.83

Table 7.7   Multiple Regression Analysis between Implementation and
Predictors

Content characteristics as implementation predictors	Full regression Beta	Full regression t-test	Stepwise regression Beta	Stepwise regression t-test
Resources	0.078	0.766		
Users	0.158	1.665	0.233	2.892**
Analyses	0.019	0.170		
Changes	0.138	1.407		
Resistance	−0.065	−0.628		
IT	0.015	0.173		
Relevance	0.048	0.449		
Responsibility	0.189	1.672	0.298	3.692**
Management	−0.071	−0.599		
Issues	0.145	1.408		

Note: The statistical significance of the t-values is for $p < 0.01$ and for $p < 0.05$.

that is, the adjusted R-square is 0.19. The F-value of 4.505 is significant at $p < 0.001$, indicating that the null hypothesis is rejected and that there is a significant relationship between content characteristics and IT strategy implementation. However, none of the content characteristics was individually significant implementation predictors. When stepwise regression (Hair et al., 1998) was applied, two of the 10 predictors have significant coefficients in the multiple regression equation. Firstly, the description of responsibility for the implementation was associated with the highest explanatory power since it achieved the highest Beta coefficient. Next, the description of user involvement during the implementation proved to be the other significant predictor. The adjusted R-square of the stepwise model is 0.19. None of the remaining eight potential predictors is significant.

Responsibility was the first hypothesis to be supported in this research: the greater the extent of description of responsibility for the implementation, the greater the extent of plan implementation (H8). Implementation participants must accept responsibility as a positive duty (Swanson, 1995), and tasks should be assigned to specific individuals (Bajjaly, 1998). Responsibility was measured by responsibility for implementation on time (Kaplan and Norton, 1996), responsibility for implementation within budget (Flynn and Goleniewska, 1993), responsibility for implementation with intended benefits (Ward *et al.*, 1996), responsibility for stepwise implementation of large projects (Kaplan and Norton, 1996), responsibility for implementation of high priority projects (Gottschalk, 1995), responsibility for short-term benefits from initial projects (Nutt, 1995), and personnel rewards from successful implementation (Argyris and Kaplan, 1994).

User involvement was the second hypothesis to be supported in this research: the greater the extent of description of user involvement during the implementation, the greater the extent of plan implementation (H2). User involvement during the implementation is the engagement of people who will employ the technology and the systems after the implementation. User involvement was measured by a multiple item scale adopted from Chan (1992).

DISCUSSION

This empirical research confirms the plan implementation link suggested by Lederer and Salmela (1996) in their theory of SISP. The total set of content characteristics of the plan has a significant impact on the extent of plan implementation, in other words, when it comes to implementing strategic IT plans, all factors are necessary and none is sufficient. With this in mind, however, description of responsibility for the implementation and description of user involvement during the implementation were the two specific content characteristics of formal IT strategy of particular significance as implementation predictors.

The most surprising result of this study, both from a theoretical and practical perspective, is the relative lack of importance of management support. All the leading research studies on which this research is based (Lederer and Seith, 1992; Earl, 1993; Galliers, 1994; Premkumar and King, 1994; Lederer and Salmela, 1996) as well as all the general business literature (e.g. Applegate *et al.*, 1996), seem to share a strong belief in the importance of management support for the implementation of IT strategy. It is interesting that management support, as reflected in management expectations, participation, monitoring, knowledge, time and enthusiasm, is of no significant importance in this study. Several explanations, however, may be offered. Firstly, there is the distinction between planning and implementing to be considered. Some argue that management is primarily involved in strategy-making, not in plan implementation (Mintzberg, 1994). Secondly, as long as responsibility for the implementation is defined, management support becomes less important (Gottschalk, 1995). Since responsibility is the relatively most important predictor in this research, the latter explanation may well carry weight. Next, the role of management is often to take on responsibility (Applegate *et al.*, 1996), suggesting that management is important through responsibility. Furthermore, the rising top management mobility in recent years in Norway may also represent some explanatory power for the relative non-importance of management support for the IT strategy implementation (Gottschalk, 1995). Finally, the existence of a plan may serve to reduce the importance of management support (Lederer and Salmela, 1996).

The three main suggestions for future research are concerned with weaknesses of the presented research. First, the research model suggested a connection between implementation of an IT strategy and the content of the strategy. Previous research has identified, as Table 7.1 indicates, that much more complicated causal relationships might exist. Secondly, the importance of various implementation predictors may depend on contingency issues such as organisation size, implementation horizon and environmental turbulence (Salmela, 1996). Finally, future research may widen the scope by including both factors and processes in both the planning phase and the implementation phase (Mintzberg, 1994; Van de Ven and Poole, 1995).

An important practical contribution can be derived from the conducted research. In practice, the CIO is often responsible for the IT strategy process, as well as the IT strategy topics and the IT strategy plan (Gottschalk, 1995a; Stephens *et al.*, 1995). When the CIO sits down to produce the formal IT strategy, this research provides clear priority on what to include in the plan document to increase the likelihood of its implementation. Description of responsibility for the implementation is important. Responsibility description should include responsibility for implementation on time, within budget, intended benefits, stepwise implementation of large projects, high priority projects and short-term benefits from initial projects. Description of user involvement during the implementation is the other important factor. User involvement description should include user training, understanding, participation, operation, development and support.

References

ALAVI, M. and HENDERSON, J.C. (1981) 'An evolutionary strategy for implementing a decision support system', *Management Science*, 27(11), 1309–23.

ALAVI, M. and JOACHIMSTHAIER, E.A. (1992) 'Revisiting DSS implementation research: a meta-analysis of the literature and suggestions for researchers', *MIS Quarterly*, 16(1), 95–116.

ALTER, S. and GINZBERG, M. (1978) 'Managing uncertainty in MIS implementation', *Sloan Management Review*, 20(1), 23–31.

APPLEGATE, L.M., MCFARLAN, F.W. and MCKENNEY, J.L. (1996) *Corporate Information Systems Management*, Chicago: Irwin.

ARGYRIS, C. and KAPLAN, R.S. (1994) 'Implementing new knowledge: the case of activity based costing', *Accounting Horizons*, 8(3), 83–105.

BAIER, V.E., MARCH, J.G. and SAETREN, H. (1986) 'Implementation and amibiguity', *Scandinavian Journal of Management Studies*, May, 197–212.

BAJJALY, S.T. (1998) 'Strategic information systems planning in the public sector', *American Review of Public Administration*, 28(1), 75–85.

BAGOZZI, R.P. (1996) 'Measurement in marketing research: basic principles of questionnaire design', in Bagozzi, R.P. (ed.), *Principles of Marketing Research*, Cambridge, MA: Blackwells, 1–49.

BARONAS, A.-M.K. and LOUIS, M.R. (1988) 'Restoring a sense of control during implementation: how user involvement leads to system acceptance', *MIS Quarterly*, 12(1), 111–24.

BOLAND, R.J. and HIRSHCHHEIM, R.A. (eds) (1987) *Critical Issues in Information Systems Research*, Chichester: John Wiley.

BRADLEY, J.H. and HAUSER, R.D. (1995) 'A framework for expert system implementation', *Expert Systems With Applications*, 8(1), 157–67.

BRANCHEAU, J.C., SCHUSTER, L. and MARCH, S.T. (1989) 'Building and implementing an information architecture', *Data Base*, Summer, 9–17.

BYRD, T.A., SAMBAMURTHY, V. and ZMUD, R.W. (1995) 'An examination of IT planning in a large, diversified public organization', *Decision Sciences*, 26(1), 49–73.

CHAN, Y.E. (1992) 'Business strategy, information systems strategy, and strategic fit: measurement and performance impacts', unpublished doctoral dissertation, University of Western Ontario.

CHAN, Y.E. and HUFF, S.L. (1994) 'The development of instruments to assess information systems and business unit strategy performance', in Venkatraman, N. and Henderson, J. (eds), *Research in Strategic Management and Information Technology*, San Francisco: JAI Press, 145–82.

COOLBAUGH, J.D. (1993) 'An analysis of strategic planning in California cities', unpublished doctoral dissertation, University of Laverne.

EARL, M.J. (1993) 'Experiences in strategic information planning', *MIS Quarterly*, 17(1), 1–24.

FALCONER, D.J. and HODGETT, R.A. (1997) 'Strategic information systems planning, an Australian experience', *Proceedings of the Americas Conference on Information Systems*, 15–17 August, Indianapolis, 837–9.

FINNEGAN, P., GALLIERS, R. and POWELL, P. (1997) 'Investigating inter-organisational information systems planning practices in Ireland and the UK', *Proceedings of the 5th European Conference on Information Systems*, June, Cork, 281–94.

FLOYD, S.W. and WOOLDRIDGE, B. (1992) 'Managing strategic consensus: the foundation of effective implementation', *Academy of Management Executive*, 6(4), 27–39.

FLYNN, D.J. and GOLENIEWSKA, E. (1993) 'A survey of the use of SISP approaches in UK organisations', *Journal of Strategic Information Systems*, 2(4), 292–319.

GALLIERS, R.D. (1993) 'IT strategies: beyond competitive advantage', *Journal of Strategic Information Systems*, 2(4), 283–91.

GALLIERS, R.D. (1994) 'Strategic information systems planning: myths, reality and guidelines for successful implementation', in Galliers, R.D. and Baker, B.S.H. (eds), *Strategic Information Management*, Oxford: Butterworth-Heinemann, 129–47.

GILL, T.G. (1996) 'Expert systems usage: task change and intrinsic motivation', *MIS Quarterly*, 20(3), 301–29.

GINZBERG, M.J. (1981) 'Key recurrent issues in the MIS implementation process', *MIS Quarterly*, 5(2), 47–59.

GOTTSCHALK, P. (1995) *Technology Management* (Teknologiledelse), Bergen: Fagbokforlaget Publishingin in Norwegian.

GOTTSCHALK, P. (1998) *Content Characteristics of Formal Information Technology Strategy as Implementation Predictors*, Oslo: Tano Aschehoug Publishing.

GRIFFITHS, T.L. and NORTHCRAFT, G.B. (1996) 'Cognitive elements in the implementation of new technology: can less information provide more benefits?', *MIS Quarterly*, 20(1), 99–110.

GUPTA, Y.P. and RAGHUNATHAN, T.S. (1989) 'Impact of information systems (IS) steering committees on IS planning', *Decision Sciences*, 20(4), 777–93.

HAIR, J.F., ANDERSON, R.E., TATHAM, R.L. and BLACK, W.C. (1998) *Multivariate Data Analysis*, 5th edn, Englewood Cliffs: Prentice-Hall.

HANN, J. and WEBER, R. (1996) 'Information systems planning: a model and empirical tests', *Management Science*, 42(7), 1043–64.

HUSSEY, D.E. (1996) 'A framework for implementation', in Hussey, D.E., *The Implementation Challenge*, Chichester: Wiley, 1–14.

JARVENPAA, S.L. and IVES, B. (1991) 'Executive involvement and participation in the management of information technology', *MIS Quarterly*, 15(2), 205–27.

JOSHI, K. (1991) 'A model of users' perspective on change: the case of information systems technology implementation', *MIS Quarterly*, 15(2), 229–42.

KAPLAN, R.S. and NORTON, D.P. (1996) 'Using the balanced scorecard as a strategic management system', *Harvard Business Review*, January–February, 75–85.

KEARNEY, A.T. (1990), 'Breaking the barriers: IT effectiveness in Great Britain and Ireland', report by A.T. Kearney for The Chartered Institute of Management Accountants, London.

KLEIN, K.J. and SORRA, J.S. (1996) 'The challenge of innovation implementation', *Academy of Management Review*, 21(4), 1055–88.

KWON, T.H. and ZMUD, R.W. (1987) 'Unifying the fragmented models of information systems implementation', in Boland, R.J. and Hirschheim, R.A. (eds), *Critical Issues in Information Systems Research*, Chichester: John Wiley, 227–48.

LEDERER, A.L. and MENDELOW, A.L. (1993) 'Information systems planning and the challenge of shifting priorities', *Information & Management*, 24(6), 319–28.

LEDERER, A.L. and SALMELA, H. (1996) 'Toward a theory of strategic information systems planning', *Journal of Strategic Information Systems*, 5(3), 237–53.

LEDERER, A.L. and SEITH, V. (1988) 'The implementation of strategic information systems planning methodologies', *MIS Quarterly*, 12(3), 445–61.

LEDERER, A.L. and SEITH, V. (1992) 'Root causes of strategic information systems planning implementation problems', *Journal of Management Information Systems*, 9(1), 25–45.

LEDERER, A.L. and SEITH, V. (1996) 'Key prescriptions for strategic information systems planning', *Journal of Management Information Systems*, 13(1), 35–62.

LEE, J. (1995) 'An exploratory study of organizational/managerial factors influencing business process reengineering implementation: an empirical study of critical success factors and resistance management', unpublished doctoral dissertation, University of Nebraska.

LEONARD-BARTON, D. and DESCHAMPS, I. (1988) 'Managerial influence in the implementation of new technology', *Management Science*, 34(10), 1252–65.

LUCAS, H.C. (1981) *Implementation: the Key to Successful Information Systems*, New York: Columbia University Press.

LUCAS, H.C., WALTON, E.J. and GINZBERG, M.J. (1988) 'Implementing packaged software', *MIS Quarterly*, 12(4), 537–49.

MARKUS, M.L. (1983) 'Power, politics and MIS implementation', *Communications of the ACM*, 26(6), 430–44.

MINTZBERG, H. (1994) *The Rise and Fall of Strategic Planning*, Englewood Cliffs: Prentice-Hall.

MONTEALEGRE, R. (1994) 'Management's role in the implementation of information technology in an agroindustrial organization of a less-developed country', unpublished doctoral dissertation, Harvard University.

NUTT, P.C. (1986) 'Tactics of implementation', *Academy of Management Journal*, 29(2), 230–61.

NUTT, P.C. (1995) 'Implementing style and use of implementation approaches', *Omega*, 23(5), 469–84.

OLSEN, R. (1995) 'Rating congruence between various management appraisal sources', unpublished doctoral dissertation, Henley Management College.

PREMKUMAR, G. and KING, W.R. (1994) 'Organizational characteristics and information systems planning: an empirical study', *Information Systems Research*, 5(2), 75–109.

RAGHUNATHAN, B. and RAGHUNATHAN, T.S. (1994) 'Adaption of a planning system success model to information systems planning', *Information Systems Research*, 5(3), 326–41.

RHODES, E. and WIELD, D. (1985) *Implementing New Technologies*, Oxford: Basil Blackwell.

SABHERWAL, R. and KING, W.R. (1995) 'An empirical taxonomy of the decision-making processes concerning strategic applications of information systems', *Journal of Management Information Systems*, 11(4), 177–214.

SALMELA, H. (1996) 'The requirements for information systems planning in a turbulent environment', doctoral dissertation, Turku School of Economics and Business Administration, Turku, Series A-1.

SEGARS, A.H. (1994) 'Strategic information systems planning: the coalignment of planning system design, its relationships with organizational context, and implications for planning system success', unpublished doctoral dissertation, University of South Carolina.

SRINIVASAN, A. and DAVIS, J.G. (1987) 'A reassessment of implementation process models', *Interfaces*, 17(3), 64–71.

STEPHENS, C.S., MITRA, A., FORD, F.N. and LEDBETTER, W.N. (1995) 'The CIO's dilemma: participating in strategic planning', *Information Strategy*, Spring, 13–17.

SWANSON, D.L. (1995) 'Addressing a theoretical problem by reorienting the corporate social performance model', *Academy of Management Review*, 20(1), 43–64.

TAYLOR, B. (1997) 'The return of strategic planning: once more with feeling', *Long Range Planning*, 30(3), 334–44.

TEO, T.S.H. (1994) 'Integration between business planning and information systems planning: evolutionary–contingency perspectives', unpublished doctoral dissertation, University of Pittsburgh.

TEO, T.S.H. and KING, W.R. (1997) 'An assessment of perceptual differences between informants in information systems research', *Omega*, 25(5), 557–66.

VAN DE VEN, A.H. and POOLE, M.S. (1995) 'Explaining development and change in organizations', *Academy of Management Review*, 20(3), 510–40.

VENKATRAMAN, N. and HENDERSON, J. (eds) (1994) *Research in Strategic Management and Information Technology*, J: JAH Press.

WARD, J. and GRIFFITHS, P. (1996) *Strategic Planning for Information Systems*, Chichester: John Wiley.

WARD, J., TAYLOR, P. and BOND, P. (1996) 'Evaluation and realisation of IS/IT benefits: an empirical study of current practice', *European Journal of Information Systems*, 4(4), 214–25.

WATSON, R.T., KELLY, G.G., GALLIERS, R.D. and BRANCHEAU, J.C. (1997) 'Key issues in information systems management: an international perspective', *Journal of Management Information Systems*, 13(4), 91–115.

WILLIAMS, K.L. (1992) 'An investigation of how organizations manage information technology initiatives', unpublished doctoral dissertation, The Florida State University.

ZMUD, R.W. and BOYNTON, A.C. (1991) 'Survey measures and instruments in MIS: inventory and appraisal', in Kraemer, K.L., Cash, J.I. and Nunamaker, J.F., *The Information Systems Research Challenge: Survey Research Methods*, Harvard Business School Research Colloquium, Harvard Business School, Boston, 149–80.

8 Sustainability Analysis for Competitive Intelligence: Success Factors for the New Economy

Gezinus J. Hidding and Jeffrey R. Williams

Most Competitive Intelligence professionals are uncomfortable with recommending strategic actions to senior management. We are comfortable with collecting the information and data, putting it together, and doing some level of analysis. We feel we are not trained to take it further. And yet it is critical. Without the ability to recommend actions based on the competitive environment our companies face, CI professionals will remain in the realm of the information provider. (Faye Brill, Ryder Systems)

THE NEW ECONOMY

Many economies around the world are extending the Industrial Age to include Information Age businesses for which the basis of competition is intellectual assets. For example, financial services, software, entertainment, media, communications, medical services, consulting, education. Thus, in the new economy, Information Age businesses co-exist with those from the Industrial and Agricultural Ages. Consequently, there is more diversity in businesses than ever before: Different products evolve through their life cycles at different speeds. But, how do you know at what speed a given business will evolve? How long will the competitive advantage (once obtained) last? How do you know what the CSF will be? What are the key measures to track over time? No wonder that, in the face of such diversity, recommending actions is getting harder.

Traditional strategy thinking cannot explain the new economy

Traditional strategy thinking does not take into account different speeds of change. It assumes that all products evolve at one and the same ('standard') speed of change. Traditional thinking is still important, but it can lead to dangerous errors when applied to businesses that evolve at different speeds. Traditional interpretations of existing measures can be wrong. For example, traditional thinking assumes that a product's market share is stable and its erosion is bad. However, market shares of many 'high-tech' gadgets, which are fast-moving businesses, generally erode rapidly. This is natural, and makes the 'management of erosion' a sign of success; a line of thinking very different from the traditional method.

Similarly, traditional thinking may disregard important measures for businesses operating at slower speeds. For example, in traditional thinking, standardisation and achievement of cost economies is assumed to be good. However, certain non-standardised, very complex products are very valuable even when their 'lot size' is small (e.g. a one-of-a-kind information technology infrastructure for a large global organisation). To make matters worse, strategy recommendations based on traditional thinking are difficult to put into action. Traditional thinking explores static cross-sectional relations; it takes 'snapshots' of a point in time. In contrast, action plays out over time, it is a 'motion picture'. It requires an analysis of the competitive dynamics over time. Consequently, if you apply traditional thinking to guide action over time, you may be gathering appropriate measures, but interpret them wrong, or you may not be gathering the 'right' measures among the enormous amounts of data CI collects.

STRATEGY CONCEPTUALISATION

Sustainability Analysis is a new method in competitive strategy that, most importantly, incorporates the different effects of time on the creation and erosion of business advantage. Its time-based logic takes obsolescence, the fact that all advantage is eventually lost, as a given and asks how long it will take and by what means value can be maximized. It does this by recasting traditional strategy thinking into 'action–reaction cycles' at the product level. Thus, SA is a competitive strategy conceptualiser (Hidding, 1988): It helps to select an appropriate way of thinking for defining and redefining a range of business problems (Williams, 1997).

As one executive commented, SA provides 'a larger picture'. It turned strategy discussions from frustrating monologues into enriching dialogues because it provided a shared language. Its logic is easy to understand and easy to translate into action, particularly, as it turns out, by hands-on middle managers.

DIFFERENT ACTION–REACTION CYCLES

For every competitive convergence, where advantage is created ('renewal'), there is a reaction – where advantage is taken away. In some businesses, the cycle of action, reaction has to be fast; in others, they can be slow. For example, drastic price reductions (on the order of 20 per cent–30 per cent) in personal computers are met by competitors almost overnight. In other markets – e.g. car rentals – moderate price reductions (of the order of 6 per cent–8 per cent) take over a year to be implemented. Thus, for some products, competitive advantage is gained or lost in very short order (e.g. Cabbage patch dolls); in others, it takes a decade (DOS disk operating system). The idea of action–reaction mirrors the manager's experience that for some products, competition is intense; in others, more relaxed (e.g. in management consulting). Similarly, as managers know, timing of entry or exit, is critical in some markets (e.g. microprocessor chips), but much less so, in other markets, see Williams (1992, 1998).

To ease explanation, we distinguish three action–reaction cycles: slow cycle, standard cycle (the topic of traditional business thinking), and fast cycle. We found that the most robust measure to classify a particular product onto an action–reaction cycle is 'product economic half-life': the amount of time that it takes for marginal profit per unit to drop to one-half of the peak amount. For slow-cycle situations, product economic half-life is on the order of 7–10 years; for standard cycle, on the order of 3–6 years; and for fast cycle, on the order of 6 months–2 years.

Based on product economic half-life and correlating measures described further below, products classified as slow cycle include operating systems (Microsoft), investment banking (Goldman

Sachs), management consulting (McKinsey), communication networks (AT&T), entertainment (Disney), hub-control airlines (USAir, Delta), patented prescription drugs (Bristol Myers Squibb). Standard cycle products include fast food (McDonalds), appliances, automobiles, tires, consulting (Anderson), food (Nestle), long-distance telephone service (AT&T), standardised financial services, e.g. credit cards (Citibank), internet brokerage (Ex-Trade). Fast cycle products include women's fashion (Liz Claiborne), toys (Nintendo), personal computers (Compaq), cellular phone handsets (Motorola), dynamic random access memory chips (Fujitsu), and fax machines (Xerox). Some products have characteristics of multiple action–reaction cycles ('hybrid'), e.g. frequent flier mileage programmes. Some are changing ('transition') to another, for example, airline service after deregulation.

By focusing on the speed of the action–reaction cycles, SA leads to increased predictability, particularly for complex organizations and/or changing market conditions. With increased predictability of market conditions, CI professionals will be better able to recommending appropriate strategic actions.

IMPLEMENTATION

Not only does SA increase predictability about what high-level strategic actions are needed, its strategic recommendations can be implemented more easily ('actionability'), (Hidding, 1992): Executives found SA's action recommendations easier to implement than recommendations resulting from Industry Structure Analysis (ISA) (Porter, 1980). Executives participating in two executive education programs filled out a questionnaire to evaluate, for given cases, the actionability of two sets of strategy recommendations (SA and ISA). For each executive's evaluation of each set of recommendations, we constructed a composite actionability score, and were thus able to compute (by executive) a difference in his or her two actionability scores. Figure 8.1 depicts, for each executive (on the horizontal axis), the difference in composite scores (on its vertical axis).

We performed several statistical tests on the detailed data from the questionnaires as well as on the composite scores. They all yielded a statistically significant difference ($p < 0.05$; for one test even $p < 0.001$) in actionability in favour of SA.

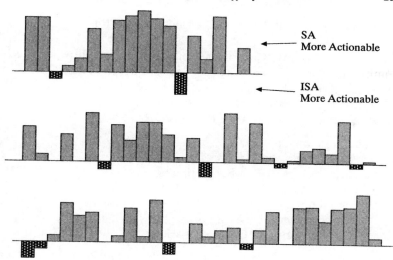

Figure 8.1   Differences in actionability scores

INTRODUCING AN EXPANDED STRATEGY LANGUAGE

SA is a new method in competitive strategy that provides a systematic focus on the effects of time on the creation and erosion of business advantage. It constitutes an expanded way of thinking where competition can evolve at different speeds. It requires the evolution to a new strategy language that recognizes dynamics and time. This new language encompasses, rather than replaces, traditional thinking. For example:

- 'First-mover advantage' evolves to 'action–reaction cycles'
- 'Capital investment' to 'investment velocity'
- 'Profitability' to 'profit margin compression'
- 'Pricing policy' to 'rate of price reduction'
- 'Entry-exit barriers' to 'speed of entry/exit'

We argue that CI that is based on traditional strategy thinking needs to be extended with language and measures that focus on dynamics over time. It needs to focus on rents, i.e. profits, and their evolution over time, and how they are tied to proposed action recommendations. Our research has yielded a number of measures of dynamics.

DYNAMICS MEASURES FOR CLASSIFICATION

We found that many types of measures correlate with product economic half-life, which was introduced earlier in this article. As part of the research described in (Hidding, 1992), we formulated, in detail, several types of measures that can be used in the classification onto the three different action–reaction cycles, for example:

- changes in annual demand
- rate of technological change
- time that buyers exploit bargaining power
- rate of capital investment
- pricing patterns over time
- speed of product innovation, or
- speed of entry or exit from the market.

If such changes and speeds play out over roughly a decade, the product is generally slow-cycle. If they play out over five years or so, the product is likely standard cycle. If they play out over two years or so, the product is likely fast cycle.

As each of these measures cannot guarantee a correct classification by itself, we prefer to classify business situations based on the collective pattern that emerges from them. For example, for products such as cellular telephones or personal computers, the product economic half life is on the order of 9 to 12 months, which generally correlates with changes in annual demand (for particular products) being drastic, and the rate of technological change being high. Also, in situations with such characteristics, prices are reduced drastically over short periods of time, and timing of entry and exit are critical.

Based on such measures, a given business situation can be classified along the spectrum of slow, standard, or fast cycle. Of course, the new strategy language we propose and the new types of measures we researched are general in nature. For organisations facing specific business situations, they need to be tailored to yield specific CI variables. In some cases, 'outlier' data point to opportunities for improving organizational fit. For example, your organisational capabilities may reveal less technical expertise than the market really demands. Or, the market is changing faster than your capabilities (e.g. pricing dynamics). Or, your strategies rely too much on traditional thinking (e.g. for brand name). Often, such inconsistencies turn out to have been the subject of much unresolved debate. By promoting a shared understanding of the fundamental differences among the different action–reaction cycles, such debate can now turned into meaningful dialogue about the future direction of the organisation.

PREDICT THE EVOLUTION

Based on the classification of the current situation, there are a number of ways to see into the future. First, the simplest is to conclude that the current action–reaction cycle will remain the same. Products come and go; but the types of success factors remain the same. In fact, action–reaction cycles mostly do stay the same; however, competitors or customers can cause drastic changes in the industry. Secondly, competitors may be causing a transition by competing in a different action–reaction cycle, i.e. they start behaving according to a faster action–reaction cycle; or a slower one. For example, a competitor may have found a new technology that changes a lot faster. Or, a competitor may slow down competition by tying its products in with a much slower-evolving business (e.g. consulting). Similarly, customer needs and desires may be changing. They may value faster-changing products more, or they may value slower-changing product more than before. Such transitions can be detected as part of your CI using the dynamics measures described above.

Thirdly, and perhaps most importantly, by your own organisation's leadership may decide to change 'what kind of organization we want to be'. As Alan Kay's motto goes: 'The best way to predict the future is to invent it'. You may want to compete in faster- or slower-changing markets. Of course, in order to preserve organisational fit, you will have to adjust your repertoire of success factors, but it may take the competition a long time to realise the fundamental change and respond successfully to it.

RECOMMEND ACTIONS BASED ON DIFFERENT SUCCESS FACTORS

Action recommendations should then be designed to reinforce the critical success factors of the action–reaction cycle(s) that are predicted or chosen for the given business. Success can be achieved in any action–reaction cycle, but always requires competitive fit, i.e. the market's needs, the organisation's capabilities and its strategies reinforce each other ('alignment'). In a slow action–reaction cycle, critical success factors include close personal relationships, a high level of expertise, high complexity of the product/service (e.g. as in custom engineering services), ties to a location, or regulation. In a standard cycle, important critical success factors include standardisation (to exploit economies of scale), orchestration of large-scale activities, bargaining power, a balance of cost leadership and differentiation (variations on standardized products and services), and market segmentation. Fast-cycle critical success factors include revolutionary new ideas, exact timing of entry and exit and rapid distribution.

MANAGING SUCCESS IN MULTIPLE ACTION–REACTION CYCLES

The most difficult situation to manage is when multiple action–reaction cycles occur simultaneously (e.g. when an organisation commercialises many different products and services). Each action–reaction cycle requires its own set of measures to track the market, your capabilities, etc. It also requires its own set of success factors in order to create, maintain, or extend a business advantage. Finally, it requires that different key performance indicators be tracked to track the action plans. Of course, simultaneously tracking such different measures presents a challenge for CI. It is, however, most challenging for the organization's leadership, who have to change their fundamental strategy thinking in response to the different cycle-demands of each business.

CONCLUSION

SA contributes to CI by providing a better ability to conceptualize business problems. It identifies the types of measures needed to understand the competitive stance of a particular product. It makes data collection more targeted, by focusing on success factors which matter most. It can provide early warnings of changing 'rules of the game', especially in complex ('hybrid'), shifting ('transition') businesses. As Sustainability Analysis expands traditional thinking, it allows CI to expand, rather than replace, the CI manager's repertoire of measures and methods. Existing CI measures and data may be interpreted in multiple ways, depending on the action–reaction cycle in which you operate, in particular to satisfy different CI needs across diverse business units.

Last, but not least, SA's strategy recommendations have been proven to be easier to translate into action. In response to the challenge outlined at the beginning of this chapter, use of SA helps to transform the role of CI professionals from mere information providers to full partners with seniour management.

Incorporating the time-based logic and language of SA will allow the CI function to remain central to problem conceptualization, intelligence gathering, strategy formulation and recommendations of strategic action, thus ensuring CI's growing value to top management in the new economy.

References

HIDDING, G.J. (1988) 'DSS conceptualizers in OR: should you apply AI?', in Mitra, G. (ed.), *Mathematical Models for Decision Support*, Berlin: Springer-Verlag, 665–94.

HIDDING, G.J. (1992) 'Strategy decision making', PhD dissertation, Ann Arbor: University Microfilms International.

PORTER, M.E. (1980) *Competitive Strategy: Techniques for Analyzing Industries and Competitors*, New York: The Free Press.

WILLIAMS, J.R. (1992) 'How sustainable is your advantage?', *California Management Review*, 34(3).

WILLIAMS, J.R. (1997) *Renewable Advantage: Creating Your Future through Economic Time*, New York: The Free Press.

Part III

Knowledge Management and Learning Organisation

9 Knowledge Management: From an IT Perspective?

Dennis Dunn and Melanie Fretwell

INTRODUCTION

The advent of the Learning Organisation (Argyris, 1982; Senge, 1990; De Geus, 1997) or the Learning Company (Pedler *et al.*, 1990) appears more than merely another management theory fad that promises unattainable benefit. Organisations must continually learn if they are to survive (De Geus, 1997) and many strive to develop strategies in support of this objective. Within these strategies it is clear that Information Technology (IT) has a leading role (Miller and Dunn, 1998) for it pervades many areas of the organisation and beyond to other elements of the supply chain. In short, IT is increasingly expected to provide the knowledge dissemination infrastructure within, and between the organisation(s) in order to support learning activities. Any comprehensive survey of the learning organisation literature and practice quickly reveals the significance of Knowledge Management (KM) (IPD, 1999) for it is through the capturing of information and sharing of knowledge that organisations can be seen to learn. The inference is clear, that to be a successful learning organisation necessitates close attention to the issue of creating organisational knowledge and of its management. Knowledge management can be said to be the policies and processes through which organisations seek to create, store and disseminate organisational knowledge, and fundamental to this endeavour has become the role of IT.

IT PERSPECTIVE

IT is well named; its organisational asset is the information that the technology holds and as information is converted (shared) to become organisational knowledge, then it seems a natural and obvious extended role for IT to manage. Fulfilling this role has brought the designation and introduction of Knowledge Based Systems

(KBS) and Knowledge Management Systems (KMS). Unlike IT, KBS may not be so well named for many such systems may contain not knowledge as the name implies, but information (Fretwell, 1999). Many organisations who believe that they have entered the domain of knowledge management may not have, and the illusion of having done so, sustained by the use of knowledge terms often developed by vendors for commercial expediency, may prove to be unrewarding and fall short of delivering the learning organisation benefits that they seek, indeed expect, from the considerable investments that some organisations appear willing to make. Critical to this issue is the juxtaposition between the information and knowledge domains and the concern of conversion from information to organisational knowledge that gives 'actants' (Callon and Latour, 1992; Collins and Yearley, 1992) the capacity to take effective action (Senge, 1998) in their organisational roles. Knowledge creation can be seen to be an essential human endeavour achieved through cognition and reasoning and while IT systems can contain elements of reasoning, codified as artificial intelligence, and be said to emulate human cognition through neural networks, they cannot (as yet) act on instinct and intuition, which are factors that seem to be present and important in human decision-making. Knowledge based systems, therefore, despite the rhetoric and impressions often afforded by technology vendors, require human endeavour at their core.

IT INFRASTRUCTURE

One important and useful way through which organisations learn is through the capture of data, processed to provide information and disseminated as organisational knowledge, much of which is achieved through the deployment of an IT infrastructure. Problematic to this endeavour is that much valuable information and knowledge is tacit, held in people's minds and surfaced (made explicit) with difficulty, if at all (Nonaka and Takeuchi, 1995). It appears therefore, in theory at least, that people might be a critical component in successful knowledge management projects. Recent research (Fretwell, 1999) which sought to illuminate the contribution that IT makes to knowledge management projects, is partially reported next. The project first surveyed a geographically dispersed target population known to have an interest in knowledge management. The analysis of these responses provided the foundation for interviews with three senior knowledge management officers of an international pharmaceutical company, based in the United Kingdom.

An e-mail questionnaire survey of professionals engaged in knowledge management project developments was undertaken. The list of recipients was compiled through a search of a number of knowledge management discussion forums, including Brint.com (http://www.brint.com) and the Federation of Enterprise Knowledge Development (http://www.fend.es). The principal disadvantage of questionnaire distribution by e-mail is that it does not normally afford any degree of personal contact with recipients, which might have an adverse effect upon the number of successful responses (Easterby-Smith *et al.*, 1991). In an attempt to overcome this factor, each recipient was sent the questionnaire individually, rather than via a distribution list, together with a personalised message of introduction to the research, their name in the body of the text message and reference to the discussion forum contribution they had made.

This attention to a relatively detailed personalised e-mail produced a 32 per cent response rate from the 112 organisational representatives in the sample size. Industry sector representation of respondents was Manufacturing 29 per cent, Business Services 26 per cent, Government/Public Services 22 per cent, Computing 15 per cent and others 8 per cent. Within these organisations almost half of the respondents (49 per cent) were working in a consultant capacity on knowledge management projects whilst the others were internal employees in IS roles and other functional specialists. The survey revealed that knowledge management projects are currently underway across many organisational departments, as shown in Table 9.1.

FINDINGS

Table 9.1   Departments undertaking Knowledge Management projects

	%
Information Systems	17
Human Resource Management	17
Development	17
Research	12
Commercial	11
Manufacturing	9
Other	17

The survey revealed a relatively even split of departments in which knowledge management projects were currently underway. The 'other' category being made up almost equally of internal consultancy, training and healthcare.

The sum total of current projects in development was 293 with an average of 11 within each organisation represented in the survey. This average may be relatively high due to the number of consultants in the target sample who may be working exclusively on knowledge management projects. It seems clear from the projects reportedly underway that the spread of knowledge management is illustrative of the varied application potential perceived by their host organisations. Also, the take-up of these project developments seems to be increasing with most respondent organisations already committed to knowledge management, and new projects still being commissioned and initiated with 36 per cent reporting projects in operation longer than 18 months. The largest proportion of projects appear to be at the project development stage (Table 9.2) with fewer projects at the initiation and analysis stages. The lowest number of projects at any one stage of the systems development life-cycle are at the completed stage, suggesting that much more is in development than has been delivered. Of the 193 projects reportedly underway in the survey only 23 (12 per cent) had been delivered to date. This appears to support the assertion that knowledge management is still presently a relatively immature organisational concept.

Table 9.2   Project Development Life-cycle

	%
Project initiation	20
Analysis	13
Development	38
Delivery	17
Completed	12

The principal function of knowledge management projects within the experience of those surveyed was to support better decision-making (64 per cent of respondents) and it could indeed be argued that this is the main reason for most projects being undertaken as organisations strive to capture and sustain competitive advantage in an increasingly turbulent business environment. To support the capturing of the knowledge of employees (52 per cent) and sharing it within the organisation (62 per cent) featured strongly as issues of functionality in knowledge management projects. Interestingly, respondents felt that capturing knowledge from outside the organisation was less significant (5 per cent) suggesting that recognition of the exploitation of environmental knowledge is relatively under developed. Organisations appear to concentrate on leveraging their own internal knowledge above all else.

The questionnaire survey inquired into responsibility for knowledge management projects (see Table 9.3).

Table 9.3 Functional Responsibility for KM Projects

	agree (%)	*disagree (%)*
Responsibility of IS	0	98
Responsibility of business functions	62	30
Driven by business processes	58	30
Mainly dependent on people	90	2
Mainly dependent on IT	30	52

Even though there is wide recognition that knowledge management projects are mainly dependent on information technology as the key deliverable, due to infrastructural considerations, it is clear that these respondents drawn from across the organisational spectrum, consider knowledge management to be much more than simply the domain of IT/IS, with the majority clearly placing responsibility upon the business functional areas for whom projects are commissioned. Indeed, some questionnaire respondents went much further indicating that it was their belief that knowledge management should be considered a business-wide strategic issue, not merely an issue for constituent parts of the organisation. Furthermore, it can be seen from Table 9.3 that knowledge management projects are viewed as being people dependent, thus supporting earlier results which indicated the people centred activities of decision-making, that is, capturing knowledge and sharing knowledge from employees were the most important in knowledge management projects.

These questionnaire findings were discussed with three senior managers of the pharmaceutical company, two having direct involvement, and one indirect, for knowledge management projects. All agreed the significance of knowledge management to enable better decision-making, particularly in an industry where the wrong decisions might cost the organisation millions of dollars in unsuitable compound (product) development. As one respondee stated, 'Increasing the chances of making good decisions is becoming increasingly important as we find ourselves operating in a highly competitive environment.' Recognised as important by those interviewed was that the organisation is able to not only capture but also retain the knowledge of its individuals so that the intellectual capital is usable beyond their employment with the company. Too much information resides in the minds of key people as tacit knowledge which if captured and codified, might have a lasting value to the organisation. However, the very act of capturing knowledge implies that individuals must be prepared to share it initially and then make use of it in the decision making process. One interviewee reported the difficulty of getting individuals to share their knowledge particularly if this is to be codified into a computer-based system and made available across the organisation as, having done so, the employee may feel vulnerable to redundancy once his expertise is readily available in a wider domain. This is perhaps understandable in the context of the apparent paradigm shift that has taken place in knowledge management, that is, from information is power to information sharing is power. As we are aware, organizational inducements, encouragement and reward systems are becoming increasingly common as ways to encourage employee participation in knowledge sharing projects, with some reported success stories notably in the professional journals. Interestingly, as in the questionnaire responses, knowledge external to organisational boundaries appears less significantly regarded by interviewees; one statement that typified this view was '. . . most information or knowledge that the organization needs is held somewhere within it, the problem is finding it and at the time when it can be useful in decision making'. This is a problematic issue and one in which both active and passive information dissemination strategies (Miller and Dunn, 1998) might offer support. Passive strategies would typically be the design of knowledge repositories that employees can tap into on a routine or regular basis, whilst active dissemination strategies would complement these repositories by pushing out knowledge to individuals or parts of the organization that might need it as a critical element to support decision-making. Interviewees further expressed concern that as the organisation presently found it difficult to leverage internal knowledge, then to also cope with external knowledge might '. . . just add to our problems'. Clearly this could be a significant organisational issue, for environment scanning and the assimilation of significant external knowledge is not just desirable but essential in competitive trading environments.

For knowledge management project deliverables those interviewed recognised the value of consultant services. Consultancy organisations were felt to be among the first to develop and implement knowledge management projects, partly in an effort to increase the knowledge-ability of their own people and organisational performance, which of course might then increase the saleability of their services and subsequent products to the marketplace. Consultants it was argued, might have a clearer understanding of what knowledge management projects are about and the changes to be made to organisational procedures for those seeking to practice it. The fact that respondents identified IT/IS as the main deliverable of knowledge management projects might suggest that many current projects are not being carried out particularly successfully in that they might be less likely to deliver meaningful outcomes that will improve organisational practice. Organisations can commission, purchase and implement IT/IS knowledge management products but still not have effective knowledge management practice. The concern becomes that unless organisations prioritise business processes as the key deliverable then many knowledge management project will be viewed unsuccessful.

DISCUSSION

The perception of KM as a predominately technical IT systems issue, particularly amongst IT professionals fuels the illusion that organisations should look first to their IS functions in consideration of knowledge management projects. Fretwell's (1999) survey, whilst small scale, clearly contradicts this view and encourages further research to encompass softer issues. Also, the recognition that the knowledge domain assigns human dependency to the endeavour presents an *a priori* case for the role of social theory to temper the ontological positions of objectivism and positivism traditional in 'hard' systems thinking that has been the cornerstone of IT, with its foundations in computer science. In recognising that knowledge creation and reasoning are traits of human cognition we may care to consider knowledge-based systems as groupings of people linked by technology to other repositories of shared information. From such recognition, it follows that the approach taken by those in the IS discipline to the considerations of such systems ought of necessity, to be from a socio-technical paradigm perspective. The information systems field is itself still relatively immature though the paradigm shift that it affords recognises, among other issues, the need for a more inclusive approach than had been evident in traditional IT. As the UKAIS have reported:

The study of information systems is a multi-disciplinary subject and addresses the range of strategic, managerial and operational activities involved in the gathering, processing, storing, distributing and use of information, and its associated technologies, in society and organizations.

(United Kingdom of Information Systems 1995)

Further, there are those whose belief is that knowledge management should not be the exclusive domain of IS at all. In the United Kingdom, IPD and others have asserted that knowledge management is in danger by being considered exclusively as an IT/IS issue.

. . . knowledge management tends to be treated mainly as an issue for information systems experts. The schemes they introduce are predominately on the supply side, focusing on data and communications systems and the processes for making people's tacit knowledge explicit and available to the rest of their organization. . . . What is missing is a more holistic approach that embraces the demand-side issues.

(IPD, 1999)

The UKAIS and IPD would, among others, appear to be in agreement that although from different perspectives, they each recognise that strategic information systems issues, like knowledge management, cannot be satisfied from a single disciplinary role. Increasingly the IT paradigm shift (Tapscott and Capston, 1993) is supported by evidence of changed necessity, to the extent that even IS professionals themselves have become conditioned to support the development of hybrid managers who can position systems developments more effectively within a wider organisational context. The research conducted by Fretwell clearly points to the need for knowledge management projects to be more than the exclusive domain of the IS function:

DOES SHARED INFORMATION EQUAL ORGANISATIONAL KNOWLEDGE?

Finally, it is important to comment upon the relationship of information to organisational knowledge for it appears to have become accepted that the one automatically creates the other. The supposition that data produces information which produces organisational knowledge is dangerously simplistic for it masks the reality that in decision-making, much more information and knowledge is relied upon than that provided by an IT-based information system, and used as the basis for people to take effective action (Senge, 1998) in their organisational lives. Some additional scrutiny and investigation of what organisational knowledge is perceived to be would be revealing and useful, for if we understood the nature and characteristics of organisational knowledge, then we have a firmer basis for understanding its successful management and the development of knowledge management projects. It may be that the emergence and growth of so called knowledge-based systems and knowledge management systems, and the designation of Chief Knowledge Officers might be an appropriate response to support organisational learning. Conversely, such developments may be adding to the problem if they are seen to be simply different packaging to familiar processes. Organisations may generally be information rich but knowledge poor, though they may not recognise themselves so. Though an apparent theoretical gap can be seen to exist between the conversion of information to organisational knowledge it might not do so in practice or, it may not matter significantly to make any appreciable difference to decision-making or organisational performance. However, it might also be that employees are indeed increasingly relying upon their knowledge-based projects and systems as decision support instruments and organisational learning mechanisms, and if this is the case, then further investigation can be seen as valuable in that our greater understanding of these issues may ultimately inform information systems design and deployment within the context of learning organisation. The case for socio-technical perspectives in knowledge management research and developments seems increasingly compelling, and indeed a predominant foci that is non IT/IS seems to grow a little stronger with each project delivered.

CONCLUSION

A large proportion of people working on knowledge management projects are consultants and many more knowledge management projects are in the development phases than have been delivered to date. Enabling better decision-making is the primary business objective of projects and this is becoming a strategic imperative for organisations operating in increasingly competitive business environments. Concentration appears still to be essentially on internal knowledge capture and sharing even though there is general and genuine awareness of the potential value and significance of external knowledge. Knowledge management projects are people dependent, this clearly has implications for openness and honesty within organisational culture (Miller and Dunn, 1998). However, successful KM projects, whilst dependent upon people also depend upon processes and technology. The combination of these three, will be critical for successful development and adoption of knowledge management projects within organisations. People issues are particularly significant within knowledge management projects as surfacing and leveraging tacit knowledge becomes the hottest issue. With reducing trends in employment longevity, human resource managers responses seem to be targeted toward employee retention policies, whilst IT strategies appear predominately focused on tacit knowledge capture for use beyond employee departure. Neither is likely to be an adequate response. If a knowledge based system is indeed a grouping of people connected to information systems and each other, then successful knowledge management strategy might start to ask questions about how that might be achieved amongst groups beyond their employment in a single organization. Such questions are unlikely to be successfully contemplated by either the HRM or IT functions in isolation.

References

ARGYRIS, C. (1982) *Reasoning, Learning and Action*, San Francisco: Jossey-Bass.
CALLON, M. and LATOUR, B. (1992) 'Don't throw the baby out with the Bath School!: A reply to Collins and Yearly', in Pickering, A. (ed.), *Science as Practice and Culture*, Chicago: University of Chicago Press.
COLLINS, H.M. and YEARLEY, S. (1992) 'Epistemological chicken', in Pickering, A. (ed.), *Science as Practice and Culture*, Chicago: University of Chicago Press.
DE GEUS, A. (1997) *The Living Company*, Boston: Harvard Business School Press.
EASTERBY-SMITH, M. THORPE, R. and LOWE, A. (1991) *Management Research: an Introduction*, London: Sage.
FRETWELL, M. (1999) 'What can Information Systems and Information Technology contribute to Knowledge Management?', MSc dissertation, Manchester Metropolitan University.
IPD (1999) *Knowledge Management: a Literature Review*, London: Institute of Personnel Development.
MILLER, K. and DUNN, D. (1998) 'Using past performance to improve

future practice: a framework for method evaluation and improvement', ISD98 Seventh International Conference, Bled, Slovenia.

NONAKA, I. and TAKEUCHI, H. (1995) *The Knowledge Creating Company*, New York: Oxford University Press.

PEDLER, M., BURGOYNE, J. and BOYDELL, T. (1991) *The Learning Company: a Strategy for Sustainable Development*, London: McGraw-Hill.

SENGE, P.M. (1990) *The Fifth Discipline. The Art and Practice of the Learning Organization*, London: Century Business.

SENGE, P.M. (1998) 'I/T and the learning organization', presentation to the BIT Conference, Manchester Metropolitan University.

TAPSCOTT, D. and CAPSTON, A. (1993) *Paradigm Shift: the New Promise of Information Technology*, New York: McGraw Hill.

UNITED KINGDOM ACADEMY OF INFORMATION SYSTEMS (1995) May, Newsletter.

10 The Process of Knowledge Harvesting™: The Key to KM

Charles Snyder and Larry Wilson

INTRODUCTION

There are several attempts at building frameworks for the emerging field of KM (see e.g. Holsapple and Joshi, 1997, 1998). Critical components of a framework must include the processes of capture, formatting, and sharing of an organisation's knowledge pertinent to the execution of its most critical processes. We have been developing software that supports KM for eight years. This software has a focus on improving an individual's ability to perform a critical process. At present, our major thrust has been on a set of processes that we label Knowledge Harvesting™ to capture expertise and put it into a software product so that widespread knowledge sharing is possible.

As the concept of harvesting is central to the following discussion, it should be defined here. Knowledge Harvesting™ is an integrated set of processes that allow the often hidden (or tacit) insights of top performers to be captured and converted into specific, actionable know-how that can be transferred to others through software. Harvesting can be considered as a subset of the broader, but ill-defined topic of knowledge transfer.

The purpose of Knowledge Harvesting™ is to capture and express expertise in a form that can be easily accessed and used by others who need the know-how in performance of their tasks. Valuable knowledge about a task or process can be made available to anyone in the organisation who needs it on a just-in-time basis. Since harvesting can be applied to nearly any kind of human knowledge that is procedurally actionable, the existing expertise or know-how can be captured and formalised into software so that the organisation can leverage it and preserve it.

The process of harvesting starts by enabling experts (top-performers) to verbalise their tacit knowledge, thereby making it explicit. Next the steps in the total process consist of capturing, organising, applying, recording, sharing, evaluating, and improving the know-how. These steps should be considered as iterative, similar to the systems development life-cycle. Software as the primary output of the harvesting process provides some distinctive advantages. The software allows individuals to simultaneously understand, learn, perform, and record performance. Thus, this learning-by-doing software can become a core organisational asset. The software presents needed know-how on a self-paced, as needed basis. It is designed so that knowledge is accessed and transferred only when needed, and only to the extent needed. Therefore it may be considered as a just-in-time Electronic Performance Support System (EPSS).

NEED FOR KM FRAMEWORKS

While the world seems to have embraced the notion of KM, there remains a dearth of proposed frameworks or models that pertain to the topic. One of the major problems is the fundamental definitional one. This problem becomes evident when one reviews the KM literature. The material that has been published to date is widely varied in terms of terminology and focus. We find several uses of the same or similar terms that have different meanings and different contexts. For example, the label of KM is used in database in a different way than in the numerous articles about intellectual asset management. In a recent book, Halal (1998) edited a collection of a wide variety of essays on creating and leading the 'knowledge enterprise'. These essays actually focus more on the organisation for organising work. Other books employ KM as a major theme, but fall short of developing clear definitions and models for KM. Perhaps the ideas of the 'knowledge enterprise' or the 'learning organization' should be examined, as they seem to play a large role in some KM writings.

Some researchers believe that KM is a part of the so-called learning organisation. The publication of Senge's popular book, *The Fifth Discipline*, (1990), led to a management movement termed as the 'learning organisation' that Senge himself has described as a management fad. Watkin (1996) reported that 300 organisations professed to be learning organisations, although apparently many were not. Senge has been quoted (Koch and Fabris, 1995, p. 32), as saying that learning is '. . . not some jazzed-up way of sharing information'.

Unfortunately, many organisations that claim to be learning organisations (or practice KM) simply deploy a Lotus Notes® database of 'best practices' and believe that they are at the forefront of the KM trend. The requirement goes far beyond building a knowledgebase with some means of access (See Vogel, 1996). KM as a label seems to be displacing the concept of the learning organisation as a management trend and this contributes to more confusion. Additionally, the rapid entry of major consulting firms into the fray has brought their own proprietary terminology as they seek differentiation and market share.

It is our belief that if KM is not to be labelled as simply a management fad *de jour*, definitions and frameworks must be promulgated so that the field itself may be defined and so that researchers may employ a common ontology in developing the construct and its subcomponents (Templeton and Snyder, 1998). Some recent efforts at building models and frameworks have been reported (see e.g. Holsapple and Joshi, 1997, 1998; Snyder *et al.*, 1998). The utility of a framework is that it describes a phenomenon in the form of key factors, constructs, or variables and their relationships. The framework might be considered as an early point or area on the research continuum. It provides the basis for further research that can become more and more rigorous as methodologies become more sophisticated. A comprehensive framework allows an organisation to gain perspective as well as provides focus to improve effectiveness.

An understanding of knowledge is a prerequisite for designing and implementing an effective KM process. To achieve a clearer understanding of what we mean by knowledge, we have included the concepts of data, information, knowledge, and expertise in the 'information food chain' and their relationship to KM.

WHAT IS KM?

It is useful to review the relation of data and information to knowledge (the 'information food chain') before discussing KM. We added expertise to the ' information food chain', reference Figure 10.1. The components are described below.

Data are defined as objective numerical or other representation in a form not processed. *Information* is processed data that is meaningful to a recipient. By processing, summarising or analysing data, organisations create information. Information should be

Data → Information → Knowledge → Expertise

Figure 10.1   The information food chain

presented to increase the knowledge of the individual, therefore, tailored to the needs of the recipient and thus, subjective. *Knowledge* is the state or fact of knowing; it is understanding gained through experience or study; the sum or range of what has been perceived, discovered or learned. Knowledge has been simply defined as the capacity and competence to perform (Snyder and Wilson, 1997). Knowledge is information whose validity has been established through tests or proof (Liebeskind, 1996). Sveiby (1997) defined knowledge as simply the capacity to act. Knowledge is similar to potential energy in that it provides an individual with the basic competence to perform. In order to actualise the potential to perform, we incorporate the concept of expertise.

Turban *et al.* (1996) defined expertise as extensive, task-specific knowledge acquired from reading, training, and experience It is expert advice or opinion; a skill or knowledge in a particular area that has been enhanced by depth of reading, training, and experience. The difference between knowledge is one of degree. A knowledgeable individual has the potential to perform; the expert possesses the added degree of knowledge that enables superiour performance. Accumulated knowledge and experience becomes expertise: the ability to apply knowledge in a variety of situations and achieve highly successful results. Why is an individual considered as an expert? We believe that the differentiating factor is in the degree of tacit knowledge held by an expert.

Knowledge is commonly believed to exist in tacit and explicit forms. Explicit knowledge is that which has been recorded and is imparted by traditional learning methods. However, explicit knowledge does not include the nuances gained through experience. Tacit knowledge is not apparent, but allows the expert to use information better. 'One can postulate that it is the vast reservoir of tacit knowledge that an expert can bring to consciousness in a situation of need that makes him/her an expert' (Snyder and Wilson, 1997, 876). The most valuable form of knowledge that exists in an organisation is this hidden asset of the experts. How is the organisation to capitalise on this asset? This is where the process model called Knowledge Harvesting™ is brought to bear. This is a process model that we have employed for several years in a variety of situations. We need to examine some of the KM definitions before discussing knowledge harvesting processes. According to Manville and Foote (1996), KM implies that there is a systematic process for assembling and controlling organisational knowledge as a resource. The knowledge harvesting^{TM} process provides the structure and means for implementing and practice of KM.

There are many definitions of KM. We provide a few definitions in Table 10.1

In our view, the emphasis should be on the process that enhances knowledge: the capacity for effective performance. New computer augmented learning applications can enhance an individual's knowl-

Table 10.1   Some definitions of KM

KM source	Definition of KM
Thomas Bertels	The management of the organisation towards the continuous renewal of the organisation knowledge base – this means, e.g. creation of supportive organisational structures, facilitation of organisation members, pushing IT – instruments with emphasis on teamwork and diffusion of knowledge (as e.g. groupware) into place.
Denham Grey	An audit of 'intellectual assets' that highlights unique sources, critical functions, and potential bottlenecks, which hinders knowledge flows to the point of use. It protects intellectual assets from decay, seeks opportunities to enhance decisions, services and products through adding intelligence, increasing value and providing flexibility.
J. Hibbard	KM is a process of locating, organising, and using the collective information and expertise within an organisation, whether it resides on paper, or in the minds of people, and distributing it wherever it benefits most.
Brain Newman	KM is the collection of processes that govern the creation, dissemination, and utilisation of knowledge.
Karl-Eric Sveiby	The art of creating value from an organisation's intangible assets.
Karl Wiig	Focusing on determining, organising, directing, facilitating, and monitoring knowledge-related practices and activities required to achieve the desired business strategies and objectives.

edge that leads to effective task performance. Technology has progressed to the point of doing what Englebart (1963) envisioned with the term 'intellectual augmentation'. Technology should play a critical role in the achievement of KM.

KNOWLEDGE HARVESTING™ MODEL

Each of the sub-processes discussed here includes tasks that should be performed by organisations that wish to deliberately manage knowledge. Knowledge harvesting™ is an integrated set of processes whereby the often hidden insights of top performers are converted into specific, actionable know-how that can be transferred to other employees via software. In the process, top performers verbalise their tacit know-how and thereby make it explicit. Tacit know-how is composed of the subjective knowledge, insights, and intuitions possessed by a person who has a depth of understanding in a particular area (Wilson, 1997). The process illustrated in Figure 10.2 should keep the knowledge refreshed, as it is an iterative, continuous lifecycle.

With KM in place, key know-how will remain even if employees leave the company ('The Facts', 1998).

One of the primary outputs of the harvesting process is software. The software is an EPSS. The EPSS allows individuals to simultaneously understand, learn, perform, and record performance in a single action (see Gery, 1991).

The process begins by *identifying* the top performers and their activities that surround accomplishment of key organisational processes. The expertise of the top performers must be *elicited* and

Figure 10.2   Harvesting processes
Source: Modified from Wilson (1997).

captured for use by others in the organisation. This captured expertise must be *organised* in order for others to *apply* the expert's knowledge to the same fundamental processes across the corporation. This is done through the EPSS that is made available throughout the enterprise. The activities of the users are *recorded*, so they can be shared throughout the organisation. An *evaluation* process is conducted in order to assess the efficacy of the EPSS. New insights are employed to *improve* the quality, efficiency, and effectiveness of the process and the application. KM relies on the people and the processes of the company. If they are not taken into consideration, the KM strategy will just result in a loss of time and effort (Stewart, 1996). The harvesting processes are ultimately aimed at the individuals performing the key tasks of the organisation. The harvesting sub-processes are discussed below.

Identify

In any categorisation, the first step is to identify the category. We now refer to this as *focus.* This is to decide just what process is the target of our harvesting efforts. In the case of KM, this would involve mapping the organisation's key processes and the individuals who possess the best know-how. In this step, the knowledge harvester is ascertaining the origin, nature, or definitive characteristics of the organisation's processes. The initiating step involves determining two things, top performing people and their critical activities.

Elicit

Once the experts and activities are identified, an understanding of these activities will be elicited from the experts. Knowledge is gathered from departments such as marketing, research and development, engineering and manufacturing (Davenport, 1996). The activities of the top performers are educed and logically mapped in the knowledge harvesting^{TM} process. As with expert systems, knowledge engineers realised that the most difficult function of creating an expert system was the process of eliciting information from key performers (experts) about the activities they performed and the rules they used in decision-making. Thus, KM encounters the same problem of uncovering the rules of decision within the activities of key performers. It is not uncommon for the experts to be reluctant to share all of their knowledge because of fear of loss of job security. Companies must make sure that these fears are allayed (Stewart, 1997). Davenport (1996) cautioned that if the company's intentions are not to downsize, then it must ensure employees of their positions within the company, thus, keeping up company morale. It is imperative that the company communicates its intentions to the top performers and provides the culture that encourages sharing of expertise.

Capture

The expertise of the top performers must be preserved to continue the success of the organisation. In the elicitation process, a great deal of information will be extracted from top performers and contained therein will be the key decision rules that need to be preserved. The capture phase distills these decision rules from the bulk of information and stores them. Examples of knowledge that might be organised and captured include best practices, patterns, software code, project experiences, and information on tools that have used (Huang, 1998). By seizing and storing the information, the Knowledge Harvesting™ process adds value to the future of the corporation. This capturing process makes a permanent copy of the memory of the organisation's top performers. We now include this as a part of the elicit phase.

Organise

The knowledge captured from top performers must be arranged in a coherent or systematic form. This procedure of structuring the knowledge into orderly and functional processes allows anyone in the organisation to retrieve the necessary information quickly and efficiently. The organisation of a corporation's key expertise provides a systematic method of producing the EPSS that allows the organization's knowledge to be carried forward for future use of various applications within the company. Our current model adds an optimise process and a share process.

Apply

The purpose of a KM system is to allow all organisational players to apply the same expert knowledge to processes as the top performers. We wish to make the stored knowledge available to everyone as appropriate. The point of a KM system is application by an individual. These individuals may request or seek assistance or advice for performance of a specific task. These applications assist the process of learning by the user. This learning is aided by context-sensitive assistance embedded in the applications. Support information such as terminology, descriptions, visual aids, and examples should be available on demand. To enhance performance, each individual may be given detailed guidance about information to gather, issues to consider, decisions to make, actions to take, or resources to consult.

Record

Once an application has been created it will require refreshing so that it can evolve with use. This sub-process records the learning that takes place with the user; causing the database of knowledge to be enhanced. This process collects and preserves information on a particular subject. It is the method of preserving the known history of performance, activities, or achievement. This preserved knowledge causes learning in an organisational context. This is a non-trivial process because the application will have to be expertly structured to glean knowledge from the action of the user and ignore everyday data and information. Every element within an application provides a place to record a response. Thus, the application keeps historical records of each learning experience and outcome (Snyder and Wilson, 1998).

The software instantly records all input information generated during the learning/doing process. Process anomalies are recorded, permitting continuous system improvements. The software application can be used by anyone allowing the organisation to make effective use of all harvested know-how. The system is user-friendly to enhance motivation to use the system, rather than rely on conventional 'cut and try' methodology. Recording means that the application will never forget what has worked in the past and why. Good documentation helps users understand how to handle a similar situation in the future or multiple instances of similar situations can be analysed as an aggregate (Snyder and Wilson, 1998).

Share

Knowledge that has been captured must be shared or its capture will be irrelevant and the effort and expense wasted. Additionally, sharing will likely lead to the seeking and capturing of other knowledge and uses of previous and new knowledge. This knowledge can be distributed throughout the organisation to individuals or groups.

A common knowledge schema is imperative to the distributed architecture and diverse functional characteristics of the devices, equipment, etc. where knowledge is advanced and documented (Snyder and Wilson, 1998). A corporate repository is developed where tangible "intellectual capital" of an organization can be accessed and exchanged. Sharing allows individuals to track activities while significantly increasing efficiency and effectiveness of existing groupware.

Buckman Laboratories is a company that has become well known for its efforts to share knowledge among its more than 1200 people in over 80 countries (Bowles, 1997; Rifken, 1996). While the idea of sharing knowledge is not new, new learning resources enable the process to be systematised across the organisation.

Evaluate

Appraisal will occur during application and sharing. This completes a feedback process. In the elicitation and capture steps some decision rules will be gathered that are of little value or whose application is lost in time. Evaluation should be continuous so that the database can be kept up to date, relevant, and as small as possible. Evaluation must be performed in order to determine the effectiveness of the software applications. Repeated use provides the basis for the next process (Snyder and Wilson, 1998). At the most basic level, learning should be evaluated by assessing the impact on individual performance. Ultimately, the evaluation must be in terms of the contribution to organisational performance.

Improve

The improved sub-process is the continuous betterment of the entire process. By improving the process or the flow of knowledge throughout the organisation, the productivity or value to individuals or groups is enhanced. Here we should seek the improvement of both the stored knowledge and its application. An overt process of improvement should cause a greater return on investment. This is because it should foster greater usage and sharing. We now refer to this process as *adapt*. Through the subprocess, we ensure refreshing and renewal of knowledge. For a state-of the-art version of the harvesting process, see *www.learnerfirst*.com.

CONCLUSIONS

Savage (1996) stated that the accelerating pace of change signals the shift from the Industrial Era to the Knowledge Era where the primary source of wealth creation is human imagination. Many others have stated essentially the same idea. Regardless of the source, the idea of KM has taken hold. To sustain KM efforts, systems implemented need to support not only just-in-time learning, but long-term learning that continuously builds individual competency and organisational memory. The software applications must be firmly grounded in learning theory, individualised, and provide supplemental memory for the user. The software should be designed to support life-long learning and sharing as well. These systems can be the basis for higher levels of individual performance, ultimately leading to superiour organisational performance. Some of these systems have been deployed and are in daily use in many organisations.

Learning tools such as the EPSS-type of application generated by the Knowledge Harvesting^{TM} process provide the mechanism for building truly sustainable knowledge management systems. These applications increase the learning rate and decrease knowledge decay and loss to the firm. The software provides the systems that can institutionalise KM and provide the basis for long-term organisational effectiveness.

References

BOWLES, J. (1997) 'Knowledge sharing at Buckman Laboratories' (advertisement), *Fortune*, 1345(3), 118–19.
DAVENPORT, T. (1996) 'Knowledge roles: the CKO and beyond', *CIO,* 9(12), 24, 26.
ENGLEBART, D. (1963) 'A conceptual framework for the augmentation of man's intellect', in Howerton, P. (ed.), *Vistas in Information Handling.*
GERY, G. (1991) *Electronic Performance Support Systems: How and Why to Remake the Workplace Through the Strategic Application of Technology,* Boston. Weingarten Publications.

HALAL, W.E. (1998) *The Infinite Resource: Creating and Leading the Knowledge Enterprise*, San Francisco. Jossey-Bass.

HOLSAPPLE, C. and JOSHI, K. (1997) 'Knowledge Management: a three-fold framework', KIKM Research Paper, 104, 1–21.

HOLSAPPLE, C. and JOSHI, K. (1998) 'In search of a descriptive framework for Knowledge Management: preliminary delphi results', *KIKM Research Paper*, 118, 1–29.

HUANG, K. (1998) 'Capitalizing, collective knowledge for winning, execution and teamwork', ⟨http:/www.ibm.com/services/articles/intelcap.html⟩.

KOCH, C. and FABRIS, P. (1995) 'Fail Safe', *CIO*, 9(5), 32–6.

LIEBESKIND, J.P. (1996) 'Knowledge, strategy, and the theory of the firm', *Strategic Management Journal*, 17 (Special Issue), 93–108.

MANVILLE, B. and FOOTE, N. (1996) 'Harvest your workers' knowledge', *Datamation*, 42(3), 78–83.

RIFKEN, G. (1996) 'Buckman Labs is nothing but net', *Fast Company*, 3, 118–27.

SAVAGE, C. (1996) *Fifth Generation Management*, Boston. Butterworth-Heineman.

SENGE, P. (1990) *The Fifth Discipline: the Art & Practice of the Learning Organization*, New York. Doubleday.

SNYDER, CHARLES A. and WILSON, LARRY T. (1997a) 'Computer augmented learning: the basis of sustained Knowledge Management', *Proceedings AIS*, 875–7.

SNYDER, CHARLES A. and WILSON, LARRY T. (1997b) 'Technology advances supporting electronic performance support systems', paper presented at SOR'97, Jena, Germany, 1–6.

SNYDER, CHARLES A., WILSON, LARRY T. and MCMANUS, DENISE J. (1998) 'Knowledge Management: a proposed process model', *Proceedings AIS Americas*, 624–5.

SPENDER, J.-C. (1993) 'Competitive advantage from tacit knowledge?: unpacking the concept and its strategic implications', *Academy of Management Best Paper Proceedings*, 37–41.

STEWART, T.A. (1997) 'Brainpower: who owns IT . . . how they profit from it', *Fortune*, 135(5), 104–110.

SVEIBY, K. (1997) *The New Organizational Wealth: Managing and Measuring Knowledge-Based Assets*, San Francisco. Brett-Koehler.

TEMPLETON, G. and SNYDER, C. (1998) 'Toward a method for providing database structure derived from an ontological specification process: the example of Knowledge Management'. *Proceedings KI'97*, 1–11.

TURBAN, E., MCLEAN, E. and WETHERBE, J. (1996) *Information Technology for Management: Improving Quality and Productivity*, New York. Wiley.

VOGEL, P. (1996) 'Know your business: build a knowledgebase', *Datamation*, 42(13), 84–7.

WATKIN, E. (1996) 'Learning is more than a label', *Beyond Computing*, 5(6), 54–5.

WILSON, LARRY T. (1997) 'Knowledge Harvesting™', ⟨www.learnerfirst.com⟩, p. 3.

11 An Ontological Approach for Integrating Enterprise, Requirements and System Knowledge

Vaios Papaioannou and
Babis Theodoulidis

INTRODUCTION

The work reported in this chapter is based on an *ontological* framework for addressing the complexity of the knowledge that is acquired in the early stages of system development in an organisational setting. This complexity arises from various factors such as diversity in views, representations, user backgrounds, domains, organisational, complexity, etc. In our view, the incorporation of Information Systems within an Enterprise must take into account *three key areas of knowledge*: *Enterprise*, *Requirements* and *Information System* (IS) knowledge. Our project, a *Hypermedia Environment for Requirements Engineering* (*HERE*) is a theoretical framework and computer based environment for enhancing the *Requirements Engineering* (RE) process by addressing the analysis management and communication of this knowledge. Our theoretical framework is mainly based on the innovative use of ontologies for integrating the Enterprise, Requirements and System knowledge into a consistent, manageable entity as well as for linking the various information elements together.

In today's modern enterprises the realisation of enterprise goals is largely dependant on their supporting IS. Moreover, the success of an IS is measured by the extent to which it meets the requirements, needs and expectations of the Enterprise. These requirements form one of the basic infrastructure elements for a system development process. They refer to the needs of the users and they include why the system is being designed, what the system is intended to accomplish, and what constraints are to be observed (Ramamoorthly *et al.*, 1984). Consequently, RE is regarded as one of the most important and critical phases of the IS development because errors that occur during the early phases of an IS development, introduce much larger problems later on, during implementation, testing and maintenance (Boehm, 1989; LAS, 1993; SEI, 1995; Standish, 1995; ARIANE5, 1996; IWSSD-8, 1996).

On the other hand, the rapid growth of IS in numbers, size, complexity, and sophistication imposed even greater demands on the research of their development methods. This complexity is reflected in the large number of RE methods that investigate a number of issues. For example the area of Enterprise Modelling is concerned with the impact of IS on organisational structure and processes (Bubenko *et al.*, 1994; Loucopoulos, 1994; Loucopoulos and Karakostas, 1995). This diversity of orientation, stakeholders and representations hinders the RE process.

In our approach, called a *HERE*, we target at this complexity by advocating that the Enterprise, Requirements and System knowledge are very critical for the IS development. Our theoretical framework and computer-based environment are based on the innovative use of ontologies for integrating the Enterprise, Requirements and System knowledge into one consistent, manageable entity. In this way we enable stakeholders to identify, capture and integrate the information gathered in the RE phase of a system development in order to analyse it, communicate it with the involved parties and store it for present or future reference.

In the following sections we will analyse further our motivations for the HERE approach which is then presented in section three. We then clarify the role of ontologies and present applications of our framework as well as our tool support. Finally we conclude the study.

REQUIREMENTS ENGINEERING

The context of the HERE project is RE for Enterprise Information Systems. RE is defined as the systematic process of developing requirements through an iterative co-operative process of analysing the problem, documenting the resulting observations in a variety of representation formats and checking the accuracy of the understanding gained (Bubenko *et al.*, 1994).

There are three main goals for the Requirements Engineering process (Pohl, 1994):

1. improving an opaque system comprehension into a complete system specification;
2. transforming informal knowledge into formal representations;
3. gaining a common agreement on the specification out of the personal views

Each of these goals is represented as a dimension in 3D cube (Figure 11.1): the *Specification* Dimension, the *Representation* Dimension, and the *Agreement* Dimension. The aim of the Requirements Engineering process can be viewed as getting from the initial input to the desired output within the three dimensions. The initial input is characterised as opaque personal views of the system represented using informal languages, whereas the desired output is characterised as formally represented, complete system specification on which agreement was gained (Pohl, 1994).

Despite the initial understanding about the area of RE and some of its intrinsic issues and problems, RE practitioners still find it very hard to engineer requirements. In today's bibliography one can find numerous studies reporting and analysing a plethora of issues and problems that are connected with RE (Roman, 1985; Christel and Kang, 1992; Pohl, 1994; Zave, 1995). For example, there still is no

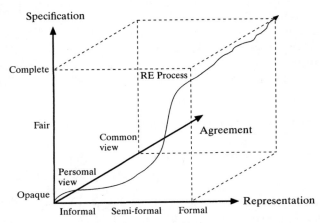

Figure 11.1   The three dimensions of Requirements Engineering (adapted from Pohl, 1994)

universal standard or description of the RE process and the full scope is not yet established.

Complexity is one of the most important problems of requirements engineering. There are different types of complexity:

- Product complexity is associated with RE products that may exist in various forms, media, etc. and may contain information covering different levels of knowledge, different views, at varying levels of formality. RE Information is very dynamic and may become difficult to inspect, manage, trace and maintain.
- Organisational complexity has to deal with the various groups of stakeholders that are involved in the RE process each one with different views, interests, domain knowledge, objectives (often conflicting), etc. This diversity is also reflected in the RE products.
- Process complexity has to do with the fact that there is no one single way of coping with the issue of requirements, nor there is one single standard to acquire, analyse, model, verify, and measure requirements.

The RE process results to products that can be viewed as information elements, which actually incorporate the knowledge, acquired though the RE process. This information may be of any capacity and varying levels of complexity. It may deal with anything from enterprise strategic goals down to system implementation descriptions and may be informal (e.g. natural language), semi-formal (e.g. dataflow diagrams) or formal (e.g. Z). The information and artifacts described are expected to be communicated to a number of *stakeholders*: requirement engineers, future system end users, domain experts, analysts, developers, testers, maintainers, etc.

More specifically RE stakeholders face the following issues regarding the RE products:

1. *Varying levels of information abstraction.* When the information to be analysed spans to more than one abstraction level, e.g. Enterprise Strategy, Enterprise Processes, Enterprise Information System, analysis may then also become complex and dependencies between one level and another may be lost. Changes at a higher level may fail to be reflected to lower levels and vice versa.
2. *Multiplicity of representation formalisms.* Information conflicts, inconsistencies and overload may occur because of the large number of existing methodologies or formalisms that may be applied. For example parts of the system development may have

been developed using structured methodologies and specifications whilst others may follow the object-oriented paradigm.

3   *Multiple views.* Information is partitioned into different viewpoints depending on the concern of the stakeholders involved. For example, a manager may be interested in strategic goal models while database operators may be interested in transaction models of their database. Furthermore, different views may introduce gaps in terminology and semantic conflicts.

These issues form the basis for the development of the HERE approach.

THE HERE APPROACH

In HERE, our view of the RE information, in an ideal situation, is essentially covering three main aspects of the Universe of Discourse (UoD):

1.   Knowledge about the *Domain Requirements*: enterprise requirements, user requirements, non-functional requirements, etc.
2.   Knowledge about the *Enterprise Domain*: the enterprise structure, its processes, actors, goals, etc.
3.   Knowledge about the *IS*: system requirements, system design, database design, process design, etc.

The HERE framework aims at the support of analysis, management and communication of the Problem Domain knowledge by integrating it into one consistent ontology (Figure 11.2).

Another critical point is the inclusion of *link ontologies*. We advocate that the conceptualisation of the relationships between the models and model constructs used to record the problem domain knowledge is as important as the elements of this knowledge themselves.

The realisation of these concepts and the communication and management of the problem domain knowledge is achieved with the HERE hypermedia environment. The HERE environment makes effective use of hyper-links, hypertext and multimedia information stored in a DBMS.

The overall architecture of the HERE environment is shown in Figure 11.3. In the HERE architecture, we identify three main components:

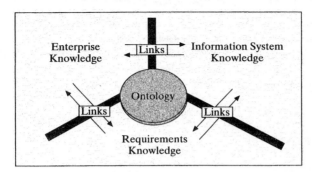

Figure 11.2   Integrating the problem domain knowledge in HERE

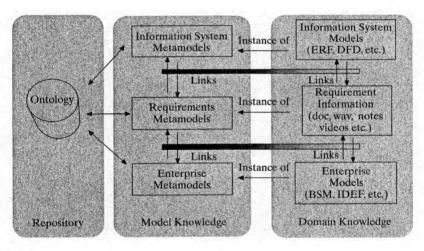

Figure 11.3   The HERE Architecture

1. The *Model Knowledge* component: includes the knowledge that describes models that may be used in order to specify domains of interest. In other words, this model contains meta-model information. This information spans over the three levels of UoD knowledge as described earlier, i.e. Enterprise, Requirements, and System knowledge.
2. The *Domain Knowledge* component: includes the knowledge that is modelled for a specific domain. The models are instances of model specifications in the Model Knowledge component.

According to their content and purpose, they also span over the Enterprise, Requirements, and System knowledge.
3. The *Repository* component: It holds all the above specifications in the form of ontologies along with all relevant data that contribute to the overall knowledge of the UoD.

Within each component, there are links, which express the interconnections that exist between elements both at the model and at the domain component.

THE ROLE OF ONTOLOGIES IN HERE

The term '*ontology*' has its origin in philosophy, where an ontology is a systematic account of existence. Recently the concept of ontology emerged as a research topic mainly in the areas of Knowledge Base System integration and Artificial Intelligence Knowledge Representation approaches (Fikes *et al.*, 1991). Although the term 'ontology' has also appeared as a conference theme in the Information – Software System development and other relative communities, only a few of their approaches have actually used ontologies solely for representing or integrating Enterprise knowledge (Fox *et al.*, 1993; Fillion *et al.*, 1995; Uschold, 1995; Uschold *et al.*, 1995).

In HERE, the concept of Ontologies was adopted within the context of Requirements Engineering. Ontologies are inventories of the kinds of things that are presumed to exist in a given domain together with a formal description of the salient properties of those things and the salient relations that hold among them. In our framework, ontologies are used to hold the knowledge about models and model instances of the UoD in one unified representation. Thus by using a common representation, ontologies become a computational medium to integrate all the domain information to describe domain knowledge in two primary realms: the *Metamodel* realm and the *Instance* realm. The first realm holds meta-level descriptions of the UoD, i.e. the constructs that will be used to describe the UoD (model knowledge component), while the second realm will actually hold this knowledge (domain knowledge component).

Ontology models differ slightly from traditional conceptual models. This is because Ontologies are driven from the need to describe the elements that exist in the UoD in a generic and explicit manner, so future references have to commit to these conceptualisations.

Traditional conceptual models on the other hand are more specific in abstracting and describing the problem domain in the context of developing a system. In this sense, the content of ontologies may be viewed as a superset of these models; for example, a specific data model of a problem domain may be based on the Ontology of the domain of interest. Thus, we view ontologies as the ideal result of the RE process where there is an effective exploitation of the domain concepts and knowledge elements.

Another special characteristic of ontologies is that they are explicit specifications of conceptualisations that are commonly agreed. Thus in HERE we view ontologies within the RE context and consider them to include the agreement dimension:

Ontology = Model + Agreement

In this view, ontologies serve as more enhanced abstractions of reality which demonstrate a higher level of conformance to the three dimensions of requirements engineering, namely specification, representation, agreement, as described by Pohl (1994) and may form a reliable basis of reference, communication, knowledge sharing and reuse.

Another important point is that the ontological descriptions are expressed in a modular, expandable, reusable manner:

- Modular: One might concentrate interest and reason about specific parts of an ontology concerning specific contexts. Specific parts of the ontology may be imported or exported.
- Expandable: Ontologies are not static. They are refined over time and may be expanded. Ontology elements may be added or deleted on demand.
- Reusable: Ontologies are regarded to be quite generic and commonly agreed, therefore they can be reused. It is in fact one of the purposes of ontologies to be the primary mediums for knowledge sharing. Once an ontology has been developed for some domain then future developments have to commit to this ontology.

Once the input is transformed into ontologies then the review, reasoning and management of the RE information becomes feasible as ontologies can then be browsed examined and managed. The fact that ontologies describe the model specifications used does not imply that the HERE ontologies replace these formalisms. The idea is for the HERE framework to provide support for the existing methodologies and formalisms and not the introduction of a new one. Applications and examples of the HERE framework are presented in the next section.

APPLYING THE HERE FRAMEWORK

The first step towards the development of an ontology for a specific model is the analysis of the main model concepts. Then the model elements can be conceptualised into an ontology in order to describe the model itself. Once the model is described as ontology at the meta-level then specific instances of the model can be used to describe individual problem domains.

In general, the top-level tasks for applying the HERE approach to a specific domain are:

1. Identify the nature of the domain and the knowledge areas required.
2. Identify the models required to describe the domain.
3. Develop or reuse (if they already exist) the ontologies that describe these models.
4. Instantiate the above models into the domain ontology instance.
5. Inspect these definitions for the purpose of analysing, communicating and managing the domain knowledge.

The last three steps can be supported by the use of the HERE computer environment.

As mentioned above, our view of the knowledge that is gathered throughout the RE process, in an ideal situation, involves three main areas: *information system knowledge*, *enterprise knowledge* and *domain requirements*. Thus, we encoded three example ontologies, the *Entity Relationship Time (ERT) Ontology* (Theodoulidis *et al.*, 1990, 1991a, 1901b; McBrien *et al.*, 1991; Ait-Braham *et al.*, 1994), the *Enterprise Ontology* (Fraser, 1994), the *Non-Functional Goal ontology* (Chung, 1991) that belong to these three domains respectively, in order to demonstrate the HERE approach. A *Link Ontology* is also developed for expressing the links that may be identified between models. These ontologies involve the definition of the above models at the meta-level using our object-oriented framework.

Ontologies in HERE are expressed according to the object-oriented paradigm. In this way the process of conceptualising and developing an ontology is more familiar within the RE and/or systems

– software engineering communities and these representations are more related to the future system development. Other benefits are the intrinsic advantages of object oriented approaches, such as easy mapping form the problem domain to the object-oriented specification, modularity, structuring, encapsulation, inheritance, etc. For example let us consider the ontological encoding of the Entity Relationship Time (ERT) model (Theodoulidis *et al.*, 1991) to describe a database schema, concerning the IS knowledge. After analysing the concepts of the ERT model then it is possible to code the facts concerning this model into an ontology. The same analysis and encoding was also applied to the enterprise ontology (Fraser, 1994; Uschold *et al.*, 1995; Stader, 1996). The original ontology was developed and coded within the scope and context of the Enterprise project. Our specification was coded based on the enterprise ontology informal specification (Uschold *et al.*, 1995) and supplemented by its ontolingua code counterpart (AIAI, 1996). In our encoding of the enterprise ontology we introduced new assumptions, we included, modified or excluded original terms, and focused mostly on the enterprise ontology sections which were more relevant to our scope.

Finally, exemplifying our approach for representing non-functional requirements knowledge we encoded the Non Functional Requirements (NFR) Framework ontology (Chung, 1991). Once the ERT, Enterprise and NFR definitions are stored at the meta-level this immediately allows the storage of information concerning specific problem domains as instances of these metamodels. For example, let us consider a university related domain. Then we expect entity instaces like students, admission officers, applications, etc. For example, we may consider the ORGANISATION_UNIT instance Computation Department of the ORGANISATION_SECTION (Enterprise Ontology): ORGANISATION_UNIT identity: computation_department managed_by: umist manages: (information_system_engineering, decision technology etc.) activities: set (admission, teaching, research, consultancy).

Similar to the development of these ontologies is also the Non Functional Requirements (NFR) framework ontology (Chung, 1991) which is also included in the HERE set of encoded ontologies.

One of the main issues for analysing the knowledge described so far is the relationship between these information elements. For example, requirements analysts would like to know the impacts of the Enterprise ontology to the Entity Relationship Time (ERT) designs and vice versa. In our evaluation, we will examine questions such as:

- Is it possible to reason about links between elements of the same model (intramodel links)?
- Is it possible to reason about links between elements of different models (intermodel links)?
- Is it possible to establish traceability links between RE artifacts?
- Is it possible to establish user-defined links?

In HERE these issues are addressed with the *Link Ontologies*. *Link Ontologies* are quite similar to the rest of the ontology models. The main difference is that the purpose of link ontologies is to identify and maintain links that may exist among concepts that have already being modelled as ontologies. In this context it is expected that the modelling, and instantiation of link ontologies takes place during the last phases of ontology modelling and instantiation.

In HERE the link ontologies are integrated with all remaining subontologies contributing to the overall ontology. In HERE we may identify three categories of link ontologies, namely model link, traceability link, and user-defined link ontologies.

By forming these link classifications and hierarchies, the HERE users are able to fully represent their knowledge concerning links among knowledge elements into clear, well structured, comprehensive, explicit models. The same models can be reused into similar situations, and tailored according to project needs. New link models or inappropriate models may be included and excluded on demand. In addition, certain stakeholders may focus on certain link models, e.g. software developers may select and reason about the links concerning the IS – software models.

THE HERE ENVIRONMENT SUPPORT

The discussion so far has only been referred to the theoretical aspects of our framework. Thus, we have seen how it is possible to provide both intentional and extensional specifications of the problem domain knowledge. In a real situation in order to take the full advantage of our work, our framework has to be supported a computer-based environment. The HERE environment realises the framework objectives into a tangible toolkit, which exploits its full potential.

The top-level objectives of the HERE environment are:

- The ability to define and manage ontologies as meta-level definitions of object models, which can be instantiated later.
- The ability to interactively examine these definitions; the ability to query ontology models.
- The ability to instantiate ontology meta-models and populate-manage the project database.
- The ability to interactively examine and query about the model instances.

The above requirements are realised via three main tool components:

1. The *Ontology Editor*: This component is responsible for defining, specifying ontologies. The users of this editor are mainly ontology engineers who develop the necessary ontologies collaborating with the domain experts who are responsible for holding the knowledge concerning the problem domain.

2. The *Ontology Manager*: It supports the population of the HERE repository with data at the domain level, that is all instances of models as described in the metamodel section (model component), and all relative RE data such as documents, videos, etc. Transactions such as insertion, deletion and update of new elements are also supported. The users of this component are expected to be requirements engineers, system designers, etc.

3. The *Ontology Browser*: It enables the examination and reasoning of the HERE repository. This component is hypermedia based, built on top of the object oriented database management system. It allows the easy exploration of the here repository elements through interactive browsing and database queries. This component is used by everyone who needs access to the central repository information.

The HERE top-level implementation architecture is WWW-based, as depicted in Figure 11.4.

The main idea is that we have a central object oriented database management system, which serves as our repository. This repository contains both meta-level (database schema) and instance-level descriptions (database instances). The repository is connected to a WWW server. Clients can communicate with the server via the Internet. All clients use a WWW interface (web browser) which allows them to interact with the central HERE repository. The clients can perform the basic operations required, i.e. define and manipulate

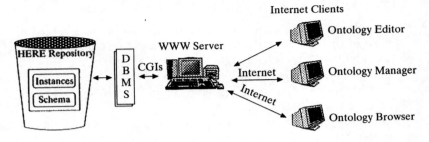

Figure 11.4   The HERE implementation overview

ontology schemas (Ontology Editor), populate ontology instances (Ontology Manager), and finally inspect the repository contents (Ontology Browser). The server can fulfil the requests of its clients by running a set of Common Gateway Interface (CGI) programs. These programs accept the requests on the server and return Hypet Text Markup Language (HTML) output to the clients.

Conclusion

The HERE approach addresses this complexity of the RE process by supporting existing practices through a complementary framework. To achieve that it gathers the information of the RE phase of a system development project in order to analyse it, communicate it with the involved parties and store it for present or future reference. As a consequence, HERE manages to minimise the complexity in terms of three dimensions:

1. *Product complexity.* HERE supports RE products in various forms, media, etc. that contain information covering different levels of knowledge, different views and at varying levels of formality.
2. *Organisational complexity.* HERE deals with the various groups of stakeholders that are involved in the RE process by accommodating each one of their different views, interests, domain knowledge and objectives.
3. *Process complexity.* HERE does not enforce one single way of coping with the issue of requirements.

Overall, HERE addresses effectively the complexity of the knowledge that is acquired in the early stages of system development in an organisational setting and in terms of three areas of knowledge: *Enterprise, Requirements*, and *IS* knowledge.

References

AIAI (1996) Ontology ENTERPRISE-V1.0 (Ontolingua code), Artificial Intelligence Applications Institute, 80 South Bridge, Edinburgh EH1 1HN, 8 November.

AIT-BRAHAM, A., THEODOULIDIS, C. and KARVELIS G. (1994) 'Conceptual modelling and manipulation of temporal databases', 13th International Conference on the Entity Relationship Approach, Manchester, December; also in *Lecture Notes in Computer Science*, 881, 296–313.

ARIANE 5 (1996) 'Flight 501 failure report by the Inquiry Board' (Chairman of the Board, Professor J.L. Lions ESA (European Space Agency)), *Public Relations Press Releases and Information Notes*, 19 July Paris.

BOEHM, B.W. (1989) *Software Risk Management*, Washington, DC: IEEE Computer Society Press.

BUBENKO, J., ROLLAND, C., LOUCOPOULOS, P. and DEANTONELLIS, V. (1994) 'Facilitating "fuzzy to formal" requirements modelling', *IEEE International Conference on Requirements Engineering*, Colorado, 18–22 April.

CHRISTEL, M. and KANG, K.C. (1992) 'Issues in requirements elicitation', Software Engineering Institute, Technical Report, CMU/SEI-92-TR-12, Carnegie Mellon University.

CHUNG (1991) 'Representation and utilisation of non-functional requirements for information system design', in R. Anderson, J.A. Bubenko, Jr. and A. Solvberg (eds), *Proceedings* of *CAiSE '91, 3rd International Conference on Advanced Information Systems Engineering*, Trondheim, Berlin: Springer-Verlag, 5–30.

FIKES R., CUTKOSKY, M., GRUBER, T. and VAN BAALEN, J. (1991) 'Knowledge sharing technology project overview', Stanford University, Knowledge Systems Laboratory, Technical Report KSL 91–71, November.

FILLION, F., MENZEL, C., BLINN, T. and MAYER, R. (1995) 'An ontology-based environment for enterprise model integration', The Workshop on Basic Ontological Issues in Knowledge Sharing at IJCAI '95, August 19–20, Montreal.

FOX, M., CHIONGLO, J.F. and FADEL, F.G. (1993) 'A common sense model of the enterprise', *Proceedings of the 2nd Industrial Engineering Research Conference*, Norcross GA: Institute for Industrial Engineers, 425–9.

FRASER, J. (1994) 'Managing Change through Enterprise Models', in Milne, R. and Montgomery, A. (eds), *Applications and Innovations in Expert Systems, II*, Boston: SGES Publications, 123–45.

GUARINO, N. and POLI, R. (1995) 'The role of formal ontology in information technology', *International Journal of Human–Computer Studies*, 43(5/6), 623–4.

IWSSD-8 (1996) *Proceedings of the 8th International Workshop on Software Specification and Design (IWSSD-8)*, Schloss Velen, 22–23 March.

LAS (1993) 'Report on the London Ambulance Service (LAS) inquiry', February 1993, version 0.99, electronically prepared by Antony Finkelstein, 30-11-95, original ISBN: 0 905133 70 6.

LOUCOPOULOS, P. (1994) 'Extending Database design techniques to incorporate enterprise requirements evolution', *The Baltic Workshop on National Infrastructure Databases: Problems, Methods, and Experiences*, Vilnius, 17–20 May.

LOUCOPOULOS, P. and KARAKOSTAS, V. (1995) *System Requirements Engineering*, London: McGraw-Hill International Series on Software Engineering.

MATTHIAS, J. and KLAUS, P. (1994) 'Requirements engineering in the Year 2001: on (virtually) managing a changing reality', *Software Engineering Journal*, November.

MCBRIEN, P., NIEZETTE, M., PANTAZIS, D., SELTVEIT, A.-H., SUNDIN, U., TZIALLAS, G. and THEODOULIDIS, C. (1991) 'A rule language to capture and model business policy specifications', *3rd Nordic Conference on Advanced Information Systems Engineering (CAiSE'91)*, Trondheim, May; also in *Lecture Notes in Computer Science*, 498, 307–18.

POHL, K. (1994) 'The three dimensions of requirements engineering: a framework and its applications', *Information Systems*, 19(3), 243–58.

RAMAMOORTHLY, C.V., PRAKASH, A., TSAI, W.T. and USUDA, Y. (1984) 'Software engineering: problems and perspectives', *IEEE Computer*, October, 191–209.

ROMAN, G.-C. (1985) 'A taxonomy of issues in requirements engineering', *IEEE computer*, April, 14–21.

SEI (1995) 'Systems engineering capability maturity model', Version 1.1A, *Software Engineering Institute* Report, CMU/SEI-95-MM-003, November.

STADER, J. (1996) 'Results of the enterprise project', in *Proceedings of Expert Systems '96, the 16th Annual Conference of the British Computer Society Specialist Group on Expert Systems*, Cambridge, December.

STANDISH (1995) 'CHAOS', The Standish Group International, Inc., ⟨http://www.standishgroup.com/chaos.html⟩.

THEODOULIDIS, C., LOUCOPOULOS, P. and WANGLER, B. (1991a) 'A conceptual modelling formalism for temporal database applications', *Information Systems*, 16(4); 401–16.

THEODOULIDIS, C. , LOUCOPOULOS, P. and WANGLE, B. (1991b) 'The time dimension in conceptual modelling', *Information Systems*, 16(3).

THEODOULIDIS, C., WANGLER, B. and LOUCOPOULOS, P. (1990) 'Requirements specification in TEMPORA', *2nd Nordic Conference on Advanced Information Systems Engineering (CAiSE'90)*. Kista, May; also in *Lecture Notes Computer Science*, 436, 264–82.

USCHOLD, M. (1995) 'Towards a methodology for building ontologies', *Workshop on Basic Ontological Issues in Knowledge Sharing*, held in conjunction with IJCAI-95.

USCHOLD, M., KING, M., MORALEE, S. and ZORGIOS, Y. (1995) 'The enterprise ontology' Artificial Intelligence Applications Institute, 80 South Bridge, Edinburgh EH1 1HN.

ZAVE, P. (1995) *Classification of Research Efforts in Requirements Engineering*', RE'95, los Alamitos, CA/York: IEEE Computer Society Press 214–16.

12 Towards a Contingency View of Infrastructure and Knowledge: an exploratory study

Claudio Ciborra and Ole Hanseth

INTRODUCTION

IT infrastructures coupled with BPR initiatives have the potential of supporting and enabling new organisational forms and help firms face the challenges of globalisation. The management literature gives prescriptions of how to set up, implement and use infrastructures to reach a new IT capability, diminish transaction costs and obtain competitive advantage. However, the scant empirical basis of such literature goes hand in hand with the lack of a theory linking the deployment of infrastructure to the nature of the business and the industry. This study of the deployment and use of infrastructures in six large multinationals prepares the ground for a contingency approach to the whole issue. The different implementation processes and applications reported by the case studies suggest that there is much more variety than a 'one best way' recommended by the literature. The theory of the firm as a repository of knowledge processes is a good candidate to explain qualitatively the empirical evidence, and provides a contingency framework that can be further tested.

Corporate infrastructure as a concept emerged in the 1980s in relation to the planning of large corporate information systems. It emphasises the standardisation of systems and data throughout the corporation as a way to reconcile the centralised IS department and resources on the one hand, and the distribution of systems and applications on the other. Today, managing an infrastructure to deliver effective IT capability means dealing with problems such as: aligning strategy with IT architecture and key business processes information requirements; (Henderson et al., 1996) universal use and access of IT resources; standardisation; interoperability of systems and applications through protocols and gateways; flexibility, resilience and security (Hanseth, 1996). Ideally, infrastructure reconciles local variety and proliferation of applications and usages of IT with centralised planning and control over IT resources and business processes. (Hanseth, 1996; Broadbent and Weill, 1997).

However, the more one looks at how large corporations are setting up and deploying complex IT infrastructures, often in connection with BPR projects (Broadbent *et al.*, 1995), the more the picture emerging is fuzzy: strategic alignment does not fully explain the dynamics of implementation (Ciborra, 1997; Sauer and Burn, 1997), and power games prevail over efficiency considerations (Knights *et al.*, 1997). At the limit, infrastructures seem to 'drift' (Ciborra, 1996), or being created by planning as well as by improvisation (Orlikowski, 1996).

In order to appreciate the key factors determining the dynamics of corporate infrastructures, an exploratory empirical study has been carried out in six multinationals: IBM, Hoffmann La Roche, Astra, SKF, Statoil and Norsk Hydro. The deployment and use of infrastructure has been followed up in a variety of corporate functions: Marketing; Production; R&D, etc. focusing on the relationships between headquarters and affiliates. A number of technologies and relevant business processes have been analysed, ranging from Lotus Notes platforms to office automation suites, SAP, Internet and Intranet, to dedicated systems, standards and protocol.

The data collected confirmed the initial awareness: infrastructures 'in action' differ significantly from the neat pictures provided by the management literature. For example, they cannot be classified in just three types (utility; dependence; enabling), (Weill *et al.*, 1996) since they drift from one use mode to another with no apparent logic; the implementation process is far from being straightforward, but is punctuated by opportunistic moves and power games (Murray and Willmott, 1997). A theory able to predict success or failure of an infrastructure project is still missing. So far, only recipes or maxims have been put forward: but what happens if a firm does not follow them? Unfortunately, reliance on previous empirical research and its conclusions has been of little help in explaining the cases at hand (Broadbent *et al.*, 1996). Namely, while IT infrastructure capabilities do vary according to industry, emerging applications such as Lotus Notes or SAP are being adopted across all industries. This tends to confound the evidence of a difference. While infrastructure varies with the intensity of business unit synergy, there can be very different ways of achieving such a synergy (e.g. by interlocking processes through BPR, or providing a common business template through access to Web sites). Since the planning process is so punctuated by surprises, chance and opportunistic adjustments, in none of the cases could a correlation be established between emphasis on strategic intent, management backing and infrastructure deployment. In one important case, Roche (see below), just the opposite has occurred: only by 'releasing' management tracking and control a (different) infrastructure could emerge.

This chapter attempts at linking the empirical study of infrastructure *in situ* with economic theory. Two streams of economic thinking are utilised: the economics of infrastructures, in particular standards (Grindley, 1995), and the theory of the firm emphasising the knowledge processing properties embedded in the firm's routines (Nelson and Winter, 1982). These theories are harnessed to understand what happens to corporate infrastructures in practice: how are they developed; where are they applied; what are their impacts and degree of success. The cases provide a rich, though initial and exploratory evidence to set out a new framework on which to build, and subsequently test, a contingency view of infrastructure. The key contingency factor is the nature of the knowledge processes in the business and the implementation process. The framework allows classifying otherwise confusing cases and generating further hypotheses to be tested.

THE ECONOMIC PERSPECTIVES

Two relevant aspects of the life of an infrastructure, i.e. its deployment and the type of business process to which it is applied, can be analysed by tapping economic theories stemming from industrial organisation and institutional economics.

The implementation process

Schematically, a typical management agenda concerning corporate infrastructure would entail the following:

- analysis of the firm's strategic context to elicit the key business drivers;
- a joint consideration for the need to improve or transform existing business processes and infrastructure;

- formulation and implementation of relevant BPR and technical change plans;
- envisioning changes in roles, responsibilities, incentives, skills, organisational structures required by BPR and infrastructure reforms. (Broadbent and Weill, 1997)

One should be wary of this 'one best way' kind of agenda since it hides a number of dilemmas. For example, one may ask: are there decreasing returns to infrastructure? (Cordella and Simon, 1997) Does more infrastructure investment in a changing business mean more sophisticated infrastructure or just facing maintenance and adaptation costs of an existing, rigid technology and organisation? Relatedly, is it better to build a flexible infrastructure that enables a wide range of unplanned business redesign options, or a highly consistent (i.e. aligned) infrastructure with the current strategic intent? Is there a trade-off between alignment and flexibility? Extensive studies of top managers' opinions do not lead to any clear-cut conclusion (Duncan, 1995).

The models of strategic alignment and the agendas that spell out what to do in order to extract the maximum IT capability from corporate infrastructure suggest (Luftman, 1996; Broadbent and Weill, 1997):

- Aligning business and technology strategies is an ongoing executive responsibility: 'strategic alignment is a journey, not an event';
- Managers must be ready to learn and adapt, no matter what is the alignment pattern selected at one point in time;
- There are barriers that due to political, cultural or economic factors impede the smooth implementation of any strategic plan concerning infrastructure.

While the management agendas tend to be precise in guiding the *formulation* of an infrastructure plan, they do not give any special advice on *implementation* and adaptation. They only provide words of caution, but these do not suffice to translate a sound plan into its production (Argyris and Schoen, 1996).

Economics of standards and network infrastructures, (Hanseth, 1996; Hanseth *et al.*, 1996) can overcome the sometimes narrow 'information engineering mindset' that lures in the managerial discourses about infrastructure. Consider the issue of pricing, as an example of how economics can broaden the implementation agenda. Pricing a collective good has several facets: how to let people use more pay more; how to avoid free riding; what is the trade off between universal service type of delivery vs. a customised service; how to reach a *critical mass* of infrastructure users? Who should benefit or pay for the positive and/or negative *externalities* generated by infrastructure use?

A balanced answer to such questions is a key factor for the take off and long-term development of any infrastructure. The pricing issue points to another important topic: the scope for control over an infrastructure is limited, and management have to live with a resource that they can govern only in part (pending the issue of transaction costs (Coase, 1962)). Also, the governance of infrastructure is a problem, not a given, since there can be multiple stakeholders with conflicting interests. The net result can be an infrastructure that expands and grows in directions and to an extent largely outside the control of any individual stakeholder. Building large infrastructures takes time. All elements are connected. New requirements appear which the infrastructure has to adapt to. A whole infrastructure cannot be changed instantly – the new has to be connected to the old. Hence, the old – the installed base – influences how the new is designed. Infrastructures develop through extending and improving the *installed base* (Hanseth, 1996).

A large information infrastructure is not just hard to change. It might also be a powerful actor influencing its own future life – its extension and size as well as its form. Consider the issue of 'standards' as a part of a more general phenomenon labelled 'self-reinforcing mechanisms' (Arthur, 1996) and 'network externalities' (Katz and Shapiro, 1986). A standard which builds up an installed base ahead of its competitors becomes cumulatively more attractive, making the choice of standards 'path dependent', and highly influenced by a small advantage gained in the early stages (Grindley, 1995).

Other key effects of self-reinforcing mechanisms are (Arthur, 1996):

- *Lock-in*: i.e. when a technology has been adopted it will be impossible to develop competing technologies.
- *Possible inefficiency*: i.e. the best solution may not necessarily win (David, 1987).

Information infrastructures are paradigmatic examples of phenomena where 'network externalities' and positive feedback (increasing return on adoption) are crucial, and accordingly technologies easily being 'locked-in' and turning irreversible. Designing and governing an infra-structure differ from designing an MIS, due to the far reaching influence of the installed base and the self-reinforcing mechanisms. The very scope of the management agenda changes. Infrastructure is not just a complex, shared tool that management are free to align according to their strategy. The economic perspective highlights a more limited and opportunistic agenda involving trade-offs and dilemmas, and a number of tactics. David (1987) points out three dilemmas in developing networking technologies:

- *Narrow policy window.* There may be only brief and uncertain 'windows in time', during which effective interventions can be made at moderate costs.
- *Blind giants.* Decision-makers are likely to have greatest power to influence the future trajectories of network technologies, just when suitable knowledge on which to make system-wide choices is most lacking;

An important remedy to help overcome the effects of positive feedback and network externalities, i.e. lock-in and inefficiency, is the construction of gateways and adapters (Katz and Shapiro, 1986; David and Bunn, 1988).

In sum, while from an engineering and managerial perspective the task is to design, build, align and control an infrastructure, the thrust of the economic understanding of the dynamics of infrastructures points out that 'cultivating' (Dahlbom and Janlert, 1996) an installed base is a more realistic option. The concept of cultivation focuses on the limits of rational, human control (Simon, 1976). Also, one should expect to find a variety of implementation processes when dealing with infrastructures: the actions of multiple stakeholders, and their limited scope; externalities and transaction costs, combined with the influence of non-linear development processes make the outcome of any implementation less predictable than the management and engineering literature would like us to believe.

THE THEORY OF THE FIRM

Why is an infrastructure useful? The management literature replies in rather generic terms: it is useful to run interlinked applications to process and communicate information seamlessly. Or, it supports streamlined processes. At the limit, it enhances coordination and decreases transaction costs. Unfortunately, the information engineering frameworks have so far paid little attention to the economics of the firm. As a consequence, theoretical developments about the role of core capabilities (Prahalad and Hamel, 1990); the resource-based view of strategy (Barney, 1991); the model of the knowledge creating company (Nonaka and Takeuchi, 1996) tend to be largely ignored, or just objects of superficial attention. This is a pity, since the common denominator of these theories is the study of the firm as a collection of people 'who know what to do'. 'Productivity derives in part from transaction and monitoring cost considerations, but it also depends on . . . the conditions that underlie the acquisition and use of knowledge' (Demsetz, 1993). Knowledge is embedded in the members' skills and the organisational routines (Nelson and Winter, 1982). Both tacit and articulated, it represents the key asset to obtain a sustainable competitive advantage. Firms can be looked at as 'treasuries of process knowledge' and of the specialised inputs and resources required to put knowledge to work (Boyton and Victor, 1991). Infrastructure is one of such key resources, since the very business processes it supports are the embodiment of the know how of the firm. If 'economic organization, including the firm, must reflect the fact that knowledge is costly to produce, maintain and use' (Demsetz, 1991), one can look at infrastructure as a device dedicated to lower such costs, by allowing its efficient processing, communication and accumulation.

The knowledge embedded in products, services and processes vary across firms and industries. In high-tech. firms workers are highly skilled, production processes are complex and products knowledge-rich. Other industries, e.g. the production of metal may rely on processes that are stable, based on routine knowledge. A firm, or an industry, can migrate from a knowledge-poor to a knowledge-rich business. Thus, Benetton operates in an industry traditionally considered mature and knowledge poor. However, it has succeeded in re-inventing the mature business by adding knowledge to its distribution chain, production process, marketing, etc. Moreover, Benetton's IT use suggests that the higher the knowledge content (in process and product), the higher the investment in infrastructure. In sum, the type of infrastructure does not vary arbitrarily; rather, it adapts in range and scope to the type of knowledge 'embedded' in the firm and the industry.

This exploratory study has focused on 'globalisation', a process making knowledge (creation, diffusion, utilisation) increasingly more important to deliver competitive products and services (Reich,

1991). Creating and getting access to knowledge requires closer collaboration inside an organisation, but even more so with outside partners – customers (Norman and Ramirez, 1994) as well as subcontractors. This collaboration of course needs to be supported by infrastructures.

THE COMPANY CASES

The company cases can now be reviewed in short, by presenting 'vignettes' with some impressionistic details about infrastructures, their application domains and implementation processes. The cases concern companies which are well known, and need only scant information about their industry, size, turnover, etc.

IBM

Since the second half of the 1990s IBM has been formulating and deploying an extensive fabric of new processes and tools in order to be able to operate efficiently on a world-wide basis as a global company. One of the most important is Customer Relationship Management (CRM).

CRM consists of an array of processes that streamline all the activities between IBM and its customers across markets, product lines and geographies. It affects more than 120000 employees world-wide and it is based on a variety of existing and new systems and applications. CRM is supposed to be the backbone for the completion of any business transaction: from the early opportunity identification to the order fulfilment and customer satisfaction evaluation. The main components of CRM, processes, roles and IT tools, represent the infrastructure of the new, global IBM. Indeed, internally CRM is nicknamed the 'plumbing' of IBM.

Various management units and practices are dedicated to the strategic management and operational deployment of CRM. Backed by full top management support its implementation has been going on for four years. However, from the initial top-down approach, management has shifted to a more opportunistic attitude, trying to fix gradually the sources of resistance emerged during the long deployment phase. The IT platform has not delivered the expected support so far, because of the huge installed base of pre- existing applications. While the development from scratch of a totally new IT infrastructure is out of question, new hope comes from commercial applications such as Lotus Notes and SAP.

SKF

SKF is a Swedish multinational that produces bearings. It is operating in more than 130 countries, with production at more than 80 different sites. Its employees are 43000. SKF has grown from its initial 15 employees in 1907 rather slowly, by successfully developing its organisation and information technology in a gradual way. For example, already in the 1970s it began securing its own global communications infrastructure (based on the SNA protocol). In the 1980s it standardised its information systems into an integrated 'common systems' set. In the 1990s it introduced process orientation in production and distribution. The infrastructure built over the last decades allows SKF to run global forecasting and supply systems through a variety of corporate applications, message transfer systems and satellite links. For example, the International Customer Service System, installed in 1981, provides a key global interface between the sales and manufacturing units. Other systems are dedicated to master production scheduling; manufacturing; and finance. What is striking is that SKF seems to have always focused on production, and has developed its infrastructure as a Management Information System for global production control. Sometimes, ambitious applications, expected to provide rich information on production processes and products, have been abandoned in favour of more basic versions.

Thanks to its hefty market share throughout the decades SKF has been able to grow gradually and build its infrastructure accordingly. On the other hand, its information systems do not strike the observer as sophisticated or state of the art. Recently, however, SKF has increased its focus on customer service, having implications for its infrastructure. Ford, for instance, wants SKF to access their stock control systems twice a day to figure out their needs for bearings. Unitor, distributing bearings (among other products) to ships requires SKF to deliver any bearing at any harbour within 24 hours and easy access to SKF's technical expertise (which means using modern telecommunications).

Norsk Hydro

Norsk Hydro (NH) is a diversified Norwegian company, founded in 1905. Since 1972 its income has grown from kr1billion to kr85billion.

Besides its original fertilisers business, it produces light metals, oil and gas. The business divisions have enjoyed a high level of autonomy. Independent IT strategies and solutions have been the common practice, although a corporate IT department has been there for quite some time. Since the late 1980s the main goals of corporate IT have been:

- unified solutions to avoid duplication of efforts among the divisions;
- infrastructure standards;
- sharing competence in systems development.

To achieve these goals institutions important for building consensus were created. Consensus was reached about the need for a common protocol (TCP/IP), and a corporate standard concerning office automation applications. Since some of the new divisions were 'allergic to mainframes', the common standard (called Bridge) referred to desktop and communication applications only. Building the Bridge platform was a slow and difficult process because of the highly decentralised way in which PCs had been purchased and applied by the divisions. Today, there are about Bridge 20 000 users. Over the years, however, with the proliferation of systems and applications (Windows, new Operating Systems, Networks, etc.), the Bridge has become an umbrella infrastructure, losing its initial focus on desktop applications. Several functions are duplicated (Lotus and Microsoft desktop products, Notes mail and cc:mail, Notes data bases and Web, etc.).

Throughout the 1990s collaboration and knowledge sharing between divisions as well as outside organisations (like engineering companies in the oil sector) has been increasingly focused. Lotus Notes and the rest of Bridge are seen as important tools supporting this. Notes use has been supported by the development of an infrastructure of more than one hundred servers. Beyond that diffusion has been based on local user initiatives. After a slow start, Notes use gained momentum. Currently about 1500 applications are in operation.

Variety does not occur among the divisions only. Even within each division solutions may differ. For example, Hydro Agri Europe, the largest division, has grown in the 1970s and 1980s through the acquisition of fertiliser companies all over Europe. In line with traditional NH management policy, the new companies were run 'hands off'. But lowering margins urged management to integrate and streamline operations across Europe through an ambitious re-engineering effort. To support this IT management initiated the development of a new infrastructure for the whole division, in which SAP played a key role. Lately, the BPR project has been discontinued and subsumed into the SAP project. The latter is proceeding slowly due the complexity involved in unifying existing work practices, the installed base of technology that still has to be in operation, and the new SAP solution.

To get the best possible services for SAP processing, it was decided to outsource IT operations. This, however, caused incredible trouble for the operations of the Bridge infrastructure.

Statoil

Statoil is the State of Norway's oil firm founded in 1972; it has 17 000 employees and operates in 25 countries. The post gulf war period and the ensuing recession in the oil industry triggered major re-organisations in most of the large oil companies. Statoil was no exception embarking in cross-functional projects to cut operational costs. Cost savings affected also IT, at the time seen as an expense item. Thus Lotus office automation software was chosen mainly for price reasons. The early adoption of Lotus Notes was due to mere chance. The upturn of the economy and a major oil field discovery gave a new self-confidence to the young company. The newly centralised IT unit (Statoil Data) benefited of the new atmosphere. The initial small-scale phenomenon of LN grew to the point of making Statoil one of the largest user of LN world-wide. The process of LN diffusion was punctuated by various episodes of mobilisation and alignment of different actors: the advanced technology group, corporate IT and functional management. Notes has been spread based on a combination of centralised push and grass root activities. Today, after several waves of consolidation, there are more than 1200 applications of LN throughout the company. Some support key processes like project management, exploration and production (including applications for knowledge transfer among functions and projects).

Astra Haessle

Astra Haessle is a relatively small (about 1500 employees) research company belonging to the Swedish multinational Astra. It is a newcomer in the pharmaceutical industry, but extremely successful thanks to its leading drug against ulcers. The company has been undergoing major BPR initiatives aimed at speeding up of the product development process. IT has been seen as a key component of such redesign. For example, a major project was launched aimed at squeezing time during the clinical trial process. A new IT infrastructure comprising hand held terminals and sophisticated networks supported remote data capture in 500 centres in 12 different countries. Though conceived and planned centrally, the project suffered from the fact that the initial analysis model was not effective in representing all the facets of the remote data capture operations. In particular the large size and the role of the installed base of computing equipment at these sites were ignored. Formally, all the projects are still on going and successful: still, very little is being deployed on a full scale.

ROCHE (1 and 2)

In Hoffmann La Roche (Roche) objects of study have been two different infrastructures in Strategic Marketing (here named Roche 1 and 2).

Roche 1

In the 1980s Strategic Marketing championed the establishment of the first corporate network. The purpose of the network and its applications, that went under the name of MedNet, was to support the new, global Marketing function.

The infrastructure was developed independently from corporate IT. This led to duplication of efforts and competence shortages at the time when standard commercial solutions were not yet available. The network was developed before Windows. This slowed down the overall development and lead to huge project costs. This caused the uneven level of adoption in the affiliates, since an affiliate had to invest significant resources to be able to use the network. After eight years of development the acceptance of the main applications (consulting medical literature; accessing clinical trials data; office automation) was low (with the exception of e-mail), and generated frustration ('we would never do it again, had we to start it today'). Some affiliates were even developing systems of their own, on distinct platforms.

MedNet was a breakthrough, but not for its expected results. Rather, it heralded a cultural revolution within Roche: IT used for networking, not just data processing. After almost 10 years from its launch MedNet was discontinued. Its negative aspects, especially costs, dictated its end. However, it survived as a network infrastructure. What was phased out was the application portfolio.

Roche 2

Today, the new infrastructure emerging in Strategic Marketing is composed of Intranet/Internet sites, conceived and developed by the 'Therapies'. A Therapy is a semi-autonomous team of highly skilled managers who craft the marketing policies world-wide, and provide product know how to the national affiliates.

With minimal coordination and direction, each Therapy has developed or is developing Web sites for internal and external communication. Style, approach and contents may vary sharply for each team. One striking features of the Web sites is their interaction with constituencies outside Roche. Namely, for some diseases external constituencies such as associations, lobbies, doctors, up to individual patients exert their voice and have a relatively high degree of horizontal communication on the Net. In response to the outside initiatives, some Therapies have created Internet Web sites directed to the public as part of a new marketing mix. When MedNet was still in existence, Internet had been kept at bay because of confidentiality concerns, in a company known for its secrecy. But, the Internet infrastructure gained ground and ultimately won because its use was backed by a global scientific community which crosses company and institutional boundaries when they need to exchange knowledge.

A NEW FRAMEWORK

The snapshots above give only a first impression of the variety of applications and business contexts. In some cases implementation is taking a number of years and the applications of the infrastructure are still incongruous in the daily work flow (IBM and Astra). Full backing from top management is no guarantee of immediate or long-term success (IBM and Roche 1, respectively), or fast implementation (IBM and Astra). A totally decentralised development process can actually lead to a self-feeding diffusion (Roche 2). While in the latter case infrastructure is an enabling one, for SKF it is simultaneously utility, dependence creating and enabling. *De facto* opportunistic implementation led to partially decentralised support of business processes in Norsk Hydro and Statoil.

One way to find a logic in such disparate results is to rely on what has emerged from the economic theories. Specifically, consider:

- the implementation process, i.e. the way the firm learns how to develop the infrastructure;
- the knowledge processes being supported or enabled by the infrastructure.

The implementation process can unfold from the 'top down', as prescribed by the management literature; be 'fragmented', when top-down initiatives get diluted by the organisational context and pursued in more adaptive, *ad hoc* ways; or, 'grass roots' where no plan or pretension of central control exists.

Knowledge processes can be of three main kinds: 'routine' knowledge characterising business processes whose execution does not need each time the processing of new knowledge; 'recombination', i.e. sharing and re-using 'standardised' knowledge packages; and 'emergent', where new knowledge has to be created continuously to cope with the requirements of knowledge-intensive processes and products.

Relying on these two dimensions a 'knowledge matrix' can be built. On this matrix the company cases can be placed, as shown in Table 12.1.

The reasons justifying in detail the qualitative classification of the cases on the knowledge matrix cannot be reported here. However, empirical evidence suggests the following relationships. The firms positioned on the diagonal seem to enjoy a good match between the way the infrastructure is developed and the nature of the business to which it is applied. In this way it is possible to reconcile apparently opposite styles of implementation (think of SKF and Roche 2),

Table 12.1   The cases classified on the knowledge matrix

Knowledge type/ Implementation process	'Routine'	'Recombination'	'Emergent'
'Top-down'	SKF	Roche 1, IBM	
'Fragmented'		Norsk Hydro, Statoil	Astra
'Grass root'			Roche 2

and their successful outcomes. The firms lying outside the diagonal seem to suffer from some form of 'mismatch'. Roche 1 has been a failure because a top down implementation was coupled with a structured way of packaging knowledge, in a business that is knowledge intensive. This can also explain why the IBM infrastructure does not fly as fast as expected, even with strong top management support.

The empirical material also illustrates a trend where the companies are moving towards the lower right corner of Table 12.1 as a part of their strategy for being more competitive globally. This corresponds to the theoretical arguments presented above. We can not conclude, however, that 'grass root' activities and absence of top management will guarantee success in infrastructure development. Although centralised management control often works poorly, coordination of infrastructure development is indeed important. What seems to work as an efficient coordinator is a powerful installed base of infrastructure gaining momentum (Hughes, 1987), serving as fertile soil for cultivating new ones. This is what happens in the rapid growth in use of Internet in Roche and Notes in Statoil and Norsk Hydro. This phenomenon is exactly the mechanism at work in the rapid development of the Internet as a universally shared infrastructure.

CONCLUSION

The study of six multinationals using large infrastructures to achieve globalisation and streamline processes confirms the scepticism towards the too coarse information engineering and managerial models found in the current literature. The reality of infrastructure projects in large corporations is more intertwined and intriguing. One way to make sense of the evidence gained from the present empirical study is to rely on a more robust theory of the firm and infrastructure building. The economic theories selected have confirmed that one is bound to find a variety of styles of implementing and using infrastructures as a resource to manage knowledge in organisations. Theorising has led to a knowledge matrix that classifies empirical cases and predicts the problems an infrastructure may encounter in different businesses. The stage is then set for further empirical research, both quantitative and qualitative, to enlarge the body of working hypotheses and confirm/disconfirm the results gained so far.

References

ARGYRIS, C. and SCHOEN, D. (1996) *Organizational Learning II*, Wokingham: Addison-Wesley.

ARTHUR, B. (1996) 'Increasing returns and the two worlds of business', *Harvard Business Review*, July–August.

BARNEY, J.B. (1991) 'Firm resources and sustained competitive advantage', *Journal of Management*, 17(1), 99–120.

BOYTON, A.C. and VICTOR, B. (1991) 'Beyond flexibility: building and managing the dynamically stable organization', *California Management Review*, 34(1), 53–66.

BROADBENT, M. and WEILL, P. (1997) 'Management by maxim: how business and IT managers can create IT infrastructures', *Sloan Management Review*, Spring, 77–92.

BROADBENT, M. WEILL, P., O'BRIAN, T. and NEO, B.S. (1996) 'Firm context and patterns of IT infrastructure capability', J.I. DeGross, S. Jarvenpaa and A. Srinivasan (eds), *Proceedings from the Seventeenth International Conference on Information Systems*, Cleveland, OH, 174–94.

BROADBENT, M., WEILL, P. and ST. CLAIR, D. (1995) 'The role of IT infrastructure in business process redesign', CISR WP278, Sloan School of Management.

CIBORRA, C.U. (1996) 'Introduction: What does Groupware Mean for the Organizations Hosting it?', in Ciborra, C. (ed.) *Groupware & Teamwork: Invisible Aid or Technical Hindrance?*, chichester: John Wiley.

CIBORRA, C.U. (1997) 'Deconstructing strategic alignment', *Scandinavian Journal of Information Systems*, 9(1), 76–82.

COASE, R. (1962) 'The problem of social cost', *Journal of Law and Economics*, 3, 1–44.

CORDELLA, A. and SIMON, K. (1997) 'Decreasing returns to infrastructure', *IRIS Proceedings*, Oslo, August, 821–834.

DAHLBOM, B. and JANLERT, S. (1996) 'Computer future', mimeo, Department of Informatics, University of Gøteborg.

DAVID, P.A. (1987) 'Some new standards for the economics in the information age', in Dasgupta, P. and Stoneman, P. (eds), Cambridge: Cambridge University Press, 206–39.

DAVID, P.A. and BUNN, J.A. (1988) 'The economics of gateways technologies', *Information Economics and Policy*, 3, 165–202.

DEMSETZ, H. (1993) 'The theory of the firm revisited', in Williamson, O.E. and Winter, S.G. (eds) New York: Oxford University Press.

DUNCAN, N.B. (1995) 'Capturing flexibility of IT infrastructure', *Journal of Management Information Systems*, 12(2), 37–57.

GRINDLEY, P. (1995) *Standards, Strategy and Policy Costs*, Oxford: Oxford University Press.

HANSETH, O. (1996) 'Information technology as infrastructure', PhD thesis, University of Gøteborg.

HANSETH, O., MONTEIRO, E. and HATLING, M. (1996) 'Developing information infrastructure standards: the tension between standardization and flexibility', *Science Technology and Human Values*, 21(4), 407–26.

HENDERSON, J.C., VENKATRAMAN, N. and OLDACH, S. (1996) 'Aligning business and IT strategies', in Luftman, J (ed.), *Strategic Alignment*, New York: Oxford University Press.

HUGHES, T.P. (1987) 'The evolution of large technical systems', in Bijker, W.E., Hughes, T.P. and Pinch, T. *The Social Construction of Technological Systems*, Cambridge, MA: MIT Press, 51–82.

KATZ, M. and SHAPIRO, C. (1986) 'Technology adoption in the presence of network externalities', *Journal of Political Economy*, 94, 822–41.

KNIGHTS, D., NOBLE, F. and WILLMOTT, H. (1997) '"We should be total slaves to the business": Aligning information technology and strategy', in Bloomfield, P. *et al.* (eds), *Information Technology and Organizations*, Oxford: Oxford University Press.

LUFTMAN, J. (ed.) (1996) *Strategic Alignment*, Oxford: Oxford University Press.

MURRAY, F. and WILLMOTT, H. (1997) 'Putting information technology in its place', in Bloomfield, P. *et al.* (eds), *Information Technology and Organizations*, Oxford, Oxford University Press.

NELSON, R.R. and WINTER, S.G. (1982) *An Evolutionary Theory of Economic Change*, Cambridge, MA. Harvard University Press.

NONAKA, I. and TAKEUCHI, J. (1996) *The Knowledge Creating Company*, Oxford: Oxford University Press.

NORMAN R. and RAMIREZ, R. (chichester: 1994) *Designing Interactive Strategies: From Value Chain to Value Constellation*, John Wiley.

ORLIKOWSKI, W.J. (1996) 'Improvising organizational transformation over time: a situated change perspective', *Information Systems Research*, 7(1), 63–92.

PRAHALAD, C.K. and HAMEL, G. (1990) 'The core competence of the corporation', *Harvard Business Review*, 68(3), 79–91.

REICH, R. (1991) *The Work of Nations*, New York: Alfred A. Knopf.

SAUER, C. and BURN, J.M. (1997) 'The pathology of strategic management', in Sauer, C. and Yetton, P.W. (eds), *Steps to the Future*, San Francisco: Jossey Bass.

SIMON, H.A. (1976) *Administrative Behaviour*, New York: Basic Books.

WEILL, P., BROADBENT, M. and ST CLAIR, D. (1996) 'IT value and the role of IT infrastructure', in Luftman, J. (ed.), *Strategic Alignment*, New York: Oxford University Press.

YIN, R.K. (1993) *Applications of Case Study Research*, Newbury Park, CA: Sage.

Part IV

Internet and Intranet Commerce

13 Aligning the Online Organisation: with What, How and Why?

Janice Burn

INTRODUCTION

This chapter looks at strategic alignment in relation to virtual organisations. It challenges the notion that the virtual organisation is the answer for the 21st century and further suggests that with the basic concepts of virtual information management being so poorly understood there are likely to be far more actual failures than virtual realities. The chapter attempts to redress some of these imbalances by providing some clear definitions of virtual organisations and different models of virtuality which can exist within the electronic market. Degrees of virtuality can be seriously constrained by the extent to which organisations have pre-existing linkages in the marketplace and the extent to which these can be substituted by virtual ones, but also by the intensity of virtual linkages which support the virtual model.

Six virtual models are proposed within a dynamic framework of change. In order to realise the flexibility promised by virtuality organisations must align themselves along the virtual strategic perspective and then match this with the virtual model for structural alignment. The virtual value which may result has then to be examined in relation to the structure/strategy alignment model and to both the virtual organisation and its component alliances. The Virtual Value Model (VVM) identifies factors which may inhibit or promote effective business value realisation. This chapter further proposes a research agenda for the 21st century which places far greater emphasis on qualitative rather than quantitative studies.

The value of going virtual is often espoused in the management literature but there is very little empirical research to show that value and 'virtuality' are directly related. Indeed, there are so many fuzzy concepts related to virtuality that any broad statement made with regard to virtual organisations must be regarded with suspicion. It could be argued that there is a degree of virtuality in all organisations but at what point does this present a conflict between control and adaptability? Is there a continuum along which organisations can position themselves in the electronic marketplace according to their needs for flexibility and fast responsiveness as opposed to stability and sustained momentum?

While there may be general agreement with regard to the advantages of flexibility the extent to which virtuality offers flexibility and the advantages which this will bring to a corporation have yet to be measured. There is an assumption that an organisation that invests in as little infrastructure as possible will be more responsive to a changing marketplace and more likely to attain global competitive advantage but this ignores the very real power which large integrated organisations can bring to the market in terms of sustained innovation over the longer term (Chesbrough and Teece, 1996). Proponents of the virtual organisation also tend to underestimate the force of virtual links. Bonds which bind a virtual organisation together may strongly inhibit flexibility and change rather than nurture the concept of the opportunistic virtual organisation (Goldman *et al.*, 1995). Aldridge (1998), suggests that it is no accident that the pioneers of electronic commerce fall into three categories:

1. Start-ups: organisations with no existing investment or legacy systems to protect;
2. Technology companies: with a vested interest in building the channel to market products and services;
3. Media companies: attracted by low set-up costs and immediate distribution of news and information.

When is a virtual organisation really virtual? One definition would suggest that organisations are virtual when producing work deliverables across different locations, at differing work cycles, and across cultures (Gray and Igbaria, 1996; Palmer and Speier, 1998). Another suggests that the single common theme is temporality. Virtual organisations centre on continual restructuring to capture the value of a short term market opportunity and are then dissolved to make way for restructuring to a new virtual entity (Byrne, 1993; Katzy, 1998). Yet others suggest that virtual organisations are characterised by the intensity, symmetricality, reciprocity and multiplexity of the linkages in their networks (Powell, 1990; Grabowski and Roberts, 1996). Whatever the definition (and this chapter hopes to resolve some of the ambiguities) there is a concensus that different degrees of virtuality exist (Hoffman *et al.*, 1995; Gray and Igbaria, 1996; Goldman *et al.*, 1995) and within this, different organisational structures can be formed (Palmer and Speier, 1998; Davidow and Malone, 1992; Miles and Snow, 1986). Such structures are normally inter-organisational and lie at the heart of any form of electronic commerce yet the organisational and management processes which should be applied to ensure successful implementation have been greatly under researched (Swatman and Swatman, 1992; Finnegan *et al.*, 1998). Further it is suggested that the relationship between tasks and structure and its effect on performance has not been studied at all in the context of virtual organisations. (Ahuja and Carley, 1998).

This chapter tries to address these aspects and remove some of the ambiguities surrounding virtual values. First, a definition of virtual organisations is developed and related to the concept of virtual culture which is the organisational embodiment of its virtuality. This may take a variety of different virtual models which will reflect the strength and structure of inter-organisational links. The chapter identifies six virtual models – the Virtual Alliance Models (VAM) and suggests that each of these will operate along a continuum and within a framework of dynamic change. In order to maximise the value derived from the VAM the organisation needs to ensure that there is a consistency between the alignment of its Virtual Strategic Positioning (VSP) and the VAM and the organisation and management of internal and external virtual characteristics. The ability of the organisation to change from one VAM to another or to extend itself as a virtual entity will reflect the extent to which an understanding of these concepts has been embedded into the knowledge management of the virtual organisation as a Virtual Organisational Change Model (VOCM). These change factors are the essential components through which virtual value can be derived and from which it can be measured as presented in the Virtual Values Model (VVM). Finally, the chapter outlines an agenda for future research which calls for far more in-depth, qualitative studies of virtual success and failure related to the real value derived from virtual operation.

VIRTUAL ORGANISATIONS AND VIRTUAL CULTURES

Virtual organisations are electronically networked organisations that transcend conventional organisational boundaries (Barner, 1996;

Berger, 1996; Rogers, 1996), with linkages which may exist both within (Davidow and Malone, 1992) and between organisations (Goldman *et al.*, 1995). In its simplest form, however, virtuality exists where IT is used to enhance organisational activities while reducing the need for physical or formalised structures (Greiner and Metes, 1996). Degrees of virtuality then exist which will reflect:

- the virtual organisational culture (strategic positioning);
- The intensity of linkages and the nature of the bonds which tie the stakeholders together (internal and external structures);
- the market (IT dependency and resource infrastructure, product, customer).

Culture is the degree to which members of a community have common shared values and beliefs (Schein, 1990). Tushman and O'Reilly (1996) suggest that organisational cultures that are accepting of technology, highly decentralised, and change-oriented are more likely to embrace virtuality and proactively seek these opportunities both within and without the organisation. Virtual culture is hence a perception of the entire virtual organisation (including its infrastructure and product) held by its stakeholder community and operationalised in choices and actions which result in a feeling of *globalness* with respect to value sharing (e.g. each client's expectations are satisfied in the product accessed), and time–space arrangement (e.g. each stakeholder has the feeling of a continuous access to the organisation and its products). The embodiment of this culture comes through the Virtual Strategic Perspective (VSP) which the organisation adopts.

Networks can be groups of organisations but also groups within organisations where the development and maintenance of communicative relationships is paramount to the successful evolution of a virtual entity. However, the ability to establish multiple alliances and the need to retain a particular identity creates a constant tension between autonomy and interdependence, competition and cooperation (Nouwens and Bouwman 1995). These relationships are often described as value-added partnerships based on horizontal, vertical or symbiotic relationships. These in turn relate to competitors, value chain collaborators and complementary providers of goods and services all of whom combine to achieve competitive advantage over organisations outside these networks. The nature of the alliances which form the virtual organisation, their strength and substitutability define the inherent virtual structure.

Markets differ from networks since markets are traditionally coordinated by pricing mechanisms. In this sense, the electronic market is no different but further 'central to the conceptualisations of the electronic marketplace is the ability of any buyer or seller to interconnect with a network to offer wares or shop for goods and services. Hence, ubiquity is by definition a prerequisite' (Steinfeld *et al.*, 1995). There are different risks associated with being a market-maker and a market-player and different products will also carry different risks. Criteria for successful electronic market development include products with low asset specificity and ease of description and a consumer market willing to buy without recourse to visiting retail stores. (Wigand and Benjamin, 1995). Necessarily, the most important asset to an electronic market is the availability of pervasive ITC infrastructures providing a critical mass of customers. A virtual organisation is both constrained and supported by the electronic market in which it operates and the stage to which its business environment has developed as an e-business (Figure 13.1).

Despite the growth of online activity many firms are nervous of the risks involved and fear a general deterioration of profit margins coupled with a relinquishment of market control. Nevertheless, as existing organisations are challenged by new entrants using direct channels to undercut prices and increase market share, solutions have to be found that enable organisations to successfully migrate into the electronic market. The authors suggest that there are six different models of virtuality which may be appropriate.

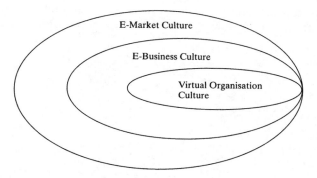

Figure 13.1   Virtual organisations and virtual cultures

MODELS OF VIRTUALITY

This chapter identifies six different forms of virtual organisations as:

1 Virtual faces
2 Co-alliance models
3 Star-alliance models – core or satellite
4 Value-alliance models – stars or constellations
5 Market-alliance models
6 Virtual brokers

Put simply, virtual faces are the cyberspace incarnations of an exist-ing non-virtual organisation (often described as a 'place' as opposed to 'space' organisation, Rayport and Sviokola, 1995) and create addi-tional value such as enabling users to carry out the same transactions over the Internet as they could otherwise do by using telephone or fax, e.g. Fleurop selling flowers or air tickets by Travelocity. The ser-vices may, however, reach far beyond this enabling the virtual face to mirror the whole activities of the parent organisation and even extend these, e.g. the web-based versions of television channels and news-papers with constant news updates and archival searches. Alterna-tively they may just extend the scope of activities by use of facilities such as electronic procurement, contract tendering or even electronic auctions or extend market scope by participating in an electronic mall with or without added enrichment such as a common payment mecha-nism. There is obviously an extremely tight link between the virtual face and the parent organisation. This model can be actualised as an e-shop, e-auction or even e-mall.

Co-alliance models are shared partnerships with each partner bringing approximately equal amounts of commitment to the virtual organisation thus forming a consortia. The composition of the con-

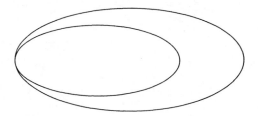

Figure 13.2   The virtual face

sortia may change to reflect market opportunities or to reflect the core competencies of each member (Preiss *et al.*, 1996). Focus can be on specific functions such as collaborative design or engineering or in providing virtual support with a virtual team of consultants. Links within the co-alliance are normally contractual for more permanent alliances or by mutual convenience on a project by project basis. There is not normally a high degree of substitutability within the life of that virtual creation.

Star-alliance models are co-ordinated networks of interconnected members reflecting a core surrounded by satellite organisations. The core comprises leaders who are the dominant players in the market and supply competency or expertise to members. These alliances commonly based around similar industries or company types. While this form is a true network, typically the star or leader is identified with the virtual face and so the core organisation is very difficult to replace whereas the satellites may have a far greater level of substitutability.

Value-alliance models bring together a range of products, services and facilities in one package and are based on the value or supply chain model. Participants may come together on a project by project basis but generally coordination is provided by the general

Figure 13.3   Co-alliance model

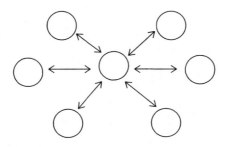

Figure 13.4   Star-alliance model

contractor. Where longer-term relationships have developed the value alliance often adopts the form of value constellations where firms supply each of the companies in the value chain and a complex and continuing set of strategic relationships are embedded into the alliance. Substitutability will relate to the positioning on the value chain and the reciprocity of the relationship.

Market-alliances are organisations that exist primarily in cyber-space, depend on their member organisations for the provision of actual products and services and operate in an electronic market. Normally they bring together a range of products, services and facilities in one package, each of which may be offered separately by individual organisations. In some cases the market is open and in others serves as an intermediary. These can also be described as virtual communities but a virtual community can be an add-on such as exists in an e-mall rather than a cyberspace organisation perceived as a virtual organisation. Amazon.com is a prime example of a market-alliance model where substitutability of links is very high.

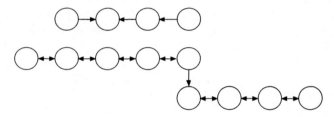

Figure 13.5   Value-alliance model

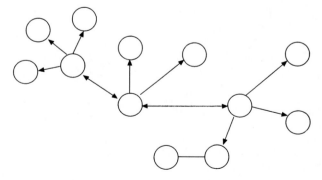

Figure 13.6   Market-alliance model

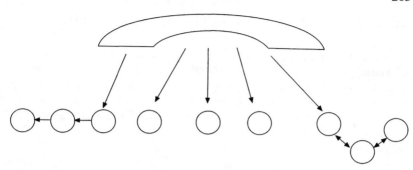

Figure 13.7   Virtual broker

Virtual Brokers are designers of dynamic networks (Miles and Snow, 1986). These prescribe additional strategic opportunities either as third-party value-added suppliers such as in the case of common web marketing events (e-Xmas) or as information brokers providing a virtual structure around specific business information services (Timmers, 1998). This has the highest level of flexibility with purpose built virtual organisations created to fill a window of opportunity and dissolved when that window is closed.

As discussed previously each of these alliances carries with it a set of tensions related to autonomy and interdependence. Virtual culture is the strategic hub around which virtual relationships are formed and virtual links implemented. In order to be flexible, links must be sub-stitutable, to allow the creation of new competencies, but links must be established and maintained if the organisation is going to fully leverage community expertise. This presents a dichotomy. The degree to which virtuality can be implemented effectively relates to the strength of existing organisational links (virtual and non-virtual) and the relationship which these impose on the virtual structure. However, as essentially networked organisations they will be constrained by the extent to which they are able to redefine or extend their virtual link-ages. Where existing linkages are strong e.g. co-located, shared culture, synchronicity of work and shared risk (reciprocity) these will both reduce the need for or perceived benefits from substitutable linkages and inhibit the development of further virtual linkages. Figure 13.8 provides a diagrammatic representation of these tensions and their interaction with the VAMs.

AUTONOMY/SUBSTITUTABILITY OF VIRTUAL LINKS

These six models are not exclusive but are intended to serve as a way of classifying the diversity of forms which an electronic business model may assume. Some of these are essentially an electronic re-implementation of traditional forms of doing business, others are add-ons for added value possibly through umbrella collaboration and others go far beyond this through value chain integration or cyber communities. What all of these have in common is that they now seek innovative ways to add value through information and change management and a rich functionality. Creating value through virtuality is only feasible if the processes which support such innovations are clearly understood.

VIRTUAL ORGANISATIONAL CHANGE MODEL

These six forms of virtual organisations all operate within a dynamic environment where their ability to change will determine the extent to which they can survive in a competitive market. Organisational theorists suggest that the ability of an organisation to change relates

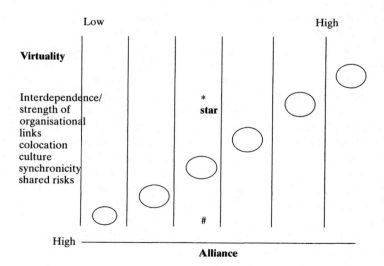

Figure 13.8   Virtual alliance models

to internal and external factors (Miles and Snow, 1978), including the organisation's technology, structure and strategy, tasks and management processes individual skills and roles and culture (Henderson *et al.*, 1996) and the business in which the organisation operates and the degree of uncertainty in the environment (Donaldson, 1995). These factors are also relevant to virtual organisations but need further refinement. Moore (1997) suggests that businesses are not just members of certain industries but parts of a complex ecosystem that incorporates bundles of different industries. The driving force is not pure competition but co-evolution. The system is seen as 'an economic community supported by a foundation of interacting organisations and individuals. . . . Over time they coevolve their capabilities and roles, and tend to align themselves with the direction set by one or more central companies' (p. 26). The ecosystems evolve through four distinct stages: Birth, Expansion, Authority, Death.

And at each of these stages the system faces different leadership, cooperative and competitive challenges.

This ecosystem can be viewed as the all embracing electronic market culture within which the e-business maintains an equilibrium. The organisational 'virtual culture' is the degree to which the organisation adopts virtual organising and this in turn will affect the individual skills, tasks and roles throughout all levels of the organisation.

Table 13.1   E-Market Ecosystem

EcoSystem stage	Leadership challenges	Cooperative challenges	Competitive challenges
Birth	Maximise customer delivered value	Find and create new value in an efficient way	Protect your ideas
Expansion	Attract critical mass of buyers	Work with suppliers and partners	Ensure market standard approach
Authority	Lead co-evolution	Provide compelling vision for the future	Maintain strong bargaining power
Renewal or death	Innovate or perish	Work with Innovators	Develop and maintain high barriers

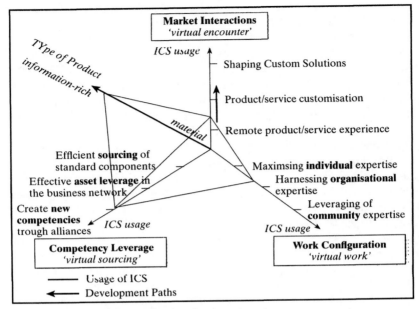

Figure 13.9   Virtual organisational management
        Source: Adapted from Venkatraman and Henderson (1998).

Venkatraman and Henderson (1998) identify three vectors of virtual organising as:

- Virtual encounters
- Virtual sourcing
- Virtual work

Virtual encounters refers to the extent to which you virtually interact with the market defined at three levels of greater virtual progression:

- Remote product/service experience
- Product/service customisation
- Shaping customer solutions

Virtual sourcing refers to competency leveraging from:

- Efficient sourcing of standard components
- Efficient asset leverage in the business network
- Create new competencies through alliances

Virtual Work refers to:

- Maximising individual experience
- Harnessing organisational expertise
- Leveraging of community expertise

Where the third levels all relate to an organisation with an 'information rich' product and the highest degree of use of ICT. If we view this as the virtual culture of the organisation then this needs to be articulated through the strategic positioning of the organisation and its structural alliances. It also needs to be supported by the knowledge management processes and the ICT. These relationships are depicted in a dynamic virtual organisation change model as shown in Figure 13.10.

The degree to which virtuality can be applied in the organisation will relate to the extent to which the VOCM factors are in alignment.

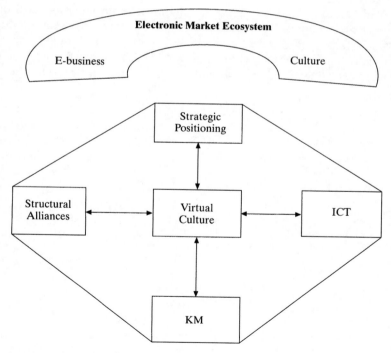

Figure 13.10   VOCM

When these are not aligned then the organisation will find itself dysfunctional in its exploitation of the virtual marketspace and so be unable to derive the maximum value benefits from its strategic position in the VAM framework.

VIRTUAL VALUES RESEARCH FRAMEWORK

The VAM framework depicted in Figure 13.8 shows the opposing structural tensions which will pull the VAM in different directions and which may therefore force the organisation into a less favourable strategic position. This same framework can be used to view the six models along a continuum which relates the extent of substitutability of virtual linkages (virtual structure) to the extent of virtuality as embedded in the organisation (virtual culture) and hence identify the strategic positioning which will be the most effective in value return.

The model in Figure 13.11 shows the ideal positioning for each of the virtual models. The organisation then needs to examine the VOCM factors in order to evaluate effectiveness and identify variables for change either within that VAM or to move beyond that VAM according to the virtual culture. A Virtual Face model is low

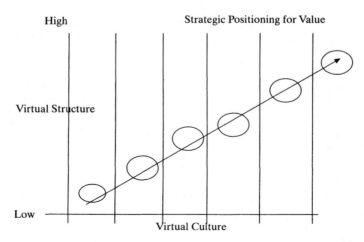

Figure 13.11   Virtual values model

in virtual culture and structure and so will typically have a strategy which relies less on ICT for virtual organising and knowledge management but should the organisation seek to form a co-alliance (*The Times* with the *New York Times*) then a greater degree of virtual organising would be required with a higher dependence on ICT. Change directions should be value led but there is as yet very little empirical research to identify how value is derived in a virtual organisation. For virtual organisations performance measurements must cross organisational boundaries and take collaboration into account but it is also necessary to measure value at the individual level since it is feasible that one could be effective without the other (Provan and Milward, 1995). There is also an interesting difference of perception. Ahuja and Carley (1998) have completed one of the few empirical studies of the relationship between structure and performance in a virtual setting and conclude that perceived outcomes were seen as highly productive when tasks and structures were 'in fit' but when measured objectively showed no correlation. This would suggest that future research cannot be based solely on quantitative measurement but also cannot rely on anecdotal evidence or subjective 'feel good' analysis. Research into virtual organisations must embrace reality at a number of different levels. The concluding section of this paper outlines where and how the author believes research efforts should be directed.

CONCLUSIONS AND RESEARCH AGENDA

A report from the OECD (OECD, 1996) finds evidence that firms and establishments adopting new organisational structures have stronger and more productive external linkages with their customers and their suppliers of inputs and services. Moreover, the combination of streamlined business processes, flat organisational hierarchies and continuous training and skill acquisition constitutes a favourable environment for innovation and improved performance. Firms' strategies based on these elements are often termed 'high performance work practices'. New work organisations have the following features in common with virtual organisations:

- More horizontal inter-firm links for outsourcing
- New work organisation complements effective use of technology
- Flatter hierarchies

- Better use of better trained, more responsive employees
- More multi-skilling and job rotation, blurred differences among traditional work activities
- More small self-managing or autonomous work groups which take more responsibility

In their 1998 surveys (OECD, 1998b) they find that organisational flexibility associated with high performance workplaces has a positive impact on firm and establishment performance. In particular, high performance workplaces are associated with higher labour productivity, better wage performance and satisfactory unit cost performance; higher sales owing to increased market shares, customer satisfaction due to better product quality and improved customer relations; and positive employment performance and lower staff turnover. Future research needs to address these issues for firms working in electronic markets in order to assess the impact of virtuality on productivity growth and performance.

First, there needs to be on-going research on the evolving nature of the commercial environment and the dynamic nature of these change processes among market actors and market structures. This will help policy makers on issues of commercial governance, which will be critical to the development of a globally networked electronic society. Further, there needs to be an acceptance of the multifarious forms which the virtual organisation can assume and the realisation that there is no 'one good way' for the virtual organisation to grow. Much of the existing literature on organisational change may be as valid in relation to virtual organisations as to traditional organisational forms but in order to assess this there must be in-depth analysis of the change process over a number of different business and electronic markets. Failures need to be evaluated and not just successes but longer term studies are needed to help understand the sustainability factors which relate to virtual organisations. Some of the more important areas for study are:

- Organisational impacts
- Competitive strategies and dynamics of the markets
- Extent to which electronic commerce is really global
- The workforce and re-engineering
- Issues of trust, confidence, privacy and consumer protection
- Contribution of the new work organisation to productivity and innovation

Secondly, there needs to be a directed effort towards evaluating information systems practices in light of virtual organisations. Strategic planning processes need to take into account the collaborative strategies as well as the individual; information systems requirements need to capture the views of the stakeholders who are now frequently the customers or even more complex the desired customer; information management needs to embrace virtual organising, knowledge management, service customisation and alliance interactions.

Thirdly, we need to apply more realistic and comprehensive measures of value benefits which encompass both objective and subjective assessments. Values apply to all the stakeholders in the virtual community and so include the customers as well as the alliance members. Sociological approaches are required to evaluate the impact of virtual access on the community and particularly to identify the repercussions for societies where web access is not a reality nor a priority.

Finally, there must be a move towards more qualitative research with multiple paradigms for research methodologies. This means that IS researchers have to become deeply involved with organisations as they manage their way through the change process.

There is a need for a continuous monitoring of the electronic marketplace. Case studies should address the sectoral and market specificity of organisational impacts (OECD, 1998a V, 18). This needs a commitment from academia to release research staff for organisationally based research work and also a definite commitment from organisations to allow researchers access to their change processes and the business impacts of such changes.

References

AHUJA, M.K. and CARLEY, K.M. (1998) 'Network structure in virtual organizations', *Journal of Computer-Mediated Communication* [On-line], 3(4) available <http://www.ascusc.org/jcmc/vol3/issue4/ahuja.html>.
ALDRIDGE, D. (1998) 'Purchasing on the net – the new opportunities for electronic commerce'. *EM – Electronic Markets*, 8(1), 34–7.
BARNER, R. (1996) 'The new millenium workplace: seven changes that will challenge managers and workers', *Futurist*, 30(2), 14–18.
BERGER, M. (1996) 'Making the virtual office a reality: sales and marketing Management', *SMT Supplement*, June, 18–22.
BYRNE, J. (1993) 'The virtual corporation', *Business Week*, 36–41.

CHESBROUGH, H.W. and TEECE, D.J. (1996) 'When is virtual virtuous?', *Harvard Business Review*, January–February, 65–73.

DAVIDOW, W.H. and MALONE, M.S. (1992) *The Virtual Corporation*, New York: Harper Business.

DONALDSON, L. (1995) *American Anti-Management Theories of Organisation*, Cambridge: Cambridge University Press.

FINNEGAN, P., GALLIERS, B. and POWELL, P. (1998) 'Systems planning in an electronic commerce environment in Europe: rethinking current approaches', *EM – Electronic Markets*, 8(2), 35–38.

GRAY, P. and IGBARIA, M. (1996) 'The virtual society', *ORMS Today*, December, 44–8.

GOLDMAN, S.L., NAGEL, R.N. and PREISS, K. (1995) *Agile Competitors and Virtual Organisations: Strategies for Enriching the Customer*, New York: Van Nostrand Reinhold.

GRABOWSKI, M. and ROBERTS, K.H. (1996) 'Human and organisational error in large scale systems', *IEEE Transactions on Systems, Man and Cybernetics*, 26(1), 2–16.

GREINER, R. and METES, G. (1996) *Going Virtual: Moving your Organisation into the 21st Century*. Englewood Cliffs, NJ. Prentice-Hall.

HENDERSON, J.C., VENKATRAMAN, N. and OLDACH, S. (1996) 'Aligning business and IT strategies', chapter 2 in Luftman Jerry N. (ed.), Oxford: Oxford University Press, 21–42.

HOFFMAN, D.L., NOVAK, T.P. and CHATTERJEE, P. (1995) Commercial scenarios for the Web: Opportunities and challenges. *Journal of Computer-Mediated Communication* [On-line], 1(3), available <http://www.ascusc.org/jcmc/vol1/issue3/hoffman.html>.

KATZY, B.R. (1998) 'Design and implementation of virtual Organisations', *HICSS*, IV, 142–9.

MILES, R.E. and SNOW, C.C. (1986) 'Organisations: new concepts for new forms', *California Management Review*, 28(3), 62–73.

MOORE, J.F. (1997) *The Death of Competition: Leadership and Strategy in the Age of Business Ecosystems*. New York. Harper Business.

NOUWENS, J. and BOUWMAN, H. (1995) 'Living apart together in electronic commerce: The use of information and communication technology to create network organizations', *Journal of Computer-Mediated Communication* [On-line] 1(3), available <http://www.ascusc.org/jcmc/vol1/issue3/nouwens.html>.

OECD (1996) *Technology, Productivity and Job Creation*, 2, Analytical Report, Paris: OECD.

OECD (1998a) *The Economic and Social Impacts of Electronic Commerce*, Paris: OECD.

OECD (1998b) *Technology, Productivity and Job Creation: Best Policy Practices*, Pairs: OECD.

PALMER, J.W. and SPEIER, C. (1998) 'Teams: virtualness and media Choice', *Proceedings of HICSS*, IV 131–40.

POWELL, W.W. (1990) 'Neither market nor hierarchy: network forms of organisation', *Research in Organisational Behaviour*, 12, 295–336.

PREISS, K., GOLDMAN, S.L. and NAGEL, R.N. (1996) *Cooperate to Compete*, New York: Van Nostrand Reinhold.

PROVAN, K. and MILWARD, H. (1995) 'A preliminary theory of inter-organisational network effectiveness: a comparative study of four community mental health system', *Adminstrative Science Quarterly*, 14, 91–114.

RAYPORT, J.F. and SVIOKOLA, J. (1995) 'Exploiting the virtual value chain', *Harvard Business Review*, 73(6), 75–86.

ROGERS, D.M. (1996) 'The challenge of fifth generation R and D', *Research Technology Management*, 39(4), 33–41.

SCHEIN, E. (1990) 'Organisational culture', *American Psychologist*, 45(2), 109–19.

STEINFELD, C., KRAUT, R. and PLUMMER, A. (1995) 'The impact of electronic commerce on buyer–seller relationships', *Journal of Computer-Mediated Communication* [On-line] 1(3), available <http://www.ascusc.org/jcmc/vol1/issue3/steinfld.html>.

SWATMAN, P.M.C. and SWATMAN, P.A. (1992) 'EDI system integration: a definition and literature survey', *The Information Society* (8), 165–205.

TIMMERS, P. (1998) 'Business models for electronic markets', *EM – Electronic Markets*, 8(2), 3–8.

TUSHMAN, M.L. and O'REILLY, III, C.A. (1996) 'Ambidextrous organisations: managing evolutionary and revolutionary change', *California Management Review*, 38(4), 8–29.

VENKATRAMAN, N. and HENDERSON, J.C. (1998) 'Real strategies for virtual organising', *Sloan Management Review*, Autumns 33–48.

WIGAND, R.T. and BENJAMIN, R.I. (1995) Electronic commerce: effects on electronic markets', *Journal of Computer-Mediated Communication* [On-line] 1(3) available <http://www.ascusc.org/jcmc/vol1/issue3/wigand.html>.

14 Economics of Content Provision on the Internet

Claudia Loebbecke

INTRODUCTION

While the Internet is considered a valuable means of communication offering the enticing possibility of interaction (one-to-one communication, e-mail), for many people the Web has turned into a primary information resource (one-to-many communication, broadcasting). Most of the information on the Web is either company (public relations) or product-specific information (marketing) to increase awareness. As with traditional marketing media, such information is offered free of charge. However, many companies who generate information (content) on the Internet, which are not their core business, are investing in new possibilities offered by the medium. They consequently face the challenge to transform these opportunities into adequate and sustainable profit (Jones and Navin-Chandra, 1995; Loebbecke, 1996; Loebbecke and Trilling, 1997).

Currently the costs of content provision on the Web is hardly covered by the contribution of Internet sales. The driving force for a Web presence is more the belief that the Web will lead to competitive advantage, or will turn into a competitive necessity in the future (see also Benjamin and Wigand, 1995). In this context, SMEs need to be distinguished from large companies. The latter can, mostly, follow a 'learning approach', being on the Web in order to 'be good at it when Web-based business really takes off'. SMEs, however, can barely invest in using and learning to use a new technology for about one to three years. In the end, they may be good at exploiting the Web, but may face the threat of bankruptcy before being able to harvest their new expertise (O'Connor and O'Keefe, 1997).

From a conceptual point of view, two situations are to be distinguished:

1. The main product offered is not digitisable (cars, coffee, computers, books) and therefore cannot be delivered via the Internet.
2. The product offered consists of information and thus can be transmitted digitally via the Internet (e.g. software, magazines, music, etc.). For such 'Online Delivered Content' (ODC) (Loebbecke, 1999), full Internet commercialisation implies a closed business cycle from 'order' via 'payment' to 'product delivery and receipt' on the net. 'Virtual enterprises' can operate from anywhere on the globe where Internet access is available; the need for a physical presence at a certain location is limited to legal requirements.

In the following the chapter will outline four ways in which companies may generate profit from providing content on the Web. The focus of this chapter lies on companies mainly dealing with non-digitisable products.

FOUR POSSIBILITIES TO PROFIT FROM PROVIDING CONTENT ON THE WEB

Internet activities, and content provision on the Web as a special kind of Internet activities, can contribute to a company's performance in four ways (Loebbecke, 1996):

1. Increased number of units sold
2. Increased margin per unit sold
3. Content sold as stand-alone product
4. Advertising income generated from Web pages

Increased number of units sold

Internet-based marketing and public relations aim at increasing awareness about a company and its product and service range. As with traditional marketing, this is costless for consumers; profit is made when the marketing costs are made up for by additional sales. Currently the largest potential in Internet-based marketing is seen in attracting new customers world-wide and in establishing distant, long-term customer relationships.

In most instances it is difficult to discover how many additional units are sold because of a Web presence. Further, some of these may be substitutes for 'traditional' sales (internal channel cannibalisation).

As long as overall world-wide or regional sales do not increase, but almost every book store and computer dealer, etc. is present on the Web (with rather different offers), it is not obvious how they all could increase their total turnover. It seems to be more like a football league: every team strengthens themselves during the summer, but by the end of the following season, there are few 'winners', and there will always be some 'losers'.

There is no doubt, however, that Internet-based turnover is predicted to grow tremendously over the next years. But with more efficient business processes and price transparency leading to decreasing margins there is not too much reason to foresee an increase in total (traditional and Internet-based) turnover.

Larger margin per unit sold

Larger margins per unit can be achieved (1) by lower costs (efficiency) or (2) by charging higher prices per unit.

Lower costs may be achieved by using the Web for various processes such as internal communications, receiving orders and payments, or providing customer service (process/business re-engineering) (Hammer and Champy, 1992). Customers could, for instance, download information from the company's Web site and special requests could be answered via (automatic) e-mail. From a more in-depth perspective, most efficiency gains will result from decreased working capital achieved by introducing electronic commerce, e.g. Internet-based activities.

Higher prices charged per unit need to be based on value-added for customers. This means that a particular book, computer or type of coffee that is advertised and sold via the Internet is more expensive than if it were sold via traditional marketing media and sales channels. This notion is the reverse of the more popular idea of selling cheaper via the Internet due to economies of scale, improved transparency, and fewer players in the value chain. The only example of a product sold at higher prices because of a Web presence that the author is aware of is TV advertising minutes, the actual product sold by (private) TV stations to companies that place their commercials (Loebbecke and Trilling, 1997).

Provided content sold as stand-alone product

While classic marketing content is not produced to be sold, companies are increasingly placing other forms of content on the Web – mainly to encourage customers to visit their sites and ultimately buy their products. They could profit from extending their 'traditional' product line to information-based products, e.g. providing access to a special database or interactive games (new business opportunity).

The most prominent examples are carefully maintained databases offered by book stores (with mixed commercial success) (e.g. Fillmore, 1997). Depending on the up-to-dateness and the content of such a database, its maintenance costs go far beyond 'putting a paper-based catalogue on the Web and just updating it quarterly'. More drastic examples can be found when visiting the content offered by TV stations (and newspapers) on the Web. News features as well as sports results go beyond what has traditionally been offered and need almost continuous updating (more than 75 per cent of sports updates have to be done between Friday 6 p.m. and Sunday midnight).

These information resources are free for consumers, who, in turn, are by no means bound, maybe not even encouraged, to watch the respective TV programme or to read the newspaper 'on paper'. Experience even shows that both the Web pages offered by TV stations and by newspapers are often accessed by those consumers who temporarily or generally do not watch/read the traditional medium.

Different approaches to selling such content offers are possible, the three most popular are: (1) charging per month, (2) charging per actual time visiting the site, and (3) charging per page accessed.

Whether such information-based products primarily reach the end-consumer directly from the company that 'has the content' or from intermediaries who repackage the content and maintain the actual sales channel on the Web, remains to be seen. Important is that whoever invests in building and maintaining the contents needs to be able to charge for it, regardless if end-consumers or intermediaries (business-to-business) pay. If intermediaries collect information themselves, manufacturers/designers lose a business opportunity; but as long as it does not involve any expenses not covered by additional income, this goes along with the overwhelming trend of specialisation and outsourcing (with specialised partners increasingly co-operating in a network or virtual organisation).

Advertising income generated from Web pages

As time for commercials is the main 'product sold' by TV stations, the market for advertising space on the Web is also booming (e.g. Quelch and Klein, 1996). Only those companies whose contents attracts a certain number of site visitors can sell additional space to others who then place their ads. While this opportunity for profit is gaining importance, it is mainly suitable for those large companies whose sites are well known and visited, e.g. TV stations, newspapers, magazines, etc. (e.g. Sterne, 1995). It does not appear to be a feasible source of income for the millions of SMEs that also offer content on the Web.

WIDENING THE PERSPECTIVE

Economic value of information and communication technology

The Internet, and specifically the Web, can be considered as a special form of ICT. Therefore, a comparison of Web usage, specifically content provision on the Web, and ICT usage seems appropriate.

For more than a decade, information systems and information technology have been considered as tools for transforming the way value activities are performed and for co-ordinating different activities (Porter and Millar, 1985).

Brynjolfsson and Hitt (1996) differentiate 'productivity', 'consumer value', and 'business profitability' as measures of IT value. Findings from investigating 370 large firms suggest that IT increases 'productivity' and 'consumer value', but not 'business profitability'. Thus, there is no inherent contradiction in the idea that IT can create value but destroy profits (see also the literature on the 'productivity paradox', e.g. Brynjolfsson, 1993).

The similarity between these research results and empirical findings about the situation of providing content on the Web is remarkable. Without doubt, the Internet contributes to productivity in the context of co-ordination and customer involvement (especially in business networks and virtual organisations where the Internet is used for co-ordination). Many of these phenomena, however, are taken as given by consumers or so widely applied that companies cannot adapt them to competitive advantages and additional profits.

Value creation via electronic commerce

Electronic commerce may be defined as any form of economic a-ctivity using electronic connections, spanning electronic markets, hierarchies and networks (Wigand, 1997). Following this definition, companies' content provision on the Web represents a form of participation in electronic commerce.

A widespread perspective of electronic commerce is built on 'markets' and 'hierarchies' (Williamson, 1975) as the two basic concepts for controlling a flow of materials and services between the members of a supply chain or electronic network. In such a framework, 'doing commerce electronically' lowers the co-ordination costs in markets and supply chains (Malone *et al.*, 1987), and hierarchies lead to strengthened commercial relationships between partners (Williamson, 1975; Pisano, 1990; Steinfeld *et al.*, 1995). The traditional 'markets' and 'hierarchies' have been complemented by new organisational forms such as electronic networks, virtual organisations, strategic corporations (Johnston and Vitale, 1988; Davidow and Malone, 1995). While the definitions of such terms vary, these concepts clearly suggest that technological infrastructures provide the opportunity for a broader range of intra- and inter-company business structures.

The current notion of enterprises engaged in electronic marketplaces focuses on achieving competitive advantage in the organisation's internal network and external relationships. 'Components of business value of electronic commerce are related to (1) improvements of products/services for specified market segments; (2) new linking mechanisms to business partners using process and technological innovations; (3) linking external relationships with internal processes; (iv) build upon a flexible, but robust telecommunication infrastructure' (van Heck and van Bon, 1997, p. 211).

Furthermore, others have stated that successful business performance in an electronic commerce environment will not arise simply by adding value across a series of business activities in a supply chain, but by redefining a whole value proposition. 'Redefining the whole value proposition', however, requires to have a value proposition, a competitive advantage which allows to sell products or services and thus to profit. Even in an electronic environment a company's offering ultimately becomes part of the end user's (or buyer's) value chain, a competitive advantage arises through differentiating the company's product or role in the supply chain.

The discussion about electronic commerce seems to follow these paradigms and to often focus on co-ordination needs and business opportunities in electronic networks and virtual organisations. It almost neglects, however, the vast number of companies ('content providers' in the narrow sense of the word) who make the Web to what it is today and who pursue the use of the new infrastructure while (mainly) sticking to their conventional business. Their issues and business needs are barely covered in the large amount of 'electronic commerce' research and publications, and even worse, the current hype about 'electronic commerce' seems to ignore the day-by-day business pressures of many players without whom the electronic marketplace would not be as it is.

Macroeconomic business impacts of the Internet-based commerce

1. *Increase in available information-based products and services*: The current Web hype is fostered by lower entrance barriers to business on the Internet. Infrastructure of large companies are no longer required to market specific products. In turn, this causes an enormous growth of information-based products and services, as well as a tremendous increase in accessibility of non-digitisable goods.
2. *Lower prices (including lower margins)*: Market transparency of suppliers, customers, and products causes cost pressures for vendors. Offers from all over the world can be found on-line, (automatically) locating and comparing potential suppliers of products or services on the Internet leads to lower transaction costs (for a detailed discussion see Barua *et al.*, 1995]. This transparency is further increased by the employment of search tools/ agents ('bargain finders'). Competition leads to constant pressure on market prices and demands for extra services to be delivered as 'add-on' to traditional service packages. For many suppliers, keeping up with market prices will mean sacrificing part of their margin.
3. *Shifts in financial flows along inter-corporate value chains*: Table 14.1 outlines two scenarios regarding potential sources of income for content providers and the according shifts in inter-corporate value chains. While large Internet players have established one of the two options, small content providers still mainly count on positive, but indirect contributions of their Internet activities to their overall cost-benefit structure. In the terminology of this paper Internet providers 'transport' the information from content

providers to customers, comparable to common carriers expecting payment for this 'intermediary' service. If they manage to enhance their service line beyond transmission, e.g. with value added services, this should allow them to charge consumers in addition to the transmission fee (Barua *et al.*, 1995).

Scenario 1: Content providers receive payment for their content directly from the consumers, who not only have to pay the Internet providers, but also the content providers for the information they access. Competition for customers among content providers would begin to develop; hence, the quality of information is likely to improve. The situation for Internet providers would mostly stay the same, unless – due to the higher 'Internet consumption price' for users – the overall Internet traffic would decrease drastically.

Scenario 2: Content providers receive payment from Internet providers who 'forward' part of their income to the content providers. Internet providers can only 'win' in this scenario if the low price of content and service in comparison to the previous scenario would lead to a drastic increase in overall Internet traffic. The situation for consumers would remain mainly the same.

Furthermore, once it will become feasible and

Table 14.1   Shifts in financial flows along inter-corporate value chains

	Content provider	Internet provider	Consumer
Currently	receives no payment for content provided	receives payment on time/volume basis	content mostly free, pays for time and volume
Scenario 1	receives payment based on content directly from the consumer	receives payment on time/volume basis	pays for content, time and volume
Scenario 2	receives a predefined 'share' from the Internet provider	receives payment on time/volume/ content basis and 'shares' with content provider	pays for time/volume

common to charge small fees for products or services, Internet providers will likely shift their strategy towards 'service providers' offering value-adding services (Barua *et al.*, 1995].

4. *Shifts in industry structures*: The integration of the Web, databases, CD-ROMs, etc. allows companies to keep up with corporate giants, or at least offers chances to compete with big organisations. One can do research on new markets, test one's ideas, build close ties to clients, and respond quickly to customers' needs without having to cover the overhead costs of large corporations. In the new marketplace, some players, such as local retailers may be eliminated from traditional value chains. New ones, e.g. for local delivery, will enter the game.

CONCLUSIONS AND FUTURE RESEARCH

Electronic media enable organisations to deliver products and services more cost-effectively and efficiently. In cases where the Internet is supposed to support the traditional business (e.g. book sales), the increasingly sophisticated services offered go beyond pure marketing efforts. They provide additional value to 'customers'. While these services constitute extra costs, they barely generate additional profits. Potential clients take advantage of these services (e.g. search the book store database) without necessarily becoming customers.

Involvement in Web-based activities and increasingly also content provision on the Web seems to have become 'compulsory' in many industry sectors. If eventually all companies achieve significantly lower cost for customised product and service delivery, the result cannot be a competitive advantage, but lower margins for the 'average player' in the sector.

At the core of Internet-based commerce, offering content on the Web has to be attractive for the providers in one of two ways: (1) strengthening a company's competitive position with respect to its traditional products (e.g. higher turnover as a consequence of Web activities, or (2) expanding towards additional, profitable product lines (e.g. selling information/content-based products and services).

In this context, future research should pursue three dimensions:

1. Additional empirical investigations of 'companies on the Web' including their total Web-driven costs and revenues would help to

better understand the current business opportunities and needs in the 'real world'.

2. Further development of concepts and business strategies for companies on the Web taking into account the short and medium term financial constraints and the macroeconomic trend that 'there won't be much business without the Web'.

3. Interdisciplinary integration of rather recent trends and findings stemming from the areas 'Internet-based business' and 'electronic commerce' with conventional IT and economics theories and research results.

'Providing content on the Web' and 'Internet-based commerce' offer outstanding opportunities to stay at the edge of business developments. After the first wave of fascination about the potential offered by the technologies, it becomes time to adapt business processes and economics to its existence. In the medium and long run, new infrastructures will provide support for a large range of traditional and innovative business ideas, and will require new business concepts. Nevertheless, the business idea itself must be economically promising, the pure fact that a company engages in the electronic marketplace has not been and will not be sufficient:

While no single company or business network can eliminate by itself the risks arising from the Web era, each of them can and needs to develop its own proactive strategies to exploit the accompanying opportunities.

T. Middelhoff, Bertelsmann AG, Member of
the Board
(translated from German)

References

BARUA, A., RAVINDRAN, S. and WHINSTON, A. (1995) 'Efficient selection of suppliers over the Internet', working Paper of the Center for Information Systems Management, Graduate School of Business, University of Texas at Austin.

BENJAMIN, R. and WIGAND, R.T. (1995) 'Electronic markets and virtual value chains on the information highway', *Sloan Management Review*, 62–72.

BRYNOLFSSON, E. (1993) 'The productivity paradox of Information Technology', *Communications of the ACM*, 35, 66–77.

BRYNJOLFSSON, E. and HITT, L. (1996) 'Paradox lost?': Firm-level evidence of the returns to Information Systems spending', *Management Science*, April.

DAVIDOW, W. and MALONE, M. (1995) *The Virtual Corporation*, New York.

FILLMORE, L. (1997) 'The difference engine in digital time: tools and strategies for selling content on the Internet', Annual Conference 1997 of the Association of American Publishers Proceedings, Washington, DC.

HAMMER, M. and CHAMPY, J.A. (1992) 'What is reengineering?', *Information Week*, 5, 10–24.

JOHNSTON, H. and VITALE, M. (1988) 'Creating competitive advantage with interorganizational systems', *MIS Quarterly*, 6, 153–65.

JONES, D. and NAVIN-CHANDRA, D. (1995) 'IndustryNet: a model for commerce on the World Wide Web', *IEEE EXPERT*, 10(5), 54–9.

LOEBBECKE, C. (1996) Content providers benefiting from commerce on the Internet: current deficiencies, proposed solutions, and foreseeable business trends', Fourth Strategic Information Systems Network (SISnet) Conference Proceedings, Lisbon.

LOEBBECKE, C. (1999) 'Electronically trading in Online Delivered Content (ODC)', Hawaii International Conference on Systems Science (HICSS).

LOEBBECKE, C. and POWELL, P. (1999) 'Electronic publishing: assessing opportunities and risks', *International Journal of Information Management*, August 1999.

LOEBBECKE, C. and TRILLING, S. (1997) 'Strategic potential of TV online services: conceptual framework and examples', *Tenth International Bled Electronic Commerce Conference Proceedings*, II, Bled, 70–92.

MALONE, T.W., YATES, J. and BENJAMIN, R.I. (1987) 'Electronic markets and electronic hierarchies', *Communications of the ACM*, 30(6), 484–97.

O'CONNOR, G. and O'KEEFE, B. (1990) 'Viewing the Web as a marketplace: the case of small companies', *Decision Support Systems*, 1997.

PISANO, G.P. (1990) 'The R&D boundaries of the firm: an empirical analysis', *Administrative Science Quarterly*, 35, 153–176.

PORTER, M. and MILLAR, V.E. (1985) 'How information gives you a competitive advantage', *Harvard Business Review*, July–Aug., 149–60.

QUELCH, J.A. and KLEIN, L.R. (1996) 'The Internet and international marketing', *Sloan Management Review*, Spring, 60–75.

STEINFELD, C., KRAUT, R. and PLUMMER, A. (1995) 'The impact of interorganizational networks on buyer-seller relationships', *Journal of Computer-Mediated Communication*, 1(3).

STERNE, J. (1995) *World Wide Web Marketing*, New York: John Wiley.

VAN HECK, E. and VAN BON, H. (1997) 'Business value of electronic value case study: the expected costs and benefits of electronic scenarios for a Dutch exporter', *Tenth International Bled Electronic Commerce Conference Proceedings*, II, 206–23.

WIGAND, R.T. (1997) 'Electronic commerce: definition, theory and context', *The Information Society*, 13(1), 1–16.

WILLIAMSON, O.E. (1975) *Markets and Hierarchies: Analysis and Antitrust Implications*, New York: Free Press.

15 Intranets: A New Breed of IT System?

James Callaghan

INTRODUCTION

Corporate Intranets – the use of Internet technology to build internal computer networks – are a relatively recent phenomenon initially made possible by the advent of web browsers such as Mosaic and Netscape in 1993/1994. Since then there has been tremendous growth in the number of companies using Intranets and if forecasts are to be believed, soon every company will have an Intranet. This chapter presents some of the findings of an in-depth case study looking at the early take-up and subsequent expansion of an Intranet within a large UK company. The case study examines the role and impact that the use of an Intranet has had to date. In addition to the cost savings that have resulted there are also 'unplanned' benefits such as enabling new ways of working, and the breakdown of barriers to communications and collaborative working. However, from an academic perspective, little work has been done on investigating the role and impact of Intranets in organisations. In an attempt to address this, this chapter treats the Intranet as just another IT system and explores the relevance and value of the existing literature. Issues addressed include the integration of IT into corporate strategy, planning and implementation, and approaches to the evaluation of the system. Each of these issues is illustrated with data from the case study. The potential contribution to the literature from the study of Intranets is also discussed.

An Intranet enables low cost access to information in a wide variety of forms without unnecessary restrictions upon location. Intranets are typically based on Internet technology which is built using open standards and multiple hardware and software platforms. Having a standard technology platform means that it is both cheaper and easier to implement than some of the existing technologies used for information publishing and distribution within organisations. However, given its relative infancy, there is almost no research literature on the actual implementation or use of Intranets. What literature there is focuses on the immediate cost savings that companies have been able to realise by using Intranets.

ISSUES ARISING FROM IT/IS LITERATURE

From a strategic perspective, IT can be viewed as a key agent of cha:.ge in the way companies operate (Scott-Morton 1991). An IT application can be defined as being strategic if it changes a firm's product or the way it competes in its industry (Ives and Learmonth, 1984) or if it has a profound effect on a company's success by influencing the company's strategy or playing a direct role in the implementation of the company's strategy (Sabherwal and King, 1991). In recent years, IT has been seen as a key enabler to organisational change strategies as it makes radical process re-design possible (Davenport and Short, 1990).

PLANNING AND IMPLEMENTING IT/IS

Strategic information systems planning remains to be one of the key IS management issues (Lederer and Salmela, 1996). The continued advances in IT, the strategic nature of the impact of IT, and the increased competitive pressures that companies are now facing, is putting the strategic IS planning process under greater pressure. Another variable that is likely to assume greater relevance in the implementation of strategic IT, is the degree to which it is integrated into existing IT and IS systems. Integration of IT systems often provides the basis for deriving strategic advantage (Benjamin and Scott-Morton, 1988).

ASSESSING WHEN BENEFITS ACCRUE

Jurison (1996) in discussing the dynamic nature of IT benefits points out that: 'there is a pattern of organisational learning in applying new technology, and that organisations go through several distinct stages before they can really exploit new technology'. Furthermore, he adds that the impact of IT on the individual precedes that on the organisation. Time lags between the implementation of IT and the delivery of benefits also make it very difficult to assess the success or effectiveness of the IT system (Brynjolfsson, 1993).

IMPACT AND EVALUATION OF IT/IS

Despite the importance of strategic IS to managers and the interest shown by researchers in the subject, the issue of evaluating and assessing the success of strategic IS and IT in general is still an area that requires further research (Lucas, 1981). Also (Jurison, 1996, p. 76) points out that many seniour managers are dissatisfied with their capabilities for evaluating IS impact on organisational performance.

THE CASE STUDY

The case study investigated the use of Intranet technology in a UK-based company of 120000 employees. The company operates in a number of industries but mainly software, multimedia and communications. Organisationally the company operates as a group of semi-autonomous divisions. There were two key reasons that led the company to experiment with and deploy an Intranet. Primarily, the company was facing increased levels of competition and needed to be able to respond more quickly and also needed to reduce its cost base. Problems with information transmission and storage of paper were resulting in major process delays and large storage and retrieval costs. Following trials in 1995 of Intranet technology, and forecasts of large cost savings, it was decided to roll out an Intranet across the company. Currently approximately 70000 employees have direct access to the Intranet.

The data collected for this case study came from a number of sources, including 25 semi-structured interviews with a variety of employees, discussions with approximately 100 users of internal newsgroups, and attendance at numerous internal workshops discussing the use and potential of Intranets. Full access was also given to the company's Intranet and documents relating to its development. The results presented in this chapter are a résumé of the data collected and of the issues that were identified.

Benefits

The benefits that the company has seen can be divided into tangible (consisting mainly of direct cost savings) and intangible (consisting of things such as increased efficiency, easier access to information and faster decision-making). Although gains in efficiency and changing the way people do things were actually part of the original intention of the Intranet it was very difficult to cost justify these benefits, so the business case for deploying an Intranet was predicated on the cost savings that would result from taking paper out of the business. In the first year of operation, realised savings were estimated to be five times the initial figures of £60 million. This was followed in 1997 by additional savings of 10 times the initial estimates. These cost savings were as a result of ceasing the paper production of items such as dense software manuals, quality management systems and pricing information. Many of these had previously been sent to every employee and a large proportion of this documentation was subject to regular updating.

Increases in efficiency resulted from saving time by having faster and easier access to information on items such as products, competitors, markets, and customers. In a number of cases additional benefits resulted from employees having access to information available on the Intranet that they would otherwise never realistically be able to obtain. Giving people access to the information they need, with confidence that it is accurate and up to date, enables them to take faster and better decisions. As an example the response time for an initial customer enquiry for a new product used to take (on average) three to four man weeks to progress to the point where a draft contract could be presented to the customer. The same process now takes approximately two man hours.

Downsides

Some negative outcomes were also evident. The rapid growth in the use of the Intranet and the opportunities that it brought about meant that although it was not built up as a business critical tool, many people began to view it as such. This led to problems in attempting to meet these expectations and trying to ensure the availability of the information. Also the fact that the Intranet began to be used as a front-end to existing IT systems and for other applications that were not envisaged initially, put greater pressure on the infrastructure and forced a re-think of how best to manage the information on the Intranet. A framework for information management, including publishing guidelines, was thus developed.

Other downsides related to the management of the process of change. There is some resistance to the use of Intranets because some people are afraid of the changes that are resulting. The removal of paper from the business has meant that many people feel concerned about how their role will change. An example of this is middle managers who feel that elements of their job will disappear because they will no longer be able to control the flow of information. A concern that was noted by a number of senior managers in the company was the worry that the use of Intranets may lead to a tendency to use the machine as a substitute for talking to people, resulting in an imbalance between personal relationships and the machine. As one manager said:

> the technology can help you manage your time better, but it is to give you time to build relationships with your customers and your colleagues – it is not about making those relationships electronic.

Current use of the Intranet and issues arising

In examining the role of the Intranet it is interesting to note that there are effectively two Intranets in use in the company. The main one is referred to as the licensed Intranet (where information has to adhere to specific guidelines and people must obtain approval to put information onto Intranet sites), and the unlicensed Intranet – referred to by some as the 'undernet' (primarily focused at the company's R&D facility), where anybody can put information onto Web pages without needing to seek permission.

Initially people searching on the Intranet could search and access information on both sets of pages. However, in recognising the growing business criticality of the Intranet, a recent initiative aimed at introducing an information management framework on the Intranet has meant that the search engines now only search on licensed pages. In migrating existing content into this framework, hyperlinks to unlicensed pages have been removed, although the unlicensed pages are still there. While it is recognised that the 'undernet' was very useful at the beginning as it allowed people to experiment with the Intranet and thus assisted with gaining momentum for widespread deployment, as the Intranet matured and as the importance to the business grew, it was recognised that a more formal controlled environment was required. The plans to migrate existing content into a managed environment initially met with protests from some people who had developed unlicensed Web sites and they set up a 'Campaign for Intranet Freedom' page to air their views. Their concern was that 'if information provision is bureaucratised, then the free sharing of information will be discouraged'.

There is a balance between creating opportunities with the Intranet and having a degree of control in place. The Internet outside is quite anarchical and it was felt that this cannot be allowed in a business situation where the Intranet is becoming business critical.

Information flow and effects on communication patterns

An Intranet facilitates much easier flows of information. It is interesting to note that in addition to supporting the flow of information across the organisation, it is also challenging the hierarchies in the company. Priour to Intranets the company had a fairly rigid structure and information flowed in a very hierarchical fashion. Many seniour managers including the Group Managing Director now encourage feedback via their personal web sites on the Intranet. Another Director has a web site with a link called 'Ask Me' where anyone in his directorate irrespective of grade can ask a question of him and get it answered. For those people who would very rarely ever meet or be able to speak to such senior managers, they can almost have a one-to-one communication. The senior managers in turn recognise that the Intranet is actually a very powerful tool for them to get across their messages. Also, they can find out what their people are concerned about or what opinions or ideas they have and find out directly without it going back up a hierarchy, and perhaps the answers being changed. As one manager commented 'it's a much more direct communication than we've ever had before'. Disseminating information and feeding back comments via Intranet pages and e-mail has obviated the need for information relays.

While bypassing the hierarchy in terms of communications and information flow has benefits, it also has the effect of exposing those middle managers who previously controlled the flow of information. Their power no longer resides in being able to control their people by controlling information. This is beginning to change the success criteria for these middle managers. Their 'power' is now about what their personal competences are, their skill sets, and their ability to manage information and relationships across boundaries. Commenting on this one senior manager said:

> I think it presents a real challenge for them but first of all they mustn't be worried about information bypassing them if it's appropriate to bypass. I think the freedom for people to contact and talk to people around the organisation is a good thing. The real trick is to make sure that you aren't being bypassed for the wrong reason. So it's a good review mechanism as well.

Discussion forums

The Intranet facilitates a number of different types of discussion forum. These include a large number of internal newsgroups of a style similar to those that exist on the Internet and a number of different bulletin board type systems based on Web pages. The newsgroups are accessible to anybody in the company that has an Intranet browser although until recently a lack of technical knowledge on how to access the groups has meant that they have tended to be used mainly by employees with a technical background. The Web page based discussion forums perform the same function as the newsgroups but have a more user-friendly interface. Examples of such systems are SIFT (Sorting Information for Tomorrow) used by HR people, and the Executive Calling System (ECS) used by executive directors to swap information with the sales force.

The main advantage of the discussion forums is that they support communities of interest across the company. For example, the use of the SIFT system is confined to the HR community and the ECS is confined to board members and very seniour managers. Through the use of such forums the communities of interest involved, in addition to building relationships, also build up knowledge in an equivalent manner to the way in which people by word of mouth build up knowledge when they are co-located. However, these forums have the added advantage of it being committed to 'print', so that you cannot in a sense be out of earshot of an 'interesting nugget'. As one manager commented: 'You can go back to it and read it and say "oh that looks an interesting topic, I can listen in on that particular topic and learn from it". So it's less ephemeral than the chit-chat of a conventional meeting place.'

The fact that the discussions are 'captured' electronically has the advantage that they can be archived and searched at a later date.

Moreover, the discussions tend to be initiated when someone is looking for information on a specific topic and very often the replies consist of others imparting their tacit knowledge. An important outcome of this is that once people 'encode' that tacit knowledge in the newsgroup this knowledge has been recorded, it has essentially become explicit knowledge and has become part of the corporate knowledge base. Other people who need this knowledge can then search through the archives and retrieve what they require. Thus, the discussion forums actually perform the role of a basic form of a KM system.

One noteworthy aspect of the use of the newsgroups is that people seem to either love them or hate them. Those who 'love' them emphasise the benefits of the groups, and the sense of 'community' or 'togetherness' that use of the newsgroups to share information engenders. One particular newsgroup 'co.misc' displayed this aspect very strongly. This newsgroup is the most heavily used and receives approximately 10 000 'hits' per day from people across the company. Even though the users of the group acknowledge that a lot of the discussion on the group is non business related they believe strongly that there are business benefits in those discussions. As one user commented the co.misc newsgroup is the

> electronic equivalent of standing around having a cup of coffee, but with everybody in the company. Although people may be having a bit of a frivolous chat, there is a sense of togetherness, a sense of shared . . . we're all in this together lads.

However, there are people in the company who disapprove of the newsgroups. These people tend to focus on the negative aspects of the newsgroups. One manager said:

> my view of them so far is that they are dominated by techie discussions or puerile discussions such as on co.misc. Some of that is shocking; I cannot believe that we're allowing people that amount of time.

Another manager offered the following 'cultural perspective' on the use of newsgroups:

> I think there's the question of how comfortable people are in sharing their problems and their views with what is actually the

whole of the company. And this company comes from a culture where, to a reasonable significant degree, information is power. And I think this newsgroup type idea challenges it because you can publicly expose yourself to 'oh didn't he know that?' and also if you give an answer it becomes public domain and then no one needs to speak to you anymore about that. And there's also a built in mindset that what I've just done 'is not normal'. In fact I felt quite weird that I was writing to somebody and every single word I wrote could be visible to whoever, whether it's the Chairman, my MD or Bill Bloggs in Aberdeen, and that felt quite weird.

People management issues

An issue related to controlling how people use the Intranet is the fear among some managers that the use of Intranets introduces a new set of people management problems. However, the evidence from the case study is that a lot of the people management issues are in a sense the same as ever, i.e. people pretending to work. As one interviewee commented 'all issues such as security and "cyberskiving" were with us before the Internet. The use of Intranets doesn't create new problems – but may expose some that you've already got'.

If the Intranet exposes existing problems it also offers an interesting new method of controlling them. An illustrative example arose on the co.misc newsgroup. One particular user who had obviously been spending too much time on the newsgroup was reported to his line manager by another user. Using the Intranet directory, this other user was able to look up the details of the 'offender's' manager and contact him directly. The offender's manager was thus able to deal with a problem that he probably was not aware existed. This 'self-policing' nature of this newsgroup is referred to in the group as being 'Petered Out' in 'honour' of the person to whom it first happened. It also occurred a number of times while this case study was being conducted.

Cultural issues

The use of Intranets in the company also raises a number of issues related to the culture in the organisation. An example of this was raised by one manager:

We have a culture that individuals are 'told' and 'provided' with information whereas the nature of the Intranet means that users have to actually go looking for it – this is a cultural change in the dissemination of information and will take time to change.

An important aspect of the use of Intranet is the ability to share easily information right across the organisation. This is leading to a greater emphasis on co-operation between different business units and getting people to work together better. However, several managers have commented that the current reward structure in the organisation actually militates against co-operation. They highlight issues such as 'traditional' competition between business units and rewarding people with individual bonuses but at the same time encouraging teamworking and working together.

The use of the Intranet to facilitate open sharing of information is seen as being extremely positive. Employees value and increasingly expect people to be open with their information and to make that information available to others. One manager commented that this change in people's attitudes to sharing information is 'a very visible sign of the organisation growing'.

KM

The benefits of using an Intranet for improving the efficiency of existing processes has been well received by the company. However, people are now beginning to explore the use of the Intranet to facilitate processes that previously were not possible. A key element of these processes is that they all involve aspects of how best to exploit the information sharing capability of the Intranet and are exploring how to use the Intranet as a platform to facilitate a company wide knowledge management system. The recent introduction of an information management framework for the Intranet is a key initial step. Many managers have recognised that as competition continues to increase they will need to find new ways to create value in their products and services and one commented that the only way they can do that is by getting better intelligence collectively in the organisation.

The importance of the Intranet

As the Intranet has rolled out across the company, its importance has grown. Senior managers talk of it as being the 'central nervous system' of the organisation, and use of the Intranet facilities is now considered to be business critical. Many users have added that Intranet is no longer just nice to have, it has become essential for them to do their job. To a certain extent people have now taken the Intranet for granted and it's difficult for them to say how they used to do things or how it's changed things because 'it's just the way they do things now'. Also in supporting and facilitating things like KM the Intranet is seen as being crucial because it allows for all pervasive connectivity.

In summing up the role of the Intranet it is believed that it's importance will continue to grow, especially as the company is now exploring the use of the Intranet to cross organisational boundaries out to customers and suppliers. One seniour manager summed it up by commenting that the current use and role of the Intranet is 'just the tip of the iceberg'.

DISCUSSION

It is evident from the case study that, for the company concerned, its Intranet is now business critical and it performs a major role in the way the company operates. It is also seen as being the key enabler of organisational change. The use of an Intranet has not only helped the company to improve the efficiency of current processes but is facilitating new processes that previously were either prohibitively expensive or were just not possible. An example of this is the use of an Intranet to support the development of a company wide KM system. So using the definitions from the literature it is safe to define the company's Intranet as a strategic IT system.

Yet, less than three years ago the Intranet was perceived as little more than an office automation tool that would allow easy access to and sharing of information across the company. It was not viewed as a strategic IT system and therefore a lot of the formal top-down planning procedures such as detailed implementation plans, formal change programmes and fully specified cost/benefit analysis, normally associated with planning and implementing a strategic IT/IS system simply did not apply. Also as a significant proportion of the hardware required to support the Intranet was already in place it is difficult to envisage what added value a detailed business analysis would have contributed. Furthermore, although formal planning processes do have benefits in that they are thorough and systematic, these benefits are at the expense of considerable time (Gogan *et al.*, 1992). It is highly likely that had such processes been applied to the Intranet then the first issue of the 'Plans and Implementation Processes for Intranet' would still be in the drafting stage! Moreover, a lot of the benefits of using the Intranet were emergent rather than planned. Examples of this include facilitating virtual team working, facilitating communities of interest across the company, and engendering a sense of togetherness among employees who have never even met except across the Intranet. It is interesting that the company has already started to realise these benefits in the time it would normally have taken to conduct a formal strategic plan for such a system. With the advent of technologies such as Intranets, there is clearly a need for new approaches to strategic IT/IS planning that will provide companies with the ability to take advantage of the benefits of new technology in shorter timescales.

The fact that the company realised benefits from using an Intranet in a remarkably short period of time means that assessing when the benefits accrue is an easier task than is normally the case with IT systems. A 'traditional' problem in researching the organisational role and impact of IT systems is that typically it can take a number of years before the impact is felt at the organisational level. However this is not the case with the Intranet studied here, where tangible benefits such as cost savings were realised within weeks and intangible benefits such as improved flows of information were in evidence within months rather than years. One manager commented that 'with Intranets things change so fast, I would say that one normal year is equivalent to 7 Intranet years'.

Thus given the shorter timescales to benefit, Intranets could prove to be a very useful area for researching the impact of IT and in particular exploring the relationship between the impact on the individual and the impact at an organisational level. Perhaps the most striking aspect of the use of Intranets is the range of resultant changes in working practices, many of which were actually unforeseen. As discussed in the case study the Intranet facilitates information sharing in the company on a scale that previously was impossible. Lack of suitable approaches for evaluating the success of IT can often prevent companies from embracing new technologies (Hollis, 1996) but with evaluating Intranets it appears to be a case of not where to start the evaluation process but rather where to stop. Perhaps one of the factors in the success of Intranets is the relative ease of use and this appears to have contributed to the very high degree of acceptance of a relatively new technology.

In the case study a number of people commented that it was the ease of use of the Intranet that led them to re-examine and improve their work patterns. Similarly the ease with which the Intranet allows integration with existing IT systems appears to be a major factor in its success and in its role as a strategic IT system. Evidence from the case study is that the integration into existing systems and the resultant 'ubiquitous' browser front end is a major advantage of the Intranet.

Comparing the findings of the case study to existing literature suggests that Intranets are almost a new 'breed'. Although there are different areas of the literature that are relevant to the study of Intranets, the findings of the case study suggest that these areas (such as strategic IT planning, assessing benefits and impacts, and evaluating the success) need to be re-examined and that Intranets provide a new perspective on the literature. Of particular interest is the fact that studying the impact of Intranets appears to require the 'integration' of a number of diverse areas of the literature. Given the recent tremendous interest of organisations in using Intranets, it appears that Intranets will provide a very fertile area for future research.

References

BENJAMIN, R. and SCOTT-MORTON, M.S. (1988) 'IT, integration, and organizational change', *Interfaces*, 18(3), 86–98.

BRYNJOLFSSON, E. (1993) 'The productivity paradox of Information Technology', *Communications of the ACM*, 36(12), 67–77.

DAVENPORT, T.H. and SHORT, J.E. (1990) 'The new industrial engi-neering: information Technology and business Process Redesign', *Sloan Management Review*, Summer, 11–27.

GOGAN, J.L., CASH, J.I., ROBINSON, J.E. (1992) 'IT-based innovation: managing a disorderly process, in Milutinovic, V. *et al.* (eds), *Proceedings of the 25th Hawaii International Conference on System Sciences*, 4, IEEE Computing Society Press, Los Alamitos, CA., 257–67.

HOLLIS, D.R. (1996) 'The shape of things to come: the role of IT', *Management Review* (AMA), June, 62.

IVES, B. and LEARMONTH, G.P. (1984) 'The Information System as a competitive weapon', *Communications of the ACM*, 27, 1193–201.

JURISON, J. (1996) 'The temporal nature of IS benefits: a longitudinal study', *Information & Management*, 30(2), 75–9.

LEDERER, A.L. and SALMELA, H. (1996) 'Toward a theory of strategic

Information Systems planning', *Journal of Strategic Information Systems*, 5(3), 237–53.

LUCAS, H.C. (1981) *Implementation: The Key to Successful Information Systems*, New York: McGraw-Hill.

SABHERWAL, R. and KING, W.R. (1991) 'Towards a theory of strategic use of information resources', *Information and Management*, 20(3), 191–212.

SCOTT-MORTON, M.S. (1991) *The Corporation of the 1990s – information Technology and Organizational Transformation*, New York: Oxford University Press.

16 Consumers in Swiss Online Grocery Shops

Pascal Sieber

INTRODUCTION

Consumer behaviour in online shops has not yet been the subject of many research projects. We know little about the demographics of online customers and even less about the factors influencing their decision to buy. Initial research results show that – in online commerce too – trustworthiness of suppliers is the factor which most influences willingness to buy (see Jarvenpaa et al., 1998). And, of course, practitioners do market research both by questionnaires and server statistics. Most well-known online shops such as Amazon.com, Dell Computers, Streamline Inc. gain competitive advantage by systematically gathering data from customers, analyzing it and using it to shape their virtual storefronts, product ranges etc. This data is most often proprietary and not available to outsiders. As a contribution to understanding the selling of consumer goods on the Internet, the research presented here takes one example, grocery shopping in Switzerland, to learn more about online customers' characteristics and behaviour. Interviews were conducted with the three leading online grocery shops in Switzerland and a survey was done with 1037 online customers.

From the consumer's point of view, online grocery shopping could be a most welcome alternative to traditional shopping. Market research in Switzerland shows that many consumers do not really enjoy everyday grocery shopping. While in 1979, 45 per cent of Swiss consumers said they liked shopping, in 1997 only 30 per cent shared this feeling (see Rosset 1998). Even more consumers feel they do not have enough spare time do to the shopping. A consumer panel organized by the Swiss Federal Statistical Office (BfS) shows that 51 per cent of Swiss citizens have major problems in finding enough time to do their shopping during opening hours. At the same time (from 1970 to 1990) the number of double-income households rose from 35 per cent to 54 per cent. There seems to be a change in the population that leverages the need for new sales channels for groceries. This is also reflected in the enormous success of different kinds of shops that are not restricted in their opening hours and can therefore sell grocery in the evenings and on Sundays (in Switzerland these are mainly Gas Stations and Railway Stations).

This was the starting point for a research project. The objectives are (1) to learn more about online grocery shopping from the suppliers' point of view and (2) to learn about consumers in online grocery shops. This chapter gives an overview of suppliers in Switzerland and describes the results of quantitative research into consumer characteristics and behaviour. Results are taken from a survey of 1037 online customers registered in the database of the market leader in online grocery shopping in Switzerland. Of course the survey has to be seen as a 'first step' towards answering the question above. There is not enough experience in buying or selling online, either from the consumer or from the grocery shop perspective, to set up sophisticated consumer panels. At the moment, demand is heavily influenced by supply because the online grocery shops in Switzerland are few in number and only very recently established.

RESEARCH DESIGN

Grocery shops

At the moment a lot of electronic grocery shopping is done in specialized shops with very narrow product ranges, such as wine merchants and chocolate shops. There are only three shops with a broad assortment of goods on the Net. One is organized decentrally (DecShopKnown), the other two have centralized their logistics for the purpose of online business (CentShopKnown and CentShopNew). Two of them are very well known grocery shops with hundreds of outlets all over Switzerland (DecShopKnown and CentShopKnown). CentShopNew, on the other hand, is a new market entrant.

To explore the field, I conducted interviews with all three shops. At DecShopKnown, which is a franchising partner of a large European grocery shop, I was able to talk to the marketing manager and his assistant who is responsible for the operation of the online shop.[1] With CentShopKnown, which is organized as a cooperative and has the largest market share in Switzerland, a new organizational unit was founded. Two marketing specialists, one with wide experience in the IS field, are now responsible for the online business. I spoke to them on several occasions.[2] At CentShopNew, the CEO and owner of 51 per cent of the capital was my interviewee.[3] Interviews took place in the working environment of the interviewees. They have been tape recorded. For each Company, a case study was written down and discussed with the interviewees to be sure there is no misunderstanding.

Grocery shoppers

In conjunction with CentShopKnown, I had the opportunity of 'sending out' a questionnaire to online customers. 'Sending out' in this case means the following:

- Customers of CentShopKnown have to register before they can use a secure server to send their orders and payment details. Therefore the population under study is known in its number and geographical distribution.
- Before shopping online, customers have to log on to the web site. This process identifies them as unique users. There is of course no authentication mechanism. We therefore do not know who exactly is using the account.
- A link to the questionnaire was provided as the first object on the screen after the login procedure. Customers had the option of either filling in the questionnaire first and shopping afterwards (or vice versa) or doing their shopping without filling in the questionnaire.
- To encourage customers to take part in our survey, all participants were entered in a competition. Five of the participants were selected at random as winners of CHF 100.

This course of action implies at least two methodological problems: (1) It is not possible to test the sample for representativeness on the basis of any criteria other than their residential area. (2) It is not a random sample but participants did self selection. Therefore we do not know if there is any systematic unrepresentativeness in the data. The return rate was more than 40 per cent. Therefore the data has been analyzed by different statistical methods although the methodological problems mentioned exist.

The objective of statistical analysis is to find out the demographical and behavioral characteristics of different groups of customers. Because of the quality of data (it is categorical, nominal) the testing of hypotheses is done by the Mann–Whitney test statistics to prove whether there are differences in the characteristics between two groups of customers. To illustrate the strength of the significant differences, Cramér's V (between 0 [no difference] and 1 [very strong difference]) and Spearman's Correlation (between −1 [strong negative difference] and +1 [strong positive difference]) are calculated. Spearman's Correlation is not a suitable measure for nominal data. Therefore both these measures have to be taken into consideration.

GROCERY SHOPS IN SWITZERLAND

In Switzerland, grocery shops have to consider three factors when thinking of going online:

1. Private households in Switzerland are comparatively well equipped with PCs and modems (e.g. see EITO 1998).
2. Because of the dense population and other historical reasons, grocery shops have many, small, outlets. Although the number of outlets fell from 7639 in 1990 to 6524 in 1997, the number of outlets per capita is still the highest in the world (see Anon. 1998).
3. Opening hours are restricted by federal law (until 7.30 p.m. on weekdays, 4 p.m. on Saturdays, closed on Sundays).

The three shops mentioned above, lead the online market at the moment. In the offline world, CentShopKnown is the market leader, DecShopKnown holds position 11 with only 2.6 per cent of the turnover of CentShopKnown. CentShopNew, of course, is not among the top 20 in the offline world since this company was launched in 1997 and only sells online.

The market volume for food and near-food in Switzerland is CHF 78.9 billion (1997), while the growth rate between 1991 and 1997 was less than 0.5 per cent p.a. There is no study available about the market volume of Internet shopping in this industry. The numbers estimated by the three market leaders for 1998 and 1999 tend to suggest that it is less than 0.1 per cent (about CHF 78.9 million) of overall turnover.

Information management

All three shops have designed information systems to support state-of-the-art electronic commerce: searchable catalogs, product descriptions and pictures, shopping basket, secure transactions (invoice, credit card), and more. Only CentShopNew already uses techniques to customize the product catalog. CentShopKnown provides consumers with cooking recipes and uses other promotional tools.DecShopKnown has integrated legacy systems in its individual shopping solution based on Netscape Enterprise Server and an MS SQL Database. CentShopKnown works with the IBM standard solution (NetCommerce) and has also integrated legacy systems. In both cases, integration was, and still is, a big problem. The online catalog is updated only once a day, the marketing managers do not have access to customer data except for some figures (such as turnover) calculated once a day. CentShopNew, by comparison, has a better situation. The whole IS solution is based on BroadVision. Financial and stock accounting, as well as the online shop are fully integrated. With the exception of CentShopNew, the information infrastructure of grocery shops in Switzerland does not yet lend itself to frequent interaction between customer and supplier. Instead they resemble offline catalogs incorporating few features to facilitate shopping acts.

Logistics

DecShopKnown forwards the orders to the outlet nearest to the delivery address (customer's address). Each outlet is responsible for fulfilling the orders. They have half an hour to do this. Afterwards an external delivery service transports the orders to the customers. On the way from the outlet to the customer, goods are not chilled. CentShopKnown fulfills the orders independent of the customer's address, at a central warehouse. From there, the orders are either transported to the distribution centers of an external delivery service or to the nearest outlet from where the customer picks it up. If the customer does not pick it up, the external delivery service takes it to the customer's address in a vehicle with a refrigeration facility.

CentShopNew has outsourced the whole logistics process to a large delivery service that not only fulfills orders but also takes care of storage. For both CentShopKnown and CentShopNew, the time frame between receiving an order and delivering it is much longer than two hours (DecShopKnown). Deliveries are made only once a day, consumers can choose between two 90-minute time slots in the evening. CentShopNew provides an express delivery service. This costs the customer a lot more than 'normal' deliveries. Response time might be one of the success factors in this market. Of course it is much more expensive to provide a short response time than it is to provide the 'only once a day' solution. DecShopKnown does not have any cost advantages when customers decide to shop online as opposed to shopping offline. CentShopKnown and CentShopNew do have better cost structures.

Marketing

Table 16.1 summarizes the Marketing Mix of the three grocery shops. It is quite obvious that there is not much differentiation between the three shops except that CentShopNew does not yet carry fresh products and that the delivery times differ a little.

CentShopNew provides the most sophisticated shopping help by leveraging one-to-one marketing mechanisms from BroadVision. 'We would be able to go much further and not only automatically generate individual shopping lists but also customize the pricing of products. But, you know, we have to be careful. Swiss people are very suspicious if you make them think that you know about their behaviour' (CEO of CentShopNew).

ECONOMIC AND COMPETITIVE ASPECTS

While DecShopKnown has invested about CHF 120,000, CentShop-Known needed more than CHF 2 million, although IBM did not calculate the total costs. At IBM they argue that this was their first project of its kind and therefore this was a learning experience. CentShopNew talks about investment of the order of CHF 3 million. They do not want to give the exact figures. All the managers involved tried to calculate net present value for their projects (Table 16.2). As the number of customers and the future investments can only be estimated very vaguely, DecShopKnown and CentShopKnown do not think they will reach break-even in the next 10 years. At the moment both make less than 0.1 per cent of their turnover from online shopping. In the next 12 years they think this figure will rise to 10 per cent.

Table 16.1   Marketing mixes (this classification is taken from
Kotler and Bliemel, 1995)

	DecShopKnown	*CentShopKnown*	*CentShopNew*
Quality of products	Low price segment and brand products	Low price segment, no brand products	High price segment, brand products only
Packing of products	Not chilled	Refrigerated	Refrigerated
Market coverage	ca. 10 per cent of Switzerland (St. Gallen, Zürich)	ca. 20 per cent of Switzerland (Zürich, Bern)	ca. 80 per cent of Switzerland (excluding some provinces)
Product range	3000 best selling products, fresh goods	2000 best selling products, fresh goods	2000 best selling products, no fresh goods
Place of delivery	Weekdays and Saturdays until 8 p.m., min. 2 hours, pick up during opening hours	Weekdays and Saturdays between 5 p.m. and 8 p.m., once a day, pick up during opening hours	Weekdays until 8 p.m., once a day, min. 3 hours (express), no pick up
Advertising	Newspapers, banner	Newspapers, TV, movies, banner	Newspapers, banner
Public relations	Local radio station	TV, newspapers	Newspapers
Online promotion	Special offers	Special offers, recipes	one-to-one-marketing
Price	Same as offline	Same as offline	Like in any other store
Discounts	None	2 per cent instead of 1 per cent for frequent customers	Individual discounts for institutional and other frequent customers
Payment methods	Invoice	Invoice, credit card	Credit card
Delivery costs	Free pick up CHF 10 home delivery	Free pick up CHF 9 home delivery pick up at Railway Station etc.	CHF 9 home delivery CHF 18 express

Table 16.2   Business strategies compared

	DecShopKnown	CentShopKnown	CentShopNew
Figures			
Investments (start to 1998)	CHF 120 000, web design	About CHF 2 million, web design	About CHF 3 million, web design, business network (re)design
Turnover (1998)	Less than CHF 100 000	CHF 3.5 million	About CHF 1 million
Workforce (number of employees / function)	3 / marketing 1 / web design	2 / marketing, web design is outsourced to IBM	2 / customer support 4 / marketing 2 / corporate finance 4 / web design
Asset Configuration	Traditional, outsourcing of transportation	Traditional, partial outsourcing of transportation	Process interdependence (concentration on customer interaction and business network design, outsourcing of warehousing and transportation)
Customer Interaction	Remote experience of products (standard web site)	Remote experience of products (standard web site)	Dynamic customization (one-to-one marketing)

CentShopNew does not have the financial resources to finance the next 12 years of loss. Therefore it plans for break-even in 4 years. From a strategy point of view, the differences between the three shops can be summarized using the 'Virtual Organizing' model of Venkatraman/Henderson (see Venkatraman/Henderson 1998), whereas the Knowledge Leverage vector is not discussed):

It is quite obvious that neither DecShopKnown nor CentShop-Known take the risk of Business Process and Business Network Redesign. Only CentShopNew operates with a business model of heavy outsourcing and automation of inter-organizational operations. On the logistics side, the only options are collection by the customer or home delivery. Other ideas like the warehouse-to-pantry or the depot-to-car model have not yet been exploited in Switzerland (see Burke 1998)

GROCERY SHOPPERS IN SWITZERLAND

Together with CentShopKnown (as this company agreed to its name being published, it will be called Migros in this chapter), an electronic questionnaire was designed and built in the web site of Migros. Approximately 10,400 customers were registered in the Migros database (October 19, 1998). Analysis of actual transactions shows that only about 2500 of them buy more than once in a three month period (from August to October 1998). These 2500 people are defined as the population under study, as follows: customers of 'Migros Online Shopping' having bought goods more than once in three months from August to October 1998. A total of 1037 questionnaires were completed between October 19 and November 1, 1998. Some answers were eliminated from the sample because the suspicion was that they did not contain reliable data (2 of the participants, for example, indicated that they work more than 150 hours a week, others claim to have more than 30 children). Depending on the question, the sample therefore consists of 1003 to 1037 (about 40 per cent of the population under study) answers from unique customers.

The following sections describe some of the data collected and test a handful of hypotheses and proposals. As stated earlier, this is the 'first step' towards learning more about consumer behaviour. Most questions were asked with the aim of testing (1) whether Migros reaches the focused customer group defined in its marketing plan and (2) to see to what extent actual online customers are satisfied by Migros' services on the Web.

DEMOGRAPHICS

Since Migros does not have data about offline customers, the sample is compared with statistical data from the Swiss Federal Statistical Office (BfS) and with a survey about Internet users in Switzerland, conducted by the Institute of Sociology at the University of Bern in August 1998. Both surveys represent highly reliable data. The BfS did a full survey, and the survey of Internet users has been tested for representativeness. Table 16.3 shows that women are still highly

Table 16.3   Demographics compared

		Internet users in Switzerland (see Franzen, 1999) n = 15624	Migros online shoppers n = 1037	Swiss citizens (see BfS, 1997) n = 7081300
Sex	Male (%)	87.3	66.8	48.8
	Female (%)	12.7	33.2	51.2
Age	20–39 years (%)	57.4	74.4	30.4
	40–64 years (%)	40.6	24.0	31.5
	65 and older (%)	1.9	0.2	14.9
	Average age (years)	38	34	–
Civil status	Never married (%)	41.0	43.2	41.9
	Married (%)	53.1	51.6	47.1
	Divorced (%)	5.4	4.9	5.1
	Widowed (%)	0.4	0.3	5.9
Household	1 person (%)	17.1	20.3	32.4
	2 persons (%)	32.4	34.9	31.7
	3 persons (%)	16.9	14.1	14.9
	4 persons (%)	23.0	18.8	14.5
	5 and more persons (%)	10.5	11.2	6.5
Education	Elementary school (%)	4.4	3.2	–
	High school (%)	38.6	42.6	–
	Undergraduate (%)	38	23.7	–
	Graduate (university degree, masters, PhD etc.) (%)	19	30.4	–

under-represented if we compare Internet users with Swiss citizens as a whole. This also holds true for online shoppers (a subgroup of Internet users). But the percentage of women among these (we might call them 'online grocery customers') is much higher than the percentage of women with Internet access. Further comparison shows that:

- Online shoppers are younger than the average Internet user.
- Online shoppers live in smaller households than average Internet users, but in larger than the average Swiss citizen.
- The educational status of online shoppers is better than that of the average Internet user.

This overview already provides some information about potential customer groups to be addressed with online shops. In the following sections, four potential target customer groups are identified. For each group one or more variables are taken into consideration to distinguish it from other customers. In each of the following sections first the target customer group is defined. This description is followed by the comparison of each group with 'other' customers. On one side demographical characteristics and on the other side behaviour characteristics are compared.

REGULAR AND NON-REGULAR SHOPPERS

From the suppliers' point of view, customers who often come back to the online store and spend large amounts are the most attractive. Therefore the sample was split in two groups: Regular Shoppers (18.9 per cent) and non-regular shoppers (81.1 per cent) (cf. Table 16.4).

The demographical comparison between regular and non-regular shoppers shows that these groups do not differ in any of the characteristics. Age, sex, number of people in the household, number of children, education and income were compared. Analysis of behaviour on the other hand, shows that Regular Shoppers spend higher amounts per shopping act, that fewer of them make the buying decision for

Table 16.4 Frequency of shopping acts

Frequency of online shopping	*Frequency*	%	
Less than once a month	424	41.3	Non-regular
1 to 2 times a month	409	39.8	Non-regular
2 to 4 times a month	154	15.0	Regular
1 to 2 times a week	40	3.9	Regular
Total	1027	100	

their whole household (when shopping offline) than is the case with others,[4] they want to do their shopping as fast as possible and they state that they have problems finding time for every-day shopping. (For details of statistical analysis see Appendix).

RUN SHOPPERS AND OTHERS[5]

To come back to the starting point of the research project, participants were asked several questions about their every-day shopping problems. To summarize the answers, two groups of shoppers have been identified: Run Shoppers and others. Run Shoppers are people (cf. Table 16.5) who

* have difficulty finding time to do their shopping during working hours,
* indicate that they have problems to take time for shopping and would be happy to save time,

Table 16.5   Run shoppers and others

Shopping as fast as possible	Freq.	%	Shopping at rush hours	Freq.	%
Yes, always	469	45.4	Strongly agree	273	26.5
Yes, frequently	347	33.6	Agree	318	30.8
Yes, rarely	18	1.7	Neither	139	13.5
No	34	3.3	Disagree	188	18.2
(Depending on time			Strongly disagree	113	11
available	166	16.1[a]	**Total**	1031	100
Total	1034	100			

Problems finding time	Freq.	%	Summary	Freq.	%
Strongly agree	361	35.1	Others	634	61.1
Agree	333	32.4	Run Shoppers	403	38.9
Neither	157	15.3	**Total**	1037	100
Disagree	121	11.8			
Strongly disagree	57	5.5			
Total	1029	100			

Note: [a] These answers have been excluded from the analysis.

- indicate that they have to do their shopping during the 'rush hours' (between 11 a.m. and 2 p.m. or between 5 p.m. and 7.30 p.m.).

Run Shoppers are a little older than others, more of them are men, they live in smaller households, have fewer children and are better educated. In their shopping behaviour they differ only little in the frequency of shopping (they do come back more often) and, of course, they do differ a lot in the three defining characteristics. All other behavioral characteristics are the same between Run Shoppers and others.

FUN SHOPPERS AND OTHERS

Fun Shoppers are people who do not really plan their shopping but are inspired by the design of the online shop and by special offers. They indicate that their buying decision is strongly influenced by spontaneous action during the shopping act (cf. Table 16.6).

Among Fun Shoppers men are over represented, they have less children and better education than others. As far as their shopping behaviour is concerned, they use shopping lists less, they more than others make the buying decision when shopping offline and they shop less frequently. So, Fun Shoppers' behavior seams to fit better to offline than to online customers.

EXTRA CUSTOMERS AND OTHERS

Extra Customers are those who normally (in offline shopping) do not make buying decisions for their whole household. When online shop-

Table 16.6 Fun shoppers and others

Spontaneous shopping online	Freq.	%	Summary	Freq.	%
Strongly agree	61	5.9	Fun shopper	273	26.5
Agree	212	20.5	Others	759	73.5
Neither	233	22.6			
Disagree	380	36.8	**Total**	1032	100
Strongly disagree	146	14.1			
Total	1032	100			

ping, on the other hand, they are the ones who make the decision. The observation that lead to the idea of creating this group of customers is as follows: About one year ago Migros asked some of their (mostly) male online customers whether they do the shopping for themselves alone or for their whole household. The answers indicated that there are many customers who take shopping lists with them to their offices. These shopping lists are written by other family members. The identified customers themselves just take advantage of 'free' Internet access in their offices, but they are not the target customers of Migros (cf. Table 16.7).

Extra Customers are younger than others, men are over represented, they live in larger households, have more children, a higher education and higher incomes than others. Apart from the fact that they make buying decisions online but not offline and they shop little more spontaneous but less frequently, their shopping behaviour does not differ from that of others.

SUMMARY OF CONSUMER ANALYSIS

Although there are significant but quite weak differences (Cramér's V ranges from 0.035 to 0.280 only) between the four different groups of customers, there are some findings of interest for online shops as regards the demographical and behavioral characteristics of online grocery shoppers:

Table 16.7 Extra customers and others

Who does the shopping offline	Who does the shopping online	Group
Other person in household	Myself	Extra Customer
Other person in household	Other person in household	others
Myself	Other person in household	others
Myself	Myself	others
Summary	*Frequency*	%
Extra Customers	221	21.3
others	816	78.7
Total	1037	100

1. Regular Shoppers spend higher amounts per shopping act than others. Marketing strategies designed to cultivate customer loyalty might therefore be particularly effective.
2. A higher percentage of Run Shoppers and of Extra Customers are men than is the case for other customers. Concentration on 'fast shopping men' might therefore be a successful customer segmentation. This suggestion is also supported by the fact that Extra Customers have higher incomes than others.
3. Fun Shoppers could be of interest to online shops, although they are less regular online shoppers at Migros. A different web site design might attract them more than Run Shoppers (see also Burke, 1998).

The web site of Migros has been designed for fast transactions but of the actual customers, Run Shoppers make up only 17.5 per cent of the most active group (Regular Shoppers). Although only little more that 38.9 per cent of all customers are Run Shoppers, this is a strong cluster of behavioral groups with statistical significance. This means that Migros attracts the focused customer group. One would expect that Run Shoppers rate Migros' web site better than others. In fact this is not the case. Their rating (from 1 [very inconvenient] to 5 [very convenient]) of 13 aspects ranging from 'do you find products easily' to 'is access time fast enough' is not significantly different from the rating of other customers. This might be interpreted as dissatisfaction of Run Shoppers, although they have been attracted by Migros' web site.

This conclusion, of course, has to be interpreted within the limits of reliability of the data. The sample might be systematically unrepresentative because Run Shoppers in particular might not have had the time to fill in the questionnaire.

CONCLUSION

This research discusses the three leading online grocery shops in Switzerland. Two of them capitalize on their brand names, the third one invested a lot more in new technologies to meet the needs of online customers. All in all, despite the different business models, the three marketing strategies do not differ greatly from one another. Moreover, the current facilities for online grocery shopping in Switzerland are far from convenient: customers still have to select single products from a catalog, then order the products and they receive them in an unsorted manner. Before cooking they have to be arranged in the right way and there are no cooking instructions (or any other help).

Potential customer groups to be addressed with online grocery shops are not yet very diverse either. However, there are significant differences in the shopping behaviour between the four groups defined for the analysis. The potential for more diverse strategies does, therefore, exist (e.g. one shop could concentrate on Fun Shoppers and design a web site especially convenient for their needs, with all kinds of special promotions and cross selling offers).

From the consumer point of view, a 'convenience store on the Internet' (this is the objective of CentShopNew) is still far enough off to justify continuing with research and learning about the trajectories of change.

Notes

1. 3 interviews each lasting approximately two hours took place between August 1998 and January 1999.
2. In all, 5 interviews lasting 2 to 3 hours took place between August 1998 and January 1999.
3. 2 interviews (one by telephone) lasting 1 and 2.5 hours respectively took place between August 1998 and January 1999.
4. 95.1 per cent of the participants indicate that they make buying decisions when shopping online for their whole households. Therefore it might be interesting to see who makes buying decisions when offline shopping. Regular Shoppers are people who normally (offline) do not make these decisions.
5. I copied the idea of calling these two groups 'fun' shoppers and 'run' shoppers from Eric van Heck (Erasmus University Rotterdam). He used these terms in a presentation at the EGS Workshop (16 December 1998) in Helsinki.
6. All statistical analysis has been done using SPSS V 9.0. The data file is available free of charge, exclusively for scientific purposes. Please contact the author if you are interested in the data.

References

ANON. (1998) Ruherer & Partner, Gottlieb Duttweiler Institut, IHA / GfM (Eds.): Detailhandel Schweiz 98. Richterswil.
BfS (1997) (ed.) Bundesamt für Statistik, *Statistisches Jahrbuch der Schweiz 1998*, Zürich.
BURKE, R.R. (1998) 'Real shopping in a virtual store,' in Bradley, S.P. and

Nolan, R.L. (eds), *Sense & Respond – Capturing Value in the Network Era*, Boston, 245–60.

EITO (1998) European Information Technology Observatory 98, Frankfurt/Main.

FRANZEN, A. (1999) *Verändert das Internet die Gesellschaft?*, Bern.

JARVENPAA, S.L., TRACTINSKY, N. and VITALE, M. (1998) *Consumer Trust in an Internet Store*, Department of Management and IS, CBA Austin, TX (working paper).

KOTLER, P. and BLIEMEL, F. (1995) *Marketing Management*, 8th edn. Stuttgart.

ROSSET, R. (1998) 'Markenwelt und Einkaufsverhalten im Wandel einer Generation (1979–1997), Ergebnisse einer Umfrage in Zusammenarbeit mit dem Schweizerischen Markenartikelverband PROMARCA,' Link Institute, Lucerne.

VENKATRAMAN, N. and HENDERSON, J.C. (1998) 'Real strategies for virtual organizing,' *Sloan Management Review*, 39(4), 33–48.

Appendix

Table 16.8 and Table 16.9 summarise the findings. For each of the rows, four hypotheses have been tested. H0 speculates that there is no difference between e.g. Run Shoppers and others as regards their age. If H0 can be rejected, Spearman's Correlation indicates the direction of difference (e.g. Run Shoppers are older than others) and Cramér's V indicates how strong the difference is (e.g. weak). Bold face indicates that the corresponding hypotheses can be rejected. Cells that are shaded are meant to indicate significant differences between the corresponding group and others because these variables were taken to define the groups. In all cases Regular, Run, Fun respectively Extra Customers are given the number 1 and others the number 0.[6]

Table 16.8   Demographic analysis

Variable		Regular	Run	Fun	Extra
Age	Sign. Mann–Whitney	0.609	0.001	0.052	0.023
[year of birth]	Cramér's V	0.040	0.152	0.105	0.100
	(Sign).	0.801	0.000	0.023	0.035
	Spearman's corr.	0.016	−0.103	−0.061	0.071
	(Sign.)	0.609	0.001	0.052	0.022
	n	1026	1035	1031	1035
Sex	Sign. Mann–Whitney	0.104	0.002	0.020	0.000
[1 male, 2 female]	Cramér's V	0.051	0.097	0.073	0.280
	(Sign).	0.104	0.002	0.020	0.000
	Spearman's corr.	0.051	−0.097	−0.073	−0.280
	(Sign.)	0.104	0.002	0.020	0.000
	n	1003	1011	1008	1011
No. of people in	Sign. Mann–Whitney	0.553	0.000	0.084	0.000
household	Cramér's V	0.027	0.216	0.096	0.313
[1, 7]	(Sign).	0.979	0.000	0.095	0.000
	Spearman's corr.	0.019	−0.206	−0.054	0.293
	(Sign.)	0.553	0.000	0.084	0.000
	n	1008	1017	1013	1017

Table 16.8   *Continued*

Variable		Regular	Run	Fun	Extra
No. of children	Sign. Mann–Whitney	0.163	0.000	0.015	0.000
[0, 10]	Cramér's V	0.091	0.210	0.084	0.183
	(Sign).	0.136	0.000	0.208	0.000
	Spearman's corr.	0.044	−0.207	−0.077	0.168
	(Sign.)	0.163	0.000	0.015	0.000
	n	1007	1016	1012	1016
Education	Sign. Mann–Whitney	0.281	0.000	0.011	0.016
[1 elementary	Cramér's V	0.042	0.136	0.122	0.083
school, 4 graduate]	(Sign).	0.608	0.000	0.002	0.069
	Spearman's corr.	−0.034	0.123	−0.080	0.076
	(Sign.)	0.281	0.000	0.011	0.015
	n	1019	1028	1024	1028
Income of	Sign. Mann–Whitney	0.726	0.105	0.460	0.000
household	Cramér's V	0.075	0.076	0.040	0.173
[1 < 2000 CHF/m.,	(Sign).	0.372	0.354	0.908	0.000
6 > 14 000 CHF/m.]	Spearman's corr.	0.011	0.052	−0.024	0.152
	(Sign.)	0.726	0.105	0.460	0.000
	n	961	969	965	969

Table 16.9   Consumer behaviour

Variable		Regular	Run	Fun	Extra
Amount spent per	Sign. Mann–Whitney	0.000	0.429	0.124	0.770
shopping act	Cramér's V	0.168	0.103	0.085	0.101
[1 < CHF 20,	(Sign).	0.000	0.140	0.380	0.159
8 > CHF 140]	Spearman's corr.	0.136	−0.025	−0.048	−0.009
	(Sign.)	0.000	0.429	0.124	0.770
	n	1021	1026	1025	1026
Use shopping lists	Sign. Mann–Whitney	0.019	0.948	0.000	0.586
[1 No, 2 mental list,	Cramér's V	0.179	0.067	0.244	0.094
3 written sometimes,	(Sign).	0.000	0.200	0.000	0.028
4 written always]	Spearman's corr.	0.073	0.002	−0.136	−0.017
	(Sign.)	0.019	0.948	0.000	0.586
	n	1024	1034	1030	1034
Decision to buy	Sign. Mann–Whitney	0.000	0.166	0.008	**0.000**
(offline vs. Online)	Cramér's V	0.113	0.043	0.083	**0.926**
[1 other person,	(Sign).	0.000	0.166	0.008	**0.000**
2 myself]	Spearman's corr.	−0.113	−0.043	0.083	**0.926**

Table 16.9   *Continued*

Variable		Regular	Run	Fun	Extra
	(Sign.)	0.000	0.166	0.008	**0.000**
	n	1022	1032	1027	**1032**
Frequency of online	Sign. Mann–Whitney	**0.000**	0.002	0.004	**0.000**
shopping	Cramér's V	**1.000**	0.099	0.100	0.131
[1 < once/month,	(Sign).	**0.000**	0.018	0.017	0.001
5 > twice/week]	Spearman's corr.	**0.730**	0.098	−0.091	−0.128
	(Sign.)	**0.000**	0.002	0.004	0.000
	n	**1027**	1027	1025	1027
Frequency of	Sign. Mann–Whitney	0.125	0.915	**0.000**	0.038
spontaneous	Cramér's V	0.104	0.053	**1.000**	0.110
shopping	(Sign).	0.025	0.577	**0.000**	0.015
[1 never,	Spearman's corr.	0.048	0.003	**−0.794**	−0.065
5 very often]	(Sign.)	0.096	0.859	**0.000**	0.036
	n	1025	1032	**1032**	1032
Shopping as fast as	Sign. Mann–Whitney	0.001	**0.000**	0.330	0.664
possible	Cramér's V	0.110	**0.263**	0.050	0.971
[1 yes, always, 4 no]	(Sign).	0.016	**0.000**	0.050	0.971
(5 [depending on	Spearman's corr.	−0.108	**0.000**	0.033	−0.015
time] was excluded	(Sign.)	0.001	**0.000**	0.330	0.664
from Analysis)	n	860	**868**	864	868
Shopping at rush	Sign. Mann–Whitney	0.203	**0.000**	0.770	0.269
hours	Cramér's V	0.054	**0.707**	0.049	0.104
[1 agree,	(Sign).	0.558	**0.000**	0.655	0.025
5 don't agree]	Spearman's corr.	−0.040	**−0.667**	0.009	0.034
	(Sign.)	0.203	**0.000**	0.770	0.269
	n	1021	**1031**	1026	1031
Problems finding	Sign. Mann–Whitney	0.000	**0.000**	0.044	0.093
time	Cramér's V	0.133	**0.583**	0.101	0.067
[1 agree,	(Sign).	0.001	**0.000**	0.034	0.324
5 don't agree]	Spearman's corr.	−0.129	**−0.558**	0.063	0.052
	(Sign.)	0.000	**0.000**	0.044	0.093
	n	1019	**1029**	1024	1029

Part V

The Millennium, Organisations and 'Humpty Dumpty'

17 The Millennium Problem: An Interesting Case of IS Failure

Paul Beynon-Davies, Ian Owens and Michael Lloyd-Williams

INTRODUCTION

The millennium problem or Y2K problem has been much discussed in the IS practitioner and general press. Surprisingly the IS academic community has remained largely silent over the issue. In this chapter we wish to examine the phenomenon of Y2K as an instance of IS failure. Taking this particular stance on the issue leads we feel to a number of interesting areas which demand further investigation. The structure of the chapter is as follows. We first review the current phenomenon of Y2K and discuss some of the relevant work in the area of IS failure. The topic of IS failure has tended to concentrate on issues of success or failure in relation to one specific organisational IS and/or project. We highlight a number of ways in which Y2K can be characterised as an unique and interesting instance of IS failure. In one sense Y2K can be characterised merely as a techno-logical failure and the responses to it merely of a technical kind. But Y2K, and the responses taken to it are of interest also on the organisational, societal, and economic level. It is therefore a phenomenon of primary concern to the IS academic. We raise a number of issues posed by our examination of Y2K which demand further investigation by IS academics. Y2K and the panic which it appears to have generated can be seen as a clear demonstration of the degree to which IS/IT is closely embedded within modern organisa-tions. However, there is preliminary evidence that Y2K is having an effect on the relationship between the IS/IT function and organisa-tions. We particularly raise questions as to its effect on IS strategy and planning, outsourcing and the IS development portfolio of organisations.

The Millennium problem or Y2K problem has been much discussed in the IS practitioner and general press. Surprisingly the IS academic community has remained largely silent over the issue (Gillies, 1997). Kappelman has recently made a call for academics to contribute to the debate and analysis in this area. He makes a distinction between what he calls technology-oriented contributions such as investigations of project management practices needed to cope with Y2K, and management-oriented contributions such as the impact Y2K is having and will have on societies and economies (Kappelman, 1997). To illustrate the paucity of material in the academic arena we conducted a small survey of past issues of seven journals which we would have expected to have some contributions on the Y2K problem: *Information Systems Journal, International Journal of Information Management, Information and Software Technology, Accounting, Management and Information Technology MIS Quarterly, European Journal of Information Systems* and *Journal Information Technology.* In each case there was not a single paper published on this topic since 1994, a period when literally thousands of practitioner articles and books have been published on Y2K. Some recent papers have appeared in the more general computing journals (such as *Communications of ACM*) particularly re-emphasising the line taken in the vast volume of practitioner literature (Berghel, 1998); (Kappelman *et al.*, 1998), but no paper has raised the focus to IS rather than for purely technological concerns.

In our survey we also examined past proceedings of one international (*European Conference on Information Systems*) and two UK conferences (*Business Information Technology, UK Academy of Information Systems*) in the IS area for the past three years. At these conferences, only a single paper raises the Y2K issue (Betts *et al.*, 1996), but again failed to raise any significant concerns of interest to the academic. We also personally contacted members of the editorial panel of two prominent IS journals (*European Journal of Information Systems, Information Systems Journal*). One editor responded as not having received any paper on this topic. The other reported having received a few submissions on this topic, but all were rejected for not making a serious contribution to the area. This lack of IS academic material on the issue of Y2K is particularly interesting in light of the degree to which journals in other professional areas have latched on to the issue. Over the last three years there has been a rush of papers in architectural, finance, electrical engineering and other disciplines. This raises the question of how we account for this lack of coverage by the IS academic fraternity of a topic which is considered of such interest by IS practitioners and most other professional groups and disciplines? A number of tentative hypotheses are expressed below:

1. One reason for the lack of academic material may be that, on the one hand Y2K is not seen as a suitably difficult computing problem; and on the other hand is not seen as a significant business problem. This would perhaps explain the lack of interest in the phenomenon on the part of computer scientists and business and management academics. It does not explain the lack of interest by IS academics in such an important topic which contributes to the shape of the IS/IT interface. Even if Y2K is treated merely as a maintenance problem, it is still a topic worthy of attention (Burton Swanson, 1992).

2. Another argument may be that academic research turns around so slowly, that people are doing research in this area but have not reported on it yet. This might account for the lack of material in the academic journals. It does not account for the lack of material at conferences since one would expect such projects to have submitted research in progress papers. One editor of an IS journal commented that by the time academics manage to report any research they have been conducting on this problem it would be too late.

3. Yet another argument may be made that the lack of IS material on Y2K is yet another instance of the gulf between IS academia and practice. Senn (1998) has recently argued that much of IS academic research is seen as untimely and mostly irrelevant on the part of IS practitioners. This surely raises questions in relation to the validity of academic IS research agendas.

In this chapter we wish to make a small contribution in the Kappelman's management-oriented focus on Y2K. We particularly wish to examine the phenomenon of Y2K as an instance of IS failure. Taking this particular stance on the issue leads we feel to the identification of a number of interesting areas which demand further investigation by the IS discipline.

The structure of the chapter is as follows:

1. We review the current phenomenon of Y2K. At its essence Y2K is that phenomenon concerned with the way in which dates have historically been stored and manipulated in computer-based systems.

2. We discuss some of the relevant work in the area of IS failure. The topic of IS failure has tended to concentrate on issues of success or failure in relation to one specific organisational IS and/or

project. Y2K is particularly interesting as a phenomenon which has an impact on a national and even world-wide level.

3. We highlight a number of ways in which Y2K can be characterised as an unique and interesting instance of IS failure. In one sense Y2K can be characterised merely as a technological failure and the responses to it merely of a technical kind. But Y2K, and the responses taken to it are of interest also on the organisational, societal, and economic level. It is therefore of primary concern to the IS academic.

4. We raise a number of issues posed by our examination of Y2K which demand further investigation by IS academics. Y2K and the panic which it appears to have generated can be seen as a clear demonstration of the degree to which IS/IT is so closely embedded within modern organisations. However, there is preliminary evidence that Y2K is having an effect on the relationship between the IS/IT function and organisations. We particularly raise questions of its effect on IS strategy and planning, outsourcing and the IS development portfolio of organisations.

Y2K

The Y2K problem has also been called the Millennium bug, the Millennium problem and the Millennium time-bomb. At its essence it is that phenomenon concerned with the way in which dates have historically been stored and manipulated in computer-based systems. The concern over Y2K was originally formulated in relation to IT systems; not only in relation to layers of software-operating systems, bespoke applications, packaged software and 'shrink-wrapped' applications – but also in relation to hardware, particularly the BIOS (basic input–output system) chips of personal computers. More latterly, the concern has been raised over the prevalence of date problems in so-called embedded systems – microprocessor-based controllers in applications ranging from washing machines to CAT scanners. The scale of the problem is a matter of some debate. Capers Jones has estimated that the Y2K problem will cost the US $70 billion to fix, while he estimates the world-wide cost of fixing the problem will be $530 billion (Jones, 1997). This includes only an estimate of the costs of software fixes and excludes costs associated with: litigation surrounding the issue, potential failures of information systems as a result of the problem and the cost of business failures which might ensue. In a more recent analysis, Kappelman (Kappelman *et al.*, 1998) puts the figure for software fixes in the US as being $136 billion while the global impact as being somewhere in the range of $323–486 billion. It is difficult to state precisely when the phenomenon began to become prominent in the practitioner literature. The conventional response of many organisations to Y2K has been to set up year 2000 projects which engage in phases such as impact analysis, planning and scheduling, conversion, testing and implementation (Kappelman and Cappel, 1996). Most large-scale companies in the UK have had a year 2000 project running for three to four years and will have completed testing of their system by April/May 1999. Many sectors have not been so organised in their response: health (Mathieson, 1998), government (Barker and Marshall, 1997), and SMEs (Maitland, 1998) are notable examples. There are also some reports that companies on the European continent may be slower in responding than their UK counterparts (Anon., 1998).

The Y2K problem has also been framed in relation to a number of interesting contemporary phenomena affecting the IS/IT industry:

1. It has been cited as a significant contributor to the current skills crisis in IS/IT. A current estimate solely for the UK is that there is a supply gap of some 30,000 IS people in the UK. Much play has also been made of the difficulties of keeping skilled IT staff and the pressure Y2K has placed on pay rates in the industry.
2. It has spawned what some have called the compliance industry. Many companies have issued so-called compliance questionnaires to their major suppliers. Many other companies have publicly announced that they will cease to trade with companies that cannot publicly state that they are Y2K compliant.
3. It is claimed that the significant investment that companies have had to make in addressing the Y2K problem has critically affected the IS development portfolio of most companies. A study recently conducted by Dataquest predicts that organisational spending on Y2K work will stifle organisational spending on important IT initiatives (Pettitt, 1998) in the short to medium-term future.

Y2K AND FAILURE

IS failure has been a significant topic of investigation for IS academics for a number of years. However, the topic of IS failure has tended to concentrate on issues of success of failure in relation to one specific organisational IS and/or project. Notable case studies such as

LASCAD (Beynon-Davies, 1995), Mandata (Sauer, 1993) and Confirm (Oz, 1994), for instance, have been built on this basis. Y2K is particularly interesting as a phenomenon which has an impact on an industrial and even world-wide level.

In one sense Y2K can be characterised merely as a technological failure and the responses to it merely of a technical kind. We might posit that this is perhaps part of the reason why IS academics have not turned their attention to it. This is supported by the way in which much of the current literature is made up of 'How to solve it' discussions relating to Y2K projects and associated software/hardware fixes. But Y2K, and the responses taken to it are of interest also on the organisational, societal, and economic level. It is therefore of primary concern to the IS academic.

At a broad level, Y2K is unique as an example of IS failure because:

1. It crosses internal IS boundaries within any one organisation. For instance, the whole idea of conducting an IS/IT inventory, an essential part of most Y2K projects, works under this supposition.
2. Y2K is a cross-organisational experience. Many inter-organisational information systems will be equally subject to Y2K. For instance, companies in the banking sector have been taking a close look at the Y2K compliance their Automated Teller Machine (ATM) networks.
3. The scale of the problem is enormous even in comparison to a costly information systems failure such as the Stock Exchange's Taurus project (Currie, 1994) (£75–£300 million). This is true both in terms of the amount of effort needed to be devoted to it and the diverse sectors it impacts upon. Y2K is a global example of IS failure that has been discussed on a whole range of levels: governments and international organisations alike. Recently estimates of the cost to the UK have ranged from £5 billion to £50 billion.
4. Y2K is unique due to the degree it has been reported both in the IS/IT industry but also more widely in the national and international media. It is particularly interesting for the way in which it constitutes a sociological phenomenon associated with issues such as millenarianism, disaster and technophobia.

IS FAILURE

Lyytinen and Hirschheim (1987) in conducting a survey of the literature on IS failure identify four major theoretical categories of such phenomena:

1. *Correspondence failure.* This is the most common form of IS failure discussed in the literature and typically reflects a management perspective on failure. It is based on the idea that design objectives are first specified in detail. An evaluation is conducted of the IS in terms of these objectives. If there is a lack of correspondence between objectives and evaluation the IS is regarded as a failure.

2. *Process failure.* This type of failure is characterised by unsatisfactory development performance. It usually refers to one of two types of failure. First, when the IS development process cannot produce a workable system. Secondly, the development process produces an IS but the project runs over budget in terms of cost, time, etc.

3. *Interaction failure.* Here, the emphasis shifts from a mismatch of requirements and system or poor development performance to a consideration of usage of a system. The argument is that if a system is heavily used it constitutes a success; if it is hardly ever used, or there are major problems involved in using a system then it constitutes a failure.

4. *Expectation failure.* Lyytinen and Hirschheim describe this as a superset of the three other types of failure. They also describe their idea of expectation failure to be a more encompassing, politically and pluralistically informed view of IS failure than the other forms. This is because they characterise correspondence, process and interaction failure as having one major theme in common: the three notions of failure portray a highly rational image of IS development; each views an IS as mainly a neutral technical artefact. In contrast, they define expectation failure as the inability of an IS to meet a specific stakeholder group's expectations. IS failures signify a gap between some existing situation and a desired situation for members of a particular stakeholder group. Stakeholders are any group of people who share a pool of values that define what the desirable features of an IS are, and how they should be obtained.

Y2K can be seen as an instance of each of these types of failure. It is a correspondence failure in that as a result of it information systems will not deliver business value. It is a process failure in that it can be portrayed as a problem associated with the design and implementation of systems. It could even be classed as an interaction failure at least after year 2000 if many of the proposed systems do not perform as expected. If we are to analyse the Y2K issue in terms of expectation failure, we need to ask the necessary question, who are the stakeholders in Y2K? The easy answer is of course to state that everybody is a stakeholder, since everybody is purported to have a notional stake in the modern information society.

STAKEHOLDER ANALYSIS

In terms of a typical IS project we may identify five major categories of stakeholder types: producers. clients, users, clientele, and regulators. Producers are the people actually producing the IS – the project organisation. Clients are supporters of IS in that they sponsor and provide resources for the continuation of an IS project. Clients normally equate to managerial groups within organisations. In terms of users, managers are rarely the *end*-users of information systems. Most IS are produced for use by other levels within the organisation. Information systems normally impact upon the customers or clientele of organisations. Finally, regulators are agencies that set environmental constraints for an IS. We may analyse the relationship of each group of stakeholders to an IS project in terms of:

1. *Degree of impact.* The degree of impact that the IS is likely to have on the stakeholder group might be expressed in terms of high impact, medium impact and low impact.
2. *Stakeholder expectations.* The key expectations that the stakeholder group has in relation to the IS may be expressed in terms of how the group 'frames' the IS. (Orlikowski and Gash, 1994). In very general terms, each stakeholder may 'frame' a technology in a negative or positive way in relation to their interests.
3. *Impact on stakeholder group.* The likely impact of the stakeholder group on the development and post-implementation trajectory of the project.
4. *The degree and type of support.* The degree and type of support needed on the part of the project organisation from the stakeholder group. In general, physical resources such as budgets are needed from clients, personnel resources are needed from users, and information resources are needed from regulators.

This categorisation of analysis criteria relevant to stakeholders allows us to employ a grid as shown in Table 17.1.

Table 17.1 Stakeholder impact and support

Degree of impact on stakeholder	High impact	Medium impact	Low impact
Stakeholder 'frame'	Negative	Ambivalent	Positive
Stakeholder impact – development trajectory	High impact	Medium impact	Low impact
Stakeholder impact – use trajectory	High impact	Medium impact	Low impact
Degree of support	High	Medium	Low
Type of support	Physical	Personnel	Information

In Table 17.2 we have attempted a preliminary analysis of the Y2K issue in terms of the framework described above.

This preliminary attempt at a stakeholder analysis for the Y2K problem indicates a number of interesting features.

1. *Producers.* The IS industry in general and internal and external IS services of relevance to a particular organisation have an inherent stake in the Y2K problem and its solution. This stakeholder group is directly involved in scoping and developing solutions for organisations. Interestingly, however, besides providing an impetus to recruitment in the industry the Y2K problem has contributed little to the current shape of the industry. In the longer term a range of predictions have been provided ranging from an IS/IT backlash to a continuing rise in the impact of the industry on general business.

2. *Clients.* Currently the Y2K problem has not provided significant problems for organisations in terms of their customer interface. The problems are likely to impact within a five year time-frame if the predicted level of business failures and litigation ensues. Kappelman (Kappelman and Cappel, 1996) has portrayed the conventional business response to learning of the Y2K problem as being: awareness, denial, anger then response. A large question is whether residual anger may be left over within the business community. We might hypothesise that Y2K and the responses to it may explain something of the continuing rise in the outsourcing trend.

3. *Users.* Users of IS have currently only been impacted by forward date problems. Again, the expected impact on the use of IS is an unknown quantity.

Table 17.2 Stakeholder analysis

Stakeholder type	Producers	Clients	Users	Clientelle	Regulators
Representative groups	IS/IT industry, internal IS services, external IS services	Organisations	IS users	Organisational customers and suppliers	Governments, trade organisations, professional bodies, Standards organisations
Degree of impact on stakeholder	Low impact	Medium– high impact	Low impact	Low impact	Low impact
Stakeholder 'frame'	Positive	Negative to ambivalent	Negative	Ambivalent	Positive
Stakeholder impact development trajectory	High impact	Low impact	Low impact	Low impact	Low impact
Stakeholder impact use trajectory	High impact	Low impact	High impact	High impact	Low impact
Degree of support	High	Medium to high	Low	Low	Low
Type of support	Effort	Personnel	None	None	None

4. *Clientele.* Both customers and suppliers generally wait to be directly impacted by the Y2K problem. It could be argued that many suppliers to organisations have already been impacted to some degree in the way they have participated in compliance questioning and subsequent agreements.

5. *Regulators.* Surprisingly perhaps, regulators like governments and professional bodies have had little impact on the trajectory of development work in this area. Governments such as that in the UK have attempted to participate in awareness raising exercises (such as Action 2000) but have contributed relatively little in the way of resources to the issue. The Prime Minister recently came under much criticism for his initiative to develop a £30 million national training scheme of 'bug busters'.

IS RESEARCH QUESTIONS ARISING FROM Y2K

We would propose that Y2K is a phenomenon that should be interesting to IS academics on many levels. It is probably not to risky to claim that Y2K and the responses to it are likely to have a profound impact on the shape of IS/IT within organisations not only in the UK but internationally. This leads us to propose that studies are needed to analyse this relationship in greater depth. In this section we detail a preliminary framework for investigating this elements of this linkage which we intend to pursue in our future research.

We propose a study which will investigate the impact that Y2K has currently had and is likely to have on three characteristics of organisations:

1. Levels and the shape of investment in IS/IT. Currently most UK organisations seem to invest somewhere between 2–7 per cent of their capital expenditure on IS/IT. How much of this has been diverted to solving the Y2K problem?
2. The structure of the internal IS service of organisations. Y2K can be seen as a problem which confirms the low opinion of the IS/IT profession on the part of general business management. UK organisations have experienced a significant degree outsourcing in relation to the IS service. To what extent has this been fuelled by an organisation's experience of the Y2K problem?

The state of IS/IT strategy within organisations. Strategy as applied to IS/IT has been much proposed by the IS academy over the last decade. Are companies now ditching strategy in the face of Y2K? How precisely has Y2K affected strategy? Have any companies explicitly addressed Y2K in their strategy? There are some suggestions that Y2K is causing organisations to defer strategic IS/IT decisions in the short term. This beggars the question as to what effect Y2K will have on the future of IS/IT strategy?

Commentators seem to suggest that the ramifications of Y2K will continue well into the next century. Longitudinal studies are therefore needed to assess the affect of Y2K on each of the elements described above. For instance, in terms of IS/IT investment, the Dataquest study reported in Pettit (1998) described five possible scenarios concerning the impact that Y2K is likely to have on organisational IS/IT spending:

1. Spending on IS/IT enjoys a significant increase between 1998 and 2001. Spending then reverts to pre-2000 levels.
2. Spending increases up until 2000 then falls as user organisations fail to reach operational sustainability.
3. Organisations realise they cannot make all their systems Y2K compliant, practise triage and abandon 30 per cent of systems that are judged to be non-critical. Y2K generates a significant loss of confidence in IS/IT at the business level and long-term spending is reduced. The IS/IT industry shrinks by 30 per cent as a result.
4. As above, in that organisations reduce their overall IS/IT spend by 30 per cent up to 2000. However, overall confidence in IS/IT is maintained and underlying growth trends for the industry continues.
5. Organisations increase spending on IS/IT to cope with Y2K, it does not affect other planned initiatives and growth in IS/IT spend continues in the longer term.

It is clearly important to determine which of these scenarios turns into reality as far as UK organisations are concerned.

Postscript

This chapter has examined the phenomenon of Y2K as an instance of information systems failure. We argued there that Y2K cannot be characterised merely as a technological failure but that it is of interest also on the organisational, societal, and economic level. The aftermath of Y2K is interesting for similar reasons. The predicted level of failure expected from Y2K has apparently not materialised in the first month of 2000. This has led to claims of a significant overspend on Y2K projects amongst companies in nations like the UK. In global terms this overspend is estimated to be in the region of $70 billion. There have been a range of reactions to this apparent overspend:

1. It is merely another example of IS/IT projects going into overspend and therefore is to be expected.
2. Spending on Y2K was a necessary expenditure that served to 'insure' or 'vaccinate' businesses from inevitable IT failure. It was therefore money well spent.
3. The small range of reported problems that have occurred are only the tip of the ice-berg. More and more date problems will come to light throughout 2000 demonstrating the importance of Y2K preparedness.

What is perhaps important from the perspective of the IS discipline is that Y2K has done something to demonstrate to organisations the centrality of IS/IT to their business. It therefore remains important to plot the effect that Y2K will have on issues like the IS strategy of organisations in the near future.

References

ANON. (1998) 'Europeans slow to tackle Y2K', *Computing*, 30 April. Barker, C. and Marshall, S. (1997) 'You're out of time', *Computing*, 22 May. 1.

BERGHEL, H. (1998) 'The Year-2000 problem and the new riddle of induction', *Communications of the ACM*, 41(3), 14–17.

BETTS, J., RACKLEY, L. and WEBB, J. (1996) '2000 and bust – IT meets its Waterloo?,' *Business Information Technology*, Manchester Metropolitan University.

BEYNON-DAVIES, P. (1995) 'Information systems failure, participatory development and risk: the case the London Ambulance Service Project', BCS special interest group on software, testing seminar, London, May.

BURTON SWANSON, E. (1992) *Maintaining Information Systems in Organisations*. Chichester. John Wiley.

CURRIE, W. (1994) 'The strategic management of a large-scale IT project in the financial services sector', *New Technology, Work and Employment*, 9(1), 19–29.

GILLIES, A. (1997) 'The year 2000 problem for general practice: an information management based analysis', *Health Informatics Journal*, 3(4), 147–53.

JONES, C. (1997) 'Global economic impacts of the year 2000 problem', in Kappleman, L., *Year 2000 Problem: Strategies and Solutions.*

KAPPELMAN, L.A. (1997) 'How can the community of IS academicians help?' in Kappelman, L., *Year 2000 Problem: Strategies and Solutions.*

KAPPELMAN, L.A. and CAPPEL, J. (1996) 'Confronting the year 2000 issue', *Journal of Systems Management*, July–Aug., 4–13.

KAPPELMAN, L. *et al.* (1998) 'Calculating the cost of year-2000 compliance', *Communications of the ACM*, 41(2), 30–9.

LYYTINEN, K. and HIRSCHHEIM, R. (1987) 'Information systems failures: a survey and classification of the empirical literature', *Oxford Surveys in Information Technology*, 4, 257–309.

MAITLAND, J. (1998) 'Lack of concern for year 2000 problem,' *PC Week*, 5 Mathieson, S. (1998) 'NHS in Y2K "underspend"', *Computing*, 7th May, 3.

MATHIESON, S. (1998) 'NHS in Y2K "Underspend"', *Computing*, 3, 5 June.

ORLIKOWSKI, W.T. and GASH, T.C. (1994) 'Technological frames: making sense of information technology in organisations', *ACM Transactions on Information Systems*, 12(2), 17–207.

OZ, E. (1994) 'When professional standards are lax: the confirm failure and its lessons', *Comm. ACM*, 37(10), 29–36.

PETTITT, J. (1998) 'Year 2000 takes initiative out of IT', *Computer Weekly*, 30 April, 20.

SAUER, C. (1993) 'Why Information Systems fail: a case study approach', Henley-on-Thames: Alfred Waller.

SENN, J. (1998) 'The challenge of relating IS research to practice', Information *Resources Management Journal*, 11(1), 23–8.

18 IS/IT Outsourcing: Conceptualising Practice and Perception

Ray Hackney and Martin Hancox

INTRODUCTION

Precise definitions of IT outsourcing differ in the literature (Glass, 1996) but there is general agreement that it is the carrying out of IT functions by third parties (Kettler and Walstrom, 1993). Expenditure on IT outsourcing is considerable, with much of it placed with a few companies (Clark *et al.*, 1995). However, there has been only a small (but increasing) number of empirical studies of IT outsourcing, a feature noted by several authors (e.g. Arnett and Jones, 1994; Sobol and Apte, 1995). In particular, there have been few British studies (Willcocks and Fitzgerald, 1993; Cronk and Sharp, 1995). Also, several conceptual frameworks are found in the literature, but more empirical work is needed to assess their validity (Corbett, 1994; Willcocks *et al.*, 1996).

The aim of the research was to assess the usefulness of four conceptual frameworks in an exploratory study of practices and perceptions of IT outsourcing in PSOs and LAs. The four conceptual frameworks used were core competencies, transaction cost economics, agency theory and partnership. They are among the most commonly found frameworks in the literature on IT outsourcing, and this suggests that they may be helpful in empirical studies. Few empirical studies have employed them, however, and it is believed no study has considered all four. The research was concerned with *sectoral* comparison, rather than in depth analysis of individual organisations. A broad division between private and public sectors can be made on the basis of funding source. PSOs (private sector organisations) receive their income from the selling of products and services. LAs (local authorities), like most public sector bodies, are principally funded from taxation or other governmental source.

RESEARCH METHOD

A qualitative research approach was employed, as the emphasis was on discovery and understanding, with the four frameworks used as sensitising concepts. Semi-structured interviews were carried out with 13 IT managers from six PSOs and seven LAs, to ascertain their experiences of and attitudes towards IT outsourcing. Each interview lasted between 75 and 135 minutes, and was tape-recorded, and then transcribed. Interviewees were heads of IT functions, or their deputies, and hence provided essentially managerial perspectives. As a result of the sampling approach explained below, each manager had considerable experience of preparing for and/or managing third party service and product provision. The use of semi-structured interviews was judged most appropriate for exploratory research because it allowed the researcher's understanding to increase incrementally throughout the series of interviews. Each interview could be informed by preceding interviews, and topics and questions revised. Also, respondents' opinions could be sought on previous respondents' ideas. The interview structure broadly followed the stages of an outsourcing evaluation and implementation exercise, with general descriptive, demographic questions asked initially to facilitate interviewer familiarity with the organisation. However, no attempt was made to build a rich description of each organisation (often associated with qualitative research), as the emphasis was on overall sectoral comparison, rather than on comparison between individual organisations.

The interviews were not built around the four conceptual frameworks, in order to avoid, as far as possible, imposing theoretical constructs on the respondents. Also, it meant that difficulties of explaining complex academic theories and terms to respondents, with associated dangers of misrepresentation by the interviewer, could be minimised. Interviews were treated as conversations, where an agenda 'merely indicates the kinds of topics, themes and questions that *might* be covered rather than the *actual* questions that were used' (Burgess, 1984, p. 110 – italics in the original). Thus interviews varied in the time and attention devoted to each topic, reflecting Patton's (1980, p. 203) belief that '*to understand the holistic world view of a group of people it is not necessary to collect the same information from each person*'. Nonetheless, a standard topic list gave interviews a high degree of commonality. As is usual with qualitative research and small samples, the central concern was not to produce findings of statistical significance which proved or disproved causal relationships; rather, it was to improve general understanding, both of the sectors under study and of the usefulness of the conceptual frameworks. A second research technique also used was documentary analysis of outsourcing vendors' marketing literature, to discover how vendors view outsourcing, and whether they regard the two sectors differently. The major source for the construction of heterogeneous samples was the *Computer Users' Yearbook* (CUYB 1994a, b), a major source of information about UK. The outsourcing vendors approached were mostly large ones which featured regularly in trade press reports, because they would have greater experience of outsourcing. Promotional material was received from eight of them.

DERIVING THE FRAMEWORKS

The four frameworks chosen have been discussed by several authors, and have in some cases been used in empirical studies, which suggests they may help to understand practices and perceptions of IT outsourcing in different settings (Richmond *et al.*, 1992; Quinn and Hilmer, 1994). For example, concentration on core competencies can be a motive for outsourcing. The transaction cost economics framework is concerned with organisational awareness of the tangible and intangible costs of market usage, which may outweigh other savings provided by outsourcing. Agency theory may help to explain how interests between a particular client and vendor may diverge, and how the relationship between them can be regulated in contractual terms. Finally, the partnership framework suggests that either at its inception or as it progresses, an arrangement between two parties can transcend organisational differences and cause the parties to work for a common purpose which may or may not be expressed in a contract. Ignoring considerable conceptual overlaps in order to avoid repetition, the chapter takes each framework in turn and outlines some key aspects in the context of IT outsourcing.

Core competencies: outline

Core competencies theory suggests activities should be performed either in-house or by suppliers. Activities which are not core competencies should be considered for outsourcing with 'best in world' suppliers. Some non-core activities may have to be retained in-house if they are part of a defensive posture to protect competitive advantage

(Quinn, 1992). Although some authors indicate characteristics of core competencies (e.g. Hamel and Prahalad, 1990): 'most of the literature on this subject is tautological – "core" equals "key" or "critical" or "fundamental"' (Quinn and Hilmer, 1994). Employees in non-core functions (even if not facing outsourcing) may feel excluded by the organisation because they are a 'non-dominant discipline' (Leonard-Barton, 1992). In the public sector, there may be particular uncertainty about what is core; Dunleavy (1994) argues that government may aim to discover its core competencies via 'a residualisation process, outsourcing until and unless the shoe pinches, or a political backlash is triggered'.

An organisation may view IT itself as a core competence. Hochstrasser and Griffiths (1991) suggest that the most successful companies have a good understanding of IT's potential. However, McLellan *et al.* (1995) report that some organisations outsource IT even though they see it as core and delivering competitive advantage. They claim that this is because IT can be considered core at the corporate level, but some of its aspects, at lower levels, might be commodities. Thus the complexity of IT, and its (at least in part) core nature, may make the contracting out of IT a particularly challenging exercise. The ability to define IT requirements and to monitor their delivery by third parties may be some of the core IT competencies that any organisation must have if it is to outsource IT successfully. Indeed, Alexander and Young (1996) argue that the very acts of specifying and managing supply contracts can themselves give competitive advantage.

Transaction cost economics: outline

In Transaction Cost Economics (TCE), an organisation chooses to source via its own hierarchy or via the market, based on relative cost, which has two components: production costs and co-ordination (transaction) costs. Economies of scale, via the market, can reduce production costs. Transaction costs are determined by several factors: asset specificity, transaction frequency, and uncertainty. Asset specificity is 'the degree to which an asset can be redeployed to alternative uses and by alternative users without sacrifice of productive value' (Williamson, 1979, p. 142). Williamson also identifies three types of transaction according to specificity. Non-specific transactions have low asset specificity, and are associated with the acquisition of commodities. Idiosyncratic transactions have high specificity. Mixed transactions have elements of both commodity and customisation. Transaction specificity can be viewed alongside transaction frequency, a second major construct of TCE, which distinguishes occasional from recurrent transactions (Williamson, 1985). Two frequency categories, multiplied by three specificity types, produce six discrete transaction types. Williamson argues that the market is better for all but transactions which are both recurrent and idiosyncratic. The third major determinant of transaction costs is uncertainty, compounded by the bounded rationality of humans and often associated with the complexity of the product to be acquired. Rather than developing specialised client-specific products, vendors may find it cheaper and safer to provide a standard product (Lowell, 1992), while organisations may prefer to acquire complex products via the internal hierarchy rather than the market (Malone et al., 1994). Throughout market usage there is also the danger of opportunism – 'lack of candour or honesty in transactions' (Williamson, 1975, p. 9). This is likely to increase if there is a small numbers situation, where only a few vendors are able and willing to contract. Transaction costs appear to be difficult to avoid, and may be unavoidably greater in some settings than in others. For example, Walsh (1995) argues that in the public sector, contract creation and monitoring are more difficult because of the sector's complexity, and because there are costs associated with bureaucracy and democracy which are hard to allocate to specific functions.

TCE has been criticised for its simplicity (e.g. Ring and Van de Ven, 1992; Walker and Poppo 1994; Willcocks and Choi, 1995). Willcocks (1995) describes TCE as 'a high level general theory, its uncalibrated constructs permitting empirical data to be fitted to support the theory all too easily'. Certainly, authors have been able to relate TCE to IT. For instance, Mylonopoulos and Ormerod (1995) give several examples of asset specificity found in IT. Transaction frequency in IT terms can be illustrated by, for example, contrasting the recurrent nature of processing a payroll every month with the occasional (indeed, unique) nature of a bespoke systems development project. Uncertainty is found in many aspects of IT (Earl, 1991; Cheon et al., 1995), and is particularly associated with systems development and unpredictable business and technological change. The difficulties and costs of both market usage and provision via the hierarchy perhaps explain why extremes of vertical integration and spot market transactions in IT are comparatively rare (Mylonopoulos and Ormerod, 1995), resulting in a range of sourcing options (Clark et al., 1995; Lacity et al., 1996).

IT transaction costs may be reduced by various methods. For example, using several vendors can reduce the damage caused by one bad contract (Cronk and Sharp, 1995); but this may increase complexity (Venkatraman and Loh, 1994) or may be impossible because of a dearth of bidders (Lacity and Hirschheim, 1995). Also, outsourcing as little as possible would be expected to minimise transaction costs, and various authors suggest ways to improve in-house performance (e.g. Hummel, 1993; Lacity and Hirschheim, 1993, 1995; Band and Scanlan, 1995). De Looff (1995) remarks that often the possibility of improvement is ignored.

Agency theory: outline

The original impetus for the development of Agency Theory (AT) was large corporations' separation of control from ownership (Karake, 1992); thus its focus was never on organisational boundaries, as with TCE theory (Jensen and Meckling, 1976). AT's primary interest is not the decision to source via the hierarchy or via the market. Although 'all contractural arrangements ... contain important elements of agency' (Ross, 1973), AT is essentially concerned with the delegation of work by one party (the principal) to another (the agent) via a contract (Eisenhardt, 1989), whether or not they are both within the same organisation. However, AT and TCE share several concepts such as opportunism, uncertainty and bounded rationality, and there is a rough correspondence between TCE's hierarchies and markets and AT's behaviour-based contracts and outcome-based contracts.

The choice of contract type depends on the agency costs, which include the principal's effort in assessing the agent's performance, and the agent's efforts in assuring the principal of his commitment (Cheon *et al.*, 1995). AT holds that human beings act through self-interest, and therefore, as contracting parties, they may have divergent goals. An important aspect of the theory is that both principal and agent wish to avoid risk when dealing with each other. The principal may prefer to place risk with the agent via an outcome-based contract, while the agent may prefer to avoid risk by having a behaviour-based contract (Eisenhardt, 1989). Outcome-based contracts are claimed to reduce agent opportunism because the rewards of both agent and principal depend on the same actions. Behaviour-based contracts need the principal to have sufficient information to identify two possible dangers: first, whether there is *adverse selection* (the agent does not possess the skills he claims); secondly, *moral hazard* – 'the agent is shirking'

(Eisenhardt, 1989). Overall risk may be reduced by sourcing via the hierarchy, but agency costs also exist in hierarchies, and may be particularly high in the public sector. For example, Walsh (1995) argues that problems between agents and principals are greater in complex organisations with many managerial layers. Also, Milgrom (1988, cited in Holmstrom and Tirole, 1989) suggests that non-market organisations are especially susceptible to 'influence costs', where employees pursue their own agenda. This might imply that within a public sector organisation, if the employees of one department were motivated by self interest, then workers in other departments would be inconvenienced and resent the action; unless, perhaps, they themselves were pursuing a similar or compatible agenda.

The technological and business complexity of IT means there may be major problems for the principal in choosing a suitable agent and in monitoring the agent's work. Only the agent knows how hard he is working, and that can be especially important in multilateral contracting (Holmstrom and Tirole, 1989), where one agent acts for several principals. This is often the case in IT outsourcing, because of the market dominance of large firms. Given the difficulties of behaviour-based contracts suggested by AT, it might be reasonable to assume that the overwhelming majority of clients would insist on outcome based contracts when acquiring IT products and services. Such a strategy can only succeed if the client can confidently specify current and future requirements. But accurate predictions by the client are not in the vendor's interests, for Lacity and Hirschheim (1995) claim that vendor account managers are rewarded according to contract profitability, which is principally achieved through charging the client extra for anything which is not in the contract.

Partnership: outline

The influential Kodak–IBM outsourcing deal had much to do with a sense of honour and a 'chemistry' between the parties (Altinkemer *et al.*, 1994), and changed the common perception of IT outsourcing from an 'arm's length' relationship to one of 'strategic partnership' (Martinsons, 1993). Partnership, often referred to as an alliance, has frequently been noted as a major feature of IT outsourcing (e.g. Gupta and Gupta, 1992; Grover and Teng, 1993; Grover *et al.*, 1994; Cheon *et al.*, 1995). However, partnership's treatment in the IS literature is largely non-theoretical (Klepper, 1995), perhaps reflecting a wide diversity of practical arrangements and the absence of a single, commonly recognised theory. Although the sharing of risk and reward is sometimes mentioned (e.g. Lacity and Hirschheim, 1995), often the emphasis is on intangibles like: trust; comfort; understanding; flexibility; co-operation; shared values, goals and problem-solving; good interpersonal relations; and regular communication (e.g. Ring and Van de Ven, 1992; Judenberg, 1994; McFarlan and Nolan, 1995; McLellan *et al.*, 1995). Partnership can reduce the risk of inadequate contractual provision (Jurison, 1995), but Willcocks and Choi (1995) argue that in the relationship between vendor and client the latter is usually overdependent on the former and that goals are not necessarily shared. A client may be more comfortable if it knows the vendor already (e.g. Huber, 1993). In partner selection, cultural compatibility is vital (e.g. Willcocks and Fitzgerald, 1994; Kern, 1997), and shared values and objectives inform all stages of the partnership development process (Klepper, 1995).

Lacity and Hirschheim (1995) and Willcocks and Fitzgerald (1994) argue that few organisations claim to be in a strategic partnership with their suppliers. The contract is more likely to favour the vendor because he has greater experience in negotiation (e.g. Lacity and Hirschheim, 1993; Willcocks and Fitzgerald, 1994; Klepper and Jones, 1997). Saunders *et al.* (1997) found that clients with 'loose' contracts were more likely to regard outsourcing as a failure; yet most respondents in their study used the vendor's standard contract as a basis for outsourcing agreement; and most did not use external technical or legal advice. Fitzgerald (1994) found that 80 per cent of clients wished they had more tightly defined contracts. McLellan and Marcolin (1994) suggest that partly the client's view of IT influences its relationship with the vendor, such that firms regarding IT as a core competence capability are more likely to look upon outsourcing as an alliance. Clients who view IT as core are also more likely to be satisfied with the outsourcing arrangements because they negotiate from a more knowledgeable position (Saunders *et al.*, 1997).

Table 18.1 shows an overview of the main findings of the research.

IMPLICATIONS FOR POLICY

In the organisations investigated, a concentration on core competencies was not an important motive for outsourcing, contrary to suggestions in vendor marketing material and in some of the literature. Perhaps this indicates a corporate managerial preference for dealing

Table 18.1 Comparison of local authorities and private sector organisations via the four conceptual frameworks

	LAs	PSOs
Core competencies	Not a major motive for IT outsourcing. CCT and financial constraints are forcing LAs to focus on front-line services. IT management acquiring new core competencies.	Not a major motive for IT outsourcing. IT management acquiring new core competencies.
Transaction cost economics	Use of market increases transaction costs. Introduction of internal market increases transaction costs, but scepticism about its benefits. Culture, and accountability and legislative requirements, suggest transaction costs likely to be higher than in private sector.	Use of market increases transaction costs. When in-house provision used, there are fewer transaction costs incurred than in LAs.
Agency theory	Market used satisfactorily most of time. Multi-lateral contracting common. Most contracts outcome-based. Not much evidence of major conflict with vendors, but is scepticism in LAs arising from vendors' primary profit motive. Imposition of CCT across (ultimately) most of an LA's departments may lead to considerable opportunity for and toleration of 'influence costs'.	Market used satisfactorily most of time. Multi-lateral contracting common. Most contracts outcome-based. Not much evidence of major conflict with vendors.
Partnerships	Great scepticism about partnership with vendors. IT departments adopting notions of partnership with users, to improve performance and retain work in-house. Partnership with private sector suppliers may be for other than commercial reasons, and may be politically delicate.	Some scepticism about partnership. Partnership less likely when outsourcing operations and infrastructure support than systems development activities.

with internal, rather than external, providers. But factors like financial pressure, and dissatisfaction with the services provided, may cause managers to change policy sometimes. Certainly, in the PSOs, the main motive for outsourcing was to drive down costs and improve service. This was also the case in LAs, and in the one LA which had pursued total outsourcing for IT, cost problems had overridden the concern of elected members that local government should be a source of employment for local people. In the private sector, IT was regarded as strategically important for the business, while in several LAs this was not the case. In particular, financial constraints had caused councillors to prioritise the purposes of local government, and in this way core competencies of LAs were viewed as the wide range of front-line services which were delivered to citizens. It may be that the person-to-person nature of delivery of some of those front-line services – e.g. education and social services – means that they are less dependent on the effective deployment of IT (at least in the eyes of the service recipients), and that therefore IT, though heavily utilised in LAs, does not play such a crucial role as in many PSOs. It may also be more than coincidental that those front-line services also provide employment for considerable numbers of people. Thus it may be possible to reconcile outsourcing of some of the less labour-intensive LA activities with maintenance of an *overall* high level of employment provided by the LA.

Many of the key concepts of transaction cost economics could be found in an analysis of IT outsourcing in the participant LAs and PSOs. The TCE perspective indicated that the market is used successfully by both types of organisation, but that third-party performance is not necessarily better than in-house performance. Where the market is used, formality increases, and thus transaction costs rise, although vendor literature stresses how smoothly vendors operate and liaise with clients. Because of culture, legislation and accountability requirements, LAs are subject to higher transaction costs than PSOs. This is particularly so when a comparison of in-house service provision in PSOs and LAs is made. The provision in PSOs is much less bureaucratic than in LAs, whose IT departments work in a quasi-market which is often regarded as bringing little benefit to compensate for the extra costs incurred.

Some of agency theory's ideas were difficult to find in the organisations investigated. For example, although there were disagreements between vendor and client, most PSOs and LAs were satisfied with most of the services they received from third parties. There was no evidence of moral hazard and little evidence of adverse selection, although sometimes vendor performance had proved disappointing. Thus vendors' literature may merely be reflecting reality when it ignores the issue of vendor–client conflict. However, in LAs, there was a greater expectation of that conflict, and this was because of concern about the private sector's profit motive.

Study of vendor literature suggests that partnership is a concept used to stress vendors' co-operative attitude, flexibility and willingness not to be constrained by precise contractual provision. Only some of the participant organisations regarded their outsourcing arrangements as partnerships, and all were aware of the primacy of the contract. Outsourcing of IT infrastructure support and operations management was less likely to be regarded as a partnership than was systems development outsourcing, which required a greater knowledge of the client's business. Because of a range of factors, including organisational culture, political leadership and public accountability, partnership with a vendor appears less likely when the client is an LA. However, in order to compete with external suppliers, LAs' internal IT departments were not just changing their working practices, but were also adopting notions of partnership, as they moved closer to their users, with whom they shared a common culture and the common goal of preserving in-house services.

CONCLUSION

Each of the four conceptual frameworks used to sensitise the investigation contributes in some way to an understanding of the practice and perception of IT outsourcing. The research has been novel in that it has employed these four conceptual frameworks in one empirical study. Equally significant is that this exploratory study has attempted a *sectoral* comparison, rather than detailed examination and associated thick description of individual organisations, as is found in much qualitative research. Also, one of the organisational types examined has not been the focus of outsourcing research before. This combination of factors has facilitated a consideration of aspects which are often missing from studies of outsourcing. These include the resentment caused by the (threatened) imposition of outsourcing from outside the organisation; the antipathy that can be felt by not-for-profit organisations towards outsourcing vendors who appear to have profit-based value systems; the tactics employed to frustrate outsourcing, including imitating some service delivery practices of out-sourcing vendors, identifying common interests with existing users, and exploiting any loopholes in the rules of the sourcing decision process; and the political dimension introduced by the involvement of different elected power centres.

References

ALEXANDER, M. and YOUNG, D. (1996) 'Strategic outsourcing', *Long Range Planning*, 29(1), 116–19.
ALTINKEMER, K., CHATURVEDI, A. and GULATI, R. (1994) 'Informa-tion Systems outsourcing: issues and Evidence', *International Journal of Information Management*, 14(4), 252–68.
ARNETT, K.P. and JONES, M.C. (1994) 'Firms that choose outsourcing: a profile', *Information and Management*, 26(4), 179–88.
BAND, D.C. and SCANLAN, G. (1995) 'Strategic control through core com-petencies', *Long Range Planning*, 28(2), 102–14.
BURGESS, R.G. (1984) *In the Field*, London. Routledge.
CHEON, M.J., GROVER, V. and TENG, J.T.C. (1995) 'Theoretical perspec-tives on the outsourcing of Information Systems', *Journal of Information Technology*, 10, 209–19.
CLARK, T.D. Jr, ZMUD, R.W. and MCCRAY, G.E. (1995) 'The outsourcing of information services: transforming the nature of business in the infor-mation industry', *Journal of Information Technology*, 10, 221–37.
CORBETT, M.F. (1994) 'Outsourcing and the new IT executive: a trends report', *Information Systems Management*, 11(4), 19–22.
CRONK, J. and SHARP, J. (1995) 'A framework for deciding what to out-source in Information Technology', *Journal of Information Technology*, 10, 259–67.
CUYB (1994a) *The Computer Users' Yearbook 1995*, 2, *Computer Services*, London. VNU Business Publications.
CUYB (1994b) *The Computer Users' Yearbook 1995*, 3, *Computer and Network Sites*, London. VNU Business Publications.
DE LOOFF, L.A. (1995) 'Information Systems outsourcing decision making: a framework: organisational theories and case studies', *Journal of Infor-mation Technology*, 10, 281–97.
DUNLEAVY, P. (1994) 'The globalisation of public services production: can government be "best in world"?', *Public Policy and Administration*, 9(2), 36–65.
EARL, M.J. (1991) 'Outsourcing information services', *Public Money and Management*, 11(3), 17–21.
EISENHARDT, K.M. (1989) 'Agency theory: an assessment and review', *Academy of Management Review*, 14(1), 57–74.
FITZGERALD, G. (1994) 'The outsourcing of Information Technology: revenge of the business manager or legitimate strategic option?', Inaugural

Lecture, Department of Computer Science, Birkbeck College, University of London, 19 October.

GLASS, R.L. (1996) 'The end of the outsourcing era', *Information Systems Management*, 13(2), 89–91

GROVER, V. and TENG, J.T.C. (1993) 'The decision To outsource Information Systems functions', *Journal of Systems Management*, 44(11), 34–8.

GROVER, V., CHEON, M. and TENG, J.T.C. (1994) 'An evaluation of the impact of corporate strategy and the role of Information Technology on IS functional outsourcing', *European Journal of Information Systems*, 3(3), 179–90.

GUPTA, U.G. and GUPTA, A. (1992) 'Outsourcing the IS Function', *Information Systems Management*, 9(3), 44–50.

HAMEL, G. and PRALAHAD, C.K. (1990) 'The core competences of the corporation', *Harvard Business Review*, 68(3), 79–91.

HOCHSTRASSER, B. and GRIFFITHS, C. (1991) *Controlling IT Investment*, London. Chapman & Hall.

HOLMSTROM, B.R. and TIROLE, J. (1989) 'The Theory of the Firm', in Schmalensee, R. and Willig, R. (eds), *Handbook of Industrial Organisation*, 1, 63–133, Amsterdam: North Holland.

HUBER, R. (1993) 'How continental bank outsourced its crown jewels', *Harvard Business Review*, 71(1), 121–9.

HUMMEL, E. (1993) 'Prevent total outsourcing', *Journal of Systems Management*, 44(7), 29–30.

JENSEN, M. and MECKLING, W. (1976) 'Theory of the firm: managerial behaviour [sic], agency costs and capital structure', *Journal of Financial Economics*, 3, 305–60.

JUDENBERG, J. (1994) 'Applications maintenance outsourcing: an alternative to total outsourcing', *Information Systems Management*, 11(4) 34–8.

JURISON, J. (1995) 'The role of risk and return in Information Technology outsourcing decisions', *Journal of Information Technology*, 10, 239–47.

KARAKE, Z.A. (1992) '*Information Technology and Management Control: An Agency Theory Perspective*', Westport, CT: Praeger.

KERN, T. (1997) 'The Gestalt of an Information Technology outsourcing relationship: an exploratory analysis', *Proceedings of the International Conference on Information Systems*, Atlanta, December.

KETTLER, K. and WALSTROM, J. (1993) 'The outsourcing decision', *International Journal of Information Management*, 13(6), 449–59.

KLEPPER, R. (1995) 'The management of partnering development in I/S outsourcing', *Journal of Information Technology*, 10, 249–58.

KLEPPER, R. and JONES, W. (1997) 'Outsourcing Information Technology systems and services', Englewood Cliffs. Prentice-Hall.

LACITY, M.C. and HIRSCHHEIM, R. (1993) '*Information Systems outsourcing: myths, Metaphors and Reality*', Chichester. John Wiley.

LACITY, M.C. and HIRSCHHEIM R. (1995) *Beyond the Information Systems Outsourcing Bandwagon – the Insourcing Response*, Chichester. John Wiley.

LACITY, M.C., WILLCOCKS, L.P. and FEENY, D.F. (1996) 'The value of selective IT sourcing', *Sloan Management Review*, 37(3), 13–25.

LEONARD-BARTON, D. (1992) 'Core capabilities and core rigidities: a paradox in managing new product development', *Strategic Management Journal*, 13, 111–25.

LOWELL, M. (1992) 'Managing your outsourcing vendors in the financial services industry', *Journal of Systems Management*, 43(5), 23–7.

MALONE, T.W., YATES, J. and BENJAMIN, R.I. (1994) 'Electronic markets and electronic hierarchies', in Allen,T.J. and Scott Morton, M.S. (eds), *Information Technology and the Corporation of the 1990s*, New York: Oxford University Press, 61–83.

MARTINSONS, M.G. (1993) 'Outsourcing Information Systems: a strategic partnership with risks', *Long Range Planning*, 26(3), 18–25.

MCFARLAN, F.W. and NOLAN, R.L. (1995) 'How to manage an IT outsourcing alliance', *Sloan Management Review*, 36(2), 9–23.

MCLELLAN, K. and MARCOLIN, B. (1994) 'Information technology outsourcing', *Business Quarterly*, 59(1), 95–99, 102–4.

MCLELLAN, K, MARCOLIN, B.L. and BEAMISH, P.W. (1995) 'Financial and strategic motivations behind IS outsourcing', *Journal of Information Technology*, 10, 299–321.

MILGROM, P. (1988) 'Employment contracts, influence activities and efficient organization design', *Journal of Political Economy*, 96, 42–60.

MYLONOPOULOS, N.A. and ORMEROD, R.J. (1995) 'A microanalytic approach to the efficient governance of IT service provision: the case of outsourcing', in Doukidis, G., Galliers, B., Jelassi, T., Kremar, H. and Land, F. (eds) *Proceedings of the Third European Conference on Information Systems*, Athens, 749–65.

PATTON, M.Q. (1980) *Qualitative Evaluation Methods*, Beverly Hills. Sage.

QUINN, J.B. (1992) *Intelligent Enterprise*, New York. Free Press.

QUINN, J.B. and HILMER, F.G. (1994) 'Strategic outsourcing', *Sloan Management Review*, 35(4), 43–55.

RICHMOND, W.B., SEIDMANN, A. and WHINSTON, A.B. (1992) 'Incomplete contracting issues in Information Systems development: Outsourcing Decision', *Support Systems*, 8(5), 459–77.

RING, P.S. and VAN DE VEN, A.H. (1992) 'Structuring cooperative relationships between organisations', *Strategic Management Journal*, 13(7), 483–98.

ROSS, S. (1973) 'The economic theory of agency: the principal's problem', *American Economic Review*, 63, 134–9.

SAUNDERS, C., GEBELT, M. and HU, Q. (1997) 'Achieving success in information systems outsourcing', *California Management Review*, 39(2), 63–79.

SOBOL, M.G. and APTE, U. (1995) 'Domestic and global outsourcing practices of America's most effective IS users', *Journal of Information Technology*, 10, 269–80.

VENKATRAMAN, N. and LOH, L. (1994) 'The shifting logic of the IS organisation: from technical portfolio to relationship portfolio', *Information Strategy*, 10(2), 5–11.

WALKER, G. and POPPO, L. (1994) 'Profit centres, single source suppliers, and transaction costs', in Allen, T.J. and Scott Morton, M.S. (eds), *Informa-*

tion Technology and the Corporation of the 1990s, New York: Oxford University Press, 298–319.

WALSH, K. (1995) *Public Services and Market Mechanisms: Competition, Contracting and the New Public Management*, Basingstoke. Macmillan.

WILLCOCKS, L. (1995) 'Editorial', *Journal of Information Technology*, 10, 203–7.

WILLCOCKS, L. and CHOI, C.J. (1995) 'Co-operative partnership and "total" IT outsourcing: from contractual obligation to strategic alliance?', *European Management Journal*, 13(1), 67–78.

WILLCOCKS, L. and FITZGERALD, G. (1993) 'Market as opportunity?: case studies in outsourcing Information Technology and services', *The Journal of Strategic Information Systems*, 2(3), 223–42.

WILLCOCKS, L. and FITZGERALD, G. (1994) *A Business Guide to Outsourcing Information Technology*, London: Business Intelligence, Ltd.

WILLCOCKS, L., FITZGERALD, G. and LACITY, M. (1996) 'To outsource IT or not?: recent research on economics and evaluation practice', *European Journal of Information Systems*, 5, pp. 143–60.

WILLIAMSON, O. (1975) *Markets and Hierarchies: Analysis and Antitrust Implications*, New York: The Free Press.

WILLIAMSON, O. (1979) 'Transaction-cost economics: the governance of contractual relations', *Journal of Law and Economics*, 22(2), 233–61.

WILLIAMSON, O. (1985) *The Economic Institutions of Capitalism*, New York: Basic Books.

19 The Evolution of BPR

Ben Light

INTRODUCTION

BPR has been one of the most discussed concepts in the business and academic literatures throughout the 1990s. Originally presented as a tightly defined concept by authors such has Hammer and Davenport, BPR has been subject to a variety of interpretations and modifications. This chapter examines how the concept of BPR has evolved from one concerned with 'clean slate' radical performance gains into one which recognises the importance of context and multidimensional BPR strategies. Finally, the chapter examines how changes in technology and the business environment are keeping the concept, which has been regarded as a fad, alive.

BPR is a strategic response to a complex and dynamic business environment and is widely recognised in the academic and business literatures (Davenport and Short, 1990; Hammer, 1990; Davenport, 1993; Hammer and Champy, 1993; Coulson-Thomas, 1994; Osterle, 1995). The emergence of BPR was the result of organisations needing to find better ways of working and improve the use of new technologies due to dramatic changes in the business environment. The organisations of North America first recognised these changes and the misalignment that had arisen between what they did and what their business pressures demanded. However, the phenomenon quickly spread on a global scale. Edwards and Peppard (1994) highlight several surveys of the early 1990s which reported the involvement of organisations in BPR projects as ranging from 36 per cent to 72 per cent. Willcocks and Smith (1995) also cite a range of surveys which indicate the pervasion of the concept at the time. The reason for the problems organisations were facing are complex and are only briefly explained here. Essentially, throughout the 20th century organisation structures evolved based upon the idea of hierarchy and control. That is, work was broken down into simple tasks in order to improve efficiency and increase managerial control. As a result, information was distributed throughout organisations in a very focused manner. Then, as computer-based information systems were introduced into organisations these mechanisms were automated. However, it became clear throughout the 1980s that merely automating existing functions and business processes was not giving a satisfactory level of payback from the investment organisations had made in adopting new technologies (Schnitt, 1993). The globalisation of markets had increased levels of competition and whether an organisation treated customers as geographically and culturally heterogeneous (Ohame, 1989) or homogenous (Levitt, 1983), they still equally required more attention due to an increasing array of alternative sources. To use a term from economics – national markets had become elastic. Those organisations that had recognised this quickly found that their existing IT and business infrastructures could not support the customer focused view they needed. Their infrastructures were geared toward improving efficiency and managing and controlling the organisation. Hence the concept of BPR evolved which argued for discontinuous thinking to overcome the historically influenced existing state of the business, or what the authors would term 'legacy systems'.

It is important to note that there are authors that have questioned the originality of the concept of BPR (Earl, 1994; Grint, 1994). While the authors recognise the merits of these analyses, here we are not concerned with the novelty of the concept. Whether the concept is new or a re-hashing or interpretation of the priour concept does not invalidate the pervasion of BPR throughout the 1990s. Th contribution of this chapter is to examine how BPR has evolved from its radical roots and into a concept which has been tailored by organisations in the light of their existing capabilities. The authors also wish to highlight the continued importance of the broad concept of BPR through an analysis of a contemporary reengineering activity, the implementation of Enterprise Resource Planning (ERP) systems.

THE 'ORIGINAL' BPR

BPR is a phenomenon that was first presented as a tightly focused concept in the early 1990s by authors such as Hammer (1990) and Davenport and Short (1990). Even then, Hammer referred to the idea as 'Business Process Reengineering' and Davenport and Short, to 'Business Process Redesign'. Since then the concept has, rightly or wrongly, been subject to interpretation, misinterpretation and copious debates resulting in numerous definitions. Hammer and Champy

(1993, p. 32), probably offer the most cited definition of BPR and the one which most accurately reflects the original concept:

> The fundamental rethinking and radical design of business processes to achieve dramatic improvements in critical contemporary measures of performance such as cost, quality, service and speed.

Hammer and Champy break down this definition into four key components or tenants. First, BPR has to be *fundamental*. That is, organisations need to think about what should be happening rather than what is happening. They need to question what is done and why it is done in a particular way. Secondly, BPR should focus on the *radical*. Any changes that are made to organisations should not manifest themselves in incremental improvements. Organisations need to completely divest themselves of existing and outdated ways of work. Thirdly, BPR projects should deliver *dramatic* results. Organisations should be looking for quantum leaps in performance 10 and 20 per cent increases should be overlooked for the more rewarding 75 and 80 per cent returns. Finally, and probably most fundamental to the concept of BPR is the idea of the *process* or *business process*. BPR projects should deal in a currency of business processes rather than functions. Examples of functions would be sales, manufacturing and distribution departments – here employees work on task within a specific area with little or no concern for how their task impacts upon the overall process of which they are part. Processes, in contrast, transcend functions. An order generation and fulfilment process may involve people working together from the purchasing, sales, manufacturing, distribution and customer services functions throughout an organisation for example.

The Ford Motor Company was one of the first widely publicised re-engineering projects (Hammer, 1990). Ford's management was concerned that it's accounts payable process was not operating efficiently and were convinced that they could reduce their existing headcount of 500 by 20 per cent. However, they realised that their process was over staffed by as much as 80 per cent when they took a view of the equivalent process in Mazda, another motor company. Ford identified that the major problem with their process was that many staff were involved in matching around 13 items on three documents, from three different sources. Ford implemented a database and all of the transactions from the purchasing of stocks, through to goods received and finally payment were conducted electronically. This eliminated the need for the large amount of document matching work and the staffing levels in the accounts payable section were reduced by 75 per cent. Instead of trying to deal with the mismatches, Ford eradicated them.

THE IMPLEMENTATION OF BPR PROJECTS

Following the successes of companies such as Ford, Xerox, AT & T, American Express and MBL, many companies decided to undertake BPR projects. However, it became clear that the concept was high on rhetoric and low on practical implementation advice. Davenport and Short (1990) outline the five steps in a BPR effort: develop business vision and process objectives, identify processes to be redesigned, understand and measure existing processes, identify IT levers and design and build a prototype of the process. However, they do not offer advice on how to do this, merely what to do. The same is true of Hammer (1990) who described the reengineering projects at Ford and MBL, and then offered a view on what organisations should do:

- organise around outcomes, not tasks;
- make sure those who use the output of the process perform the process;
- subsume information processing work into the real work that produces the information;
- treat geographically dispersed resources as though they were centralised;
- link parallel activities instead of integrating their results;
- put the decision point where the work is performed, and build control into the process;
- capture information once and at the source.

It became clear that managers were spending too much time trying to implement BPR projects without knowing what they were doing. Instead of making re-engineering work, they were producing further organisational problems (Hall *et al.,* 1993). This problem spawned a large number of 'how to do' re-engineering books and articles. A wide array of methods and tools for the implementation of BPR projects subsequently evolved. Many of these originated form the big consultancy firms such as Cap Gemini, Ernst and Young, Andersen Consulting and PriceWaterhouse. Kettinger *et al.*, (1997) have conducted a large study into these methodologies, techniques and tools. The results of their study offer a framework for determining which are the most appropriate for a project's characteristics. As part their study, they identified at least 72 techniques in use on BPR projects and that these generally were 'borrowed' from other disciplines. Adoptions included process modelling techniques such as IDEF diagramming, concepts from the quality management movement, work design thinking, and aspects of socio-technical systems design such as soft systems methodology. They also identified a growing set of 102 tools which were being used to structure the project and manage the associated information.

In addition to the evolution of the methods and tools other advice on implementation emerged which can be categorised as belonging to the 'critical success factors for BPR' family. That is, what needs to be paid attention to in order to achieve a successful BPR project implementation. An exemplar of this mode of the literature is the work of Bashein *et al.* (1994) which examines the preconditions for BPR success. They argue that there are several positive and negative preconditions that relate to BPR projects and offer ways of generating the positive pre-conditions and dealing with the negative ones. A summary of their thinking is shown in Figure 19.1.

Examples of other works in this mode refer to similar themes such as the need for IS and business partnerships (Martinez, 1995), the requirement for, and communication of a clearly defined vision (Barrett, 1994) and cultural change (Bartlett and Ghoshal, 1995). However, even given these guidelines, managers in organisations still faced difficulties when trying to implement BPR projects. The authors argue that this is largely due to the explicit lack of the acknowledgement of context within which the BPR projects were implemented as will now be discussed.

THE MULTI-DIMENSIONAL NATURE OF BPR

From the discussions on the classic concept of BPR and the nature of implementation, it is acutely clear that one of the main difficulties with traditional thinking on BPR is its promotion as a generic concept. That is, as offering a 'one size fits all' solution that ignores the nature of the current situation or 'legacy systems'. The standard approaches typically assume a green-field site. For example, Hammer and Champy

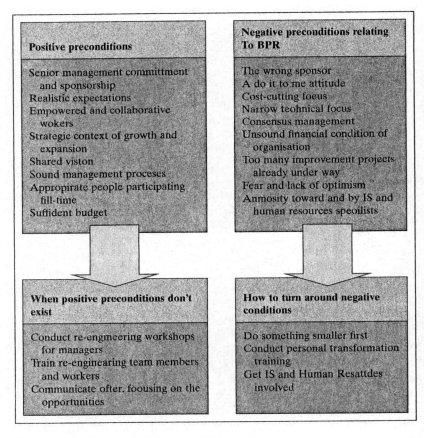

Figure 19.1   The preconditions for BPR project success

(1993) state that re-engineering should begin with no assumptions or givens, should ignore what is and concentrate on what should be. Furthermore, Davenport and Short (1990) argue that it is important to understand and measure existing processes which appears a step in the right direction. However, it transpires that this is purely to ensure that the existing business processes are not replicated and to provide a baseline for future improvement.

Consequently, more recent analyses of the BPR concept have highlighted the importance of the broader strategic and IT contexts in which BPR projects are managed. For example Galliers (1998) states that BPR is concerned with profit maximisation, argues that little thought is given to more pluralistic outcomes and that there is minimal concern for cultural and contextual issues other than viewing them as obstacles to change. Similarly, Coulson-Thomas (1994) suggests that approaches tend to be insufficiently tailored to situations, circumstances and contexts. It is clear that the way a company is organised, the manner in which work is conducted and the existing operational systems are all factors that need to be taken account of on a BPR project otherwise problems may be encountered (Avison and Fitzgerald, 1995). Moreover, several other authors writing on the challenges of re-engineering all suggest that the existing state of the business and IT infrastructure will affect the outcomes of a BPR project (Hall *et al.*, 1993; Bashein *et al.*, 1994; Martinez, 1995; Grover *et al.*, 1998). Consequently, concepts of BPR that do not take account of legacy systems are potentially flawed. Some of the early innovators in the field have developed the original BPR frameworks to take into account the importance of the legacy issues (e.g. Davenport *et al.*, 1995). Davenport and Stoddard (1994) state that in practice a 'blank sheet of paper' is rarely found and that one of the key factors for a firm they studied not taking a clean slate approach was the need for the replacement of legacy systems. A broadening of the BPR philosophy in practice has emerged and is typified by the work of Grover and Kettinger (1995 p.vi). They identify that in reality BPR is generally adapted as necessary by organisations and state that

> the revolution of reengineering, the requirement to sustain and integrate process change, the need to reconcile alternative process improvement and management approaches, and the recognition of organizational constraints to implementation, all serve to broaden the concepts of BPR, recognizing the need for the radical, the incremental, the continuous and the contingent.

Organisations are now recognising and using the dimensions of BPR to facilitate change in a way that is sympathetic to their legacy systems and business pressures. It is clear from the brief review of the BPR literature that most of the early BPR thinking supported a philosophy of radical change to the business model of the firm or industry underpinned by the innovative application of information technology.

Whilet this approach encourages new ideas to be raised, the results have been mixed. The importance of the current systems and business practices was often underestimated and has undoubtedly impeded the implementation of new concepts.

The situation is summarised by Ward and Griffiths (1996, p. 239):

> In many companies IT has become a constraint to redesign, because in the past IT was often used to automate badly designed processes and they are now expensively petrified in silicon!

This quote illustrates the importance of organisational change associated with most IT projects, but particularly with BPR projects. Typical process models of organisations are cross-functional but existing systems are likely to re-enforce functional boundaries (Bartholemew, 1994). For some organisations, this problem is particularly acute because the systems have been developed and modified over several decades. This results in information systems that are characterised by high levels of entropy and technical complexity making them extremely difficult and expensive to change. However, the systems may be so business critical and so heavily embedded within the IT infrastructure of the firm that BPR has to be enacted using the existing system in the best way possible. It is clear that BPR is a contextual problem, and that the different business and IT histories of individual organisations influence the planning and implementation of BPR projects. Ponce-de-Leon *et al.* (1995) have made inroads into this area by developing a taxonomy of BPR strategies which is comprised of a BPR dimension and an IT applications delivery strategy dimension as shown in Figure 19.2. They argue that re-engineering projects will differ in two respects: the organisational scope and in how the IT application is delivered. Whilst this illustrates a good deal of the potential complexities associated with BPR, the nature of BPR and IT strategies, coupled with the impact of legacy systems, or context, is not adequately explained.

This work also highlights another important factor through its focus upon scope. Originally BPR was aimed at improving internal organisational processes. However, the concept has since been extended to those processes that cross organisational boundaries (Short and Venkatraman, 1992; Venkatraman, 1994). This strengthens the argument for the need to consider the context within which the BPR project is being implementation.

IT Applications Delivery Strategy

		Vendor Driven ⟷ User Driven		
		Vendor developed application solution	**Application adaptation**	**Customised application**
Narrow focus	Intrafunctonal (localised teams)	Functional localised vendor constrained work-flow BPR	Functional semi-customised localized work-flow BPR	Functional customised localised work-flow BPR
(BPR Scope ↑)	Interfunctional (cross functional teams)	Cross functional vendor constrained BPR	Cross functional semi-customised BPR	Cross functional customised BPR
Broad focus	Interorganisational (cross business teams)	Strategic business network vendor constrained BPR	Strategic business network semi-customised BPR	Strategic business network, redefinition customised BPR

Figure 19.2   BPR strategies

BPR IN PRACTICE

Given the problems encountered by organisations and the criticisms raised in the literature regarding BPR, the authors have developed a framework for understanding the contextual nature of BPR as shown in Figure 19.3 (Light and Holland, 1998). The framework is not presented as a prescription for organisations rather, as a way of articulating and understanding the BPR as a multidimensional and contextual concept.

The framework allows a distinction to be made between relatively simple, single business process initiatives and much more complex strategies as identified by Dixon *et al.* (1994). Examples of the former include the Fords accounts payable processes (Hammer, 1990) and the pilot project at CIGNA Reinsurance (Caron *et al.*, 1994). Examples of more complex strategies include the transformation of Monsanto (Edmondson *et al.*, 1997) and Cable Systems International (Appleton, 1997) and Guilbert Niceday (Gibson *et al.*, 1999) following ERP implementations.

To explain the framework, it can be seen that organisations have business and IT legacy systems. The business legacy is the composite characteristics of an organisation such as its structure, culture, busi-

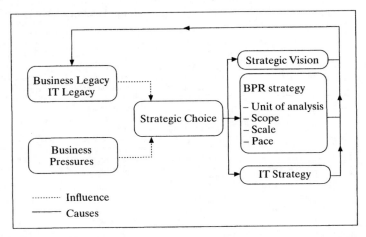

Figure 19.3   The contextual and multidimensional nature of BPR

ness processes and strategy which result from the impact of internal and external forces (Johnson, 1992). The IT legacy is the IT based system/s that are inhibiting organisational operations and performance due to a combination of factors such as their age, size and complexity (Bennett, 1994; Sneed, 1995; Ward, 1995; Adolph, 1996; Kim, 1997). The IS literature typically focuses on the technical dimension of legacy systems and pays little attention to the business dimension. It is also worth noting that in some instances the business and IT legacy may well contain valuable aspects. The fundamental problem of business and IT legacy for organisations is therefore twofold: understanding and managing their inhibiting effects and identifying their inherent opportunities.

Organisations will also face business pressures which, for brevity, we will group into globalisation, deregulation, IT and competitive forces (Porter, 1980). The combination and nature of the legacy systems and business pressures will influence the strategic choice. Strategic choice is the decision-making process that organisations go through when formulating strategy. Johnson and Scholes (1993) state that this will involve generating strategic options, evaluating those options and making a selection upon the basis of this. This process will result in the development of a strategic vision and supporting IT and BPR Strategies.

The strategic vision is the intended plan for the transformation of an organisation in order to obtain competitive advantage. It is highly interconnected with the business processes as competitive advantage originates from differences between organisations and the ways these are purposefully articulated in strategies (Porter, 1996). The IT strategy is the method of support for strategic vision that is provided by information technology (Earl, 1989). There are numerous IT strategies, each with implementation issues that need consideration based on the other characteristics of the framework. IT strategies include the adoption of standard packages, ringfencing – building around existing systems, business process rooted strategies such as outsourcing, bespoke development and the maintenance or modification of existing systems.

Finally, the BPR strategy aims to reorganise capabilities in order to realise the strategic vision. BPR strategies are composed of four dimensions: the unit of analysis that is the focus of change, the scope of the change, the scale of the change and the implementation strategy. The unit of analysis includes the individual, the team, the business function, the organisation and the market network. The scope of the change is the number of business processes included in the project ranging from individual processes such as recruitment right through to all business processes contained in an organisation. The scale of the change is the size of the proposed change ranging from minor enhancements to total re-engineering of a process (Cule *et al.*, 1995). The scale of the change is related to the starting position of the organisation. That is, what may be a major scale of change for one organisation may be a smaller one for another depending upon their legacy systems. The pace of change refers to the speed of implementation from incremental through to big bang approaches.

THE FUTURE: BPR AND ERP SYSTEMS

Although organisations are continuing to implement broad BPR or business process change projects, one of the most influential factors upon the sustenance of the concept of BPR throughout the 1990s has been the wide-scale adoption of ERP systems. As such, it is essential to examine the link between these two areas. ERP systems are process oriented and highly integrated standard software systems which are used to automate core corporate activities such as finance, logistics and human resources. The ERP applications market has grown enormously over the past five years and is at present is estimated to be around $20 billion (AMR Research, 1999). Interestingly, the key reasons for the adoption of ERP systems are closely allied to those for the evolution of BPR – the need to deal with legacy systems in a complex and dynamic business environment. Historically most international firms have managed their IT systems on a country by country basis with a few notable exceptions such as Hewlett Packard (Lee and Billington, 1995) and Ford (Treece *et al.*, 1995). This was due in part to the natural historical evolution of local nationally based strategies and systems, and also because there was no obvious single solution that was globally acceptable. Companies are now looking to improve the management of global operations and employ innovative supply chain based competitive strategies such as time based competition (Vessey, 1991), the formation of new types of industrial structures (Malone *et al.*, 1987, 1989; Konsynksi and McFarlan, 1990) and mass customisation strategies (Feitzinger and Lee, 1997). However, many existing systems have become so difficult and costly to maintain, inflexible and misaligned with a global business strategy that firms have taken a clean slate approach towards their IT and have implemented ERP systems. Managers of ERP projects that have spoken with the authors have suggested that ERP is the new BPR. The reason for this is because a key aspect of any ERP project is the need for most organisations to undertake some form of BPR exercise (Holland and Light, 1999). ERP systems are process-oriented and, due to their highly interconnected nature, require organisations that implement these types of system to adopt a process oriented philosophy. Therefore, if an organisation has not undergone an organisation wide reengineering exercise, and their structure still represents the functional silos model, they will do so. Even if there are elements of a process orientation within an organisation, it is likely that the a certain level of reengineering will occur. This has considerable implications for competitive advantage. The persuasiveness of these systems means that many companies may have reengineered their business processes to align them with an implicit business process map which is almost identical to their competitors who have also implemented an ERP strategy. Consequently, further 'high level' reengineering projects are now taking place. Examples of these include radical changes to supply chains, distribution channels, relationships with customers and the nature of the products and services offered by organisations.

CONCLUSION

Dramatic changes in the business environment throughout the 1980s have forced organisations to examine outdated modes of work and formulate new externally focussed strategies based on new business models. Many business management concepts have emerged, such as TQM and outsourcing, in order to facilitate this transformation but BPR has probably been the most influential. BPR emerged as a tightly defined concept geared toward a clean slate, radial approach. However, the original ideas were high on rhetoric did not take account of the practical situation in organisations where factors such as the evolution of national historical preferences for ways of work, organisational cultures and IT infrastructures had become inextricably linked with the existence of organisations. From the confusion and implementation failures, a variety of methodologies, tools and techniques have been developed for the implementation of BPR projects. Common to the more sophisticated of the approaches has been the recognition of the strategic and operational contexts of organisations. As a result the concept of BPR has survived and has been broadened to become more commonly associated with multidimensional process change efforts such as ERP implementations. Re-engineering is no longer just a matter of fundamental and radical improvements in performance, it has become a mechanism for fundamentally thinking about and transforming the nature of businesses and even industries.

Acknowledgement

The author would like to thank the Engineering and Physical Sciences Research Council, which have supported the research reported in this paper under the Systems Engineering for Business Process Change programme of research.

References

ADOLPH, W.S. (1996) 'Cash cow in the tar pit: reengineering a legacy system', *IEEE Software*, May, 41–7.
AMR Research (1999) 'AMR research predicts ERP market will reach $66.6 billion by 2003', Press Release, 18 May <http://www.amrresearch.com>
APPLETON, E.L. (1997) 'How to survive ERP', *Datamation*, Mar., 50–3.
AVISON, D.E. and FITZGERALD, G. (1995) *Information Systems Develop-*

ment: Methodologies, Techniques and Tools, 2nd edn, London: McGraw-Hill.

BARRETT, J.L. (1994) 'Process visualisation: getting the vision right is key', *Information Systems Management*, Spring, 14–23.

BARTHOLEMEW, D. (1994) 'Technology a hurdle?: survey says top execs see IT inhibiting corporate reengineering', *Business Week (Bonus Issue: The Information Revolution)*, 18 May.

BARTLETT, C.A. and GHOSHAL, S. (1995) 'Rebuilding behavioral context: turn process reengineering into people rejuvenation', *Sloan Management Review*, Autumn 11–23.

BASHEIN, B.J., MARKUS, M.L. and RILEY, P. (1994) 'Preconditions for BPR success and how to prevent failures', *Information Systems Management*, Spring, 7–13.

BENNETT, K. (1994) 'Legacy systems: coping with success', *IEEE Software*, 12, (1), 19–23.

CARON, J.R., JARVENPAA, S.L. and STODDARD, D.B. (1994) 'Business reengineering at CIGNA Corporation: experiences and lessons learned from the first five years', *Management Information Systems Quarterly*, September, 233–50.

COULSON-THOMAS, C. (ed.) (1994) *Business Process Re-engineering: Myth And Reality*, London: Kogan Page.

CULE, P.E. (1995) in Grover, V. and Kettinger, W.J. (eds), *BPR: Reengineering Concepts, Methods And Technologies*, Idea Publishing Group, London.

DAVENPORT, T.H. (1993) *Process Innovation: Reengineering Work Through Information Technology*, Boston: Harvard, Business School Press.

DAVENPORT, T.H. (1995) in Grover, V. and Kettinger, W.J. (eds), *BPR: Reengineering Concepts, Methods And Technologies* London: Idea Publishing Group.

DAVENPORT, T.H. and SHORT, J.E. (1990) 'The new industrial engineering: information technology and business process redesign', *Sloan Management Review*, Summer, 11–27.

DAVENPORT, T.H. and STODDARD, D.B. (1994) 'Reengineering: business change of mythic proportions?', *Management Information Systems Quarterly*, June, 121–7.

DIXON, J.B., ARNOLD, P., HEINEKE, J., KIM, J.S. and MULLIGAN, P. (1994) 'Business process reengineering: improving in new strategic directions', *Calafornia Management Review*, Summer, 93–108.

EARL, M.J. (1989) *Management Strategies for Information Technology*, London: Prentice-Hall.

EARL, M.J. (1994) 'How new is business process redesign?', *European Management Journal*, 12, 20–30.

EDMONDSON, G., BAKER, S. and CORTESE, A. (1997) 'Silicon Valley on the Rhine', *Business Week*, 3 November, 40–7.

EDWARDS, C. and PEPPARD, J.W. (1994) 'Business Process Redesign: hype, hope or hypocrisy', *Journal of Information Technology*, 9(4), 251–66.

FEITZINGER, E. and LEE, H.L. (1997) 'Mass customization at Hewlett-Packard: The power of Postponement', *Harvard Business Review*, January–February, 116–21.

GALLIERS, R.D. (1998) in Galliers, R.D. and Baets, W.R. (eds), *Information Technology And Organizational Transformation: Innovation For The 21*st *Century Organization*, Chichester: John Wiley.

GIBSON, N., HOLLAND, C. and LIGHT, B. (1999) A fast track SAP R/3 implementation at Guilbert Niceday, *Electronic Markets*, June.

GRINT, K. (1994) 'Reengineering history: social resonances and Business Process Reengineering', *Organization*, 1(1), 179–201.

GROVER, V. and KETTINGER, W.J. (eds) (1995) *BPR: Reengineering Concepts, Methods and Technologies*, London: Idea Publishing Group.

GROVER, V., SEUNG RYUL, J. and TENG, J.T.C. (1998) 'Survey of reengineering challenges', *Information Systems Management*, Spring, 53–9.

HALL, G., ROSENTHAL, J. and WADE, J. (1993) 'How to make reengineering really work', *Harvard Business Review*, November–December, 119–31.

HAMMER, M. (1990) 'Reengineering work: don't automate, obliterate', *Harvard Business Review*, July–August, 104–12.

HAMMER, M. and CHAMPY, J. (1993) *Reengineering The Corporation*, New York: Harper Business.

HOLLAND, C. and LIGHT, B. (1999) 'A critical success factors model for ERP implementation', *IEEE Software*, 16(3), 31–6.

JOHNSON, G. (1992) 'Managing strategic change: strategy, culture and action', *Long Range Planning*, 25(1), 28–36.

JOHNSON, G. and SCHOLES, K. (1993) *Exploring Corporate Strategy*, 3rd edn, London: Prentice-Hall.

KETTINGER, W.J., TENG, J.T.C. and GUHA, S. (1997) 'Business process change: a study of methodologies, techniques, and tools', *Management Information Systems Quarterly*, March, 55–80.

KIM, Y.G. (1997) 'Improving legacy systems maintainability', *Information Systems Management*, Winter, 7–11.

KONSYNSKI, B.R. and MCFARLAN, F.W. (1990) 'Information partnerships – shared data, shared scale', *Harvard Business Review*, 68(5), 114–20.

LEE, H.L. and BILLINGTON, C. (1995) 'The evolution of supply-chain management models and practice at Hewlett-Packard', *Interfaces*, 25(5), 42–63.

LEVITT, T. (1983) 'The globalization of markets', *Harvard Business Review*, May–June, 92–102.

LIGHT, B. and HOLLAND, C. (1998) 'The influence of legacy Information Systems on Business Process Reengineering Strategies', *Proceedings of the 8th Annual BIT Conference*, 4–5 November, Manchester.

MALONE, T.W., YATES, J. and Benjamin, R.I. (1987) 'Electronic markets and electronic hierarchies', *Communications of the ACM*, 30(6), 484–97.

MALONE, T.W., YATES, J. and BENJAMIN, R.I. (1989) 'The logic of electronic markets', *Harvard Business Review*, 67(3), 166–72.

MARTINEZ, E.V. (1995) 'Successful reengineering demands IS/business partnerships', *Sloan Management Review*, Summer, 51–60.

OHAME, K. (1989) 'Managing in a borderless world', *Harvard Business Review*, May–June, 152–61.

OSTERLE, H. (1995) *Business in the Information Age: Heading for new Processes*, Berlin: Springer.

PONCE-DE-LEON, J.A., RAI, A. and MELCHER, A. (1995) in Grover, V.

and Kettinger, W.J. (eds), *BPR: Reengineering Concepts, Methods And Technologies,* London: Group.

PORTER, M.E. (1980) *Competitive Strategy,* New York: Free Press.

PORTER, M.E. (1996) 'What is strategy?', *Harvard Business Review,* November–December, 61–78.

SCHNITT, D.L. (1993) 'Reengineering the organization using Information Technology', *Journal of Systems Management,* January, 14–42.

SHORT, J.E. and VENKATRAMAN, N. (1992) 'Beyond Business Process Redesign: redefining Baxter's business network', *Sloan Management Review,* Autumn, 7–21.

SNEED, H.M. (1995) 'Planning the reengineering of legacy systems', *IEEE Software,* January, 24–34.

TREECE, J.B. KERWIN, K. and DAWLEY, H. (1995) 'Alex Trotman's daring global strategy', *Business Week,* 3 April, 36–44.

VENKATRAMAN, N. (1994) 'IT-enabled business transformation: from automation to business scope redefinition', *Sloan Management Review,* Winter, 73–87.

VESSEY, J.T. (1991) 'The new competitors: they think in terms of "speed-to-market"', *Academy of Management Executive,* 5(2), 23–33.

WARD, J.M. (1995) *Principles of Information Systems Management,* London: Routledge.

WARD, J. and GRIFFITHS, P. (1996) *Strategic Planning for Information Systems,* 2nd edn, Chichester: John Wiley.

WILLCOCKS, L. and SMITH, G. (1995) 'IT-enabled Business Process Reengineering: organizational and human dimensions', *Journal of Strategic Information Systems,* 4(3), 279–301.

20 Networks, Failures, Futures and Adaptivity: ICT as 'Humpty Dumpty'

Mark Stubbs, Gareth Griffiths and Dave Tucker

Humpty Dumpty sat on a wall
Humpty Dumpty had a great fall
All the King's horses
And all the King's men
Couldn't put Humpty together again

INTRODUCTION

Increasingly, ICTs are being taken for granted. When their behaviour does not surprise us, we find them unremarkable. It is convenient to treat things this way. Usually, we are not amazed when databases, mobile telephones or Internet browsers link us with the electronic representations of disembodied others. We rarely marvel that these representations have travelled across space and time (from the past into the present) to be with us. It just happens. ICTs have become part of the fabric of society. Admittedly, we struggle to predict what they will be like in the future. But, we find it equally difficult to imagine a future without them.

At work we may come across a disembodied customer to whom we feel an obligation to respond. With a few key strokes we may exercise some capacity to do so. We might neither know nor care how (exactly) such things are possible. For many of us, the complex and precarious arrangements of materials and people that facilitate such interactions have disappeared. More or less dependable tools stand in their place, and we work with them and around them. These tools have enabled, and then become deeply embedded in, the production and reproduction of our highly interconnected modern world (Lash and Urry,

307

1994). We talk of global coupling of economies, the media, food distribution networks, medicine, sport, and many other communities of practice which shape our lives. Yet, in many ways, this networked world is beyond us.

For most of us, the scale at which ICTs operate is outside our day-to-day experience. We might talk about ICTs in terms of hardware and software, and say that software is intangible – it cannot be grasped physically. (Some dictionaries remind us that intangible expresses something that cannot be grasped mentally, and perhaps this also strikes a chord.) We content ourselves with grasping only hardware. Even then, we tend only to grasp surfaces, the outer casings of complex mechanisms which are too small, too numerous, and too fast to comprehend. Within these mechanisms, things are happening at the nano level, outside our unaided sensory range. Increasingly, such mechanisms are being linked directly with one another, allowing nano-level changes to spread out across the globe at speeds that make us feel our world has become small. We talk of layers of abstraction distancing our day-to-day existence from this interwoven realm of the super tiny and the super fast. We assume that expert others have attended to matters appropriate to the layers below the surface we see. We are content to work with 'black boxed' tools.

Only when the behaviour of one of our 'black-boxes' disappoints are we forced to recognise our dependence on layers below the familiar surfaces. Our usual reaction is to seek experts versed in these previously hidden domains, who are willing and able to fix our disappointment. Consider, for instance, that most familiar of 'black-boxes': the television set. A fault quickly translates a taken-for-granted piece of furniture into the focal point of a web of time-absorbing interactions, involving numerous telephone conversations, discussions about warranties, visits by repair people, decisions about replacement, and so on. Failure unmasks this complexity and reminds us that our 'black box' was a precarious illusion. However, if our disappointment is mild or some expert rescues us before it has chance to become otherwise, such failure is merely an annoyance. We accept it. We may soon forget about it. The 'black-box' gets remade.

It is comforting to make sense of ICT in terms of 'black-boxed' tools – strategic weapons, data mining gear, or whatever else happens to be in vogue. Developments in specific technologies occur at such staggering rates that even those who assume responsibility for explaining the subject to others cannot keep up. Pressures build to move away from specifics, to find increasingly abstract and more durable representations with which will people can work. Those who do not wish to understand the technology but wish only to use it productively can find the rate of change bewildering to the point of alienation. It is extremely tempting to think of complex technology in terms of black-boxed productivity tools. It is also made to be so. Well-resourced advertising campaigns suggest that those who do not join the IT band-wagon will be missing out on something of great benefit and impor-tance. Understanding is not presented as a prerequisite for ownership. Often the reverse is implied. Television and magazine advertisements depict families standing around their home PC, happy and smiling with the pleasure the new technology brings to them all. Commercials aimed at businesses emphasise how the technology is enabling 'smarter' rather than 'harder' work, the implication being that the business is inferiour without the technology. That these claims seem at odds with personal experience and some respected studies (e.g. Roach, 1986; Strassman, 1997) seems not to matter.

IT vendors work hard to sustain the 'black box'/productivity tool image. They recognise that many end users (and would-be end-users) are not, and do not wish to be, technically competent – they want a tool that works and is easy to use. Consequently much effort is devoted to making the hardware increasingly easy to install and con-figure, ensuring software has 'user friendly' interfaces, and so on. Ten years ago, installing new software was a laborious task requiring the user to make endless changes to computer files with alien-sounding names such as 'config.sys' and 'autoexec.bat'. While the user may not have understood fully what s/he was doing, s/he was at least aware of the changes made because s/he had done them. The black-box was partly transparent. Should there be a problem, steps could possibly be retraced and the computer returned to its previous state. Today, the software is so sophisticated that the user is 'freed' from the frustra-tion of installation – it virtually installs itself. Hardware is now called 'plug and play'. These modern 'black boxes' have become easier and more opaque. Changes made to the configuration are intangible. But so what, if it works?

Our experience is that these modern black boxes do not always work. We are told that this is not a problem, we must simply ring the customer service number of the vendor who will guide us to the solu-tion. We dial the number and are greeted by an electronic voice who kindly places our call in a queue and 'soothes' us with music. Some-times, given sufficient patience, we get through to a human being and feel relieved. We expect our problems will soon be over, we imagine we have reached an expert who can help us. Unfortunately, it is rare not to become disappointed at this point. 'Try this. If it doesn't work, then get back to me', we hear. We try. More often than not it does not quite fix our problem. Regarding ourselves as unlucky somehow seems easier to live with than letting go of the thought that there are experts out there who understand and can fix our particular black boxes. Perhaps, just for a moment, we allow ourselves to think about just how many possibilities for error lie below the surfaces we see. We remember that our hardware and software has been purchased at different times, from different vendors. We remember newspaper articles about the fluid ICT job market and how difficult it is to keep knowledge within an organisation when individuals leave. Yet somehow it feels unproductive to think of our black boxes as precarious. We don't want to think that putting them back together when they come apart could involve a search for nano-needles in macro haystacks. So we get on with other things. We muddle through. We manage to get a fix from somewhere or work around the problem. Like pain, our disappointments and concerns are soon forgotten. Sometimes, we look at others and are amazed at the levels of annoyance they can experience without challenging the way they work with ICT – just ask some of our students about data loss ! But somehow, despite all this, the potential of ICT is no less captivating. The benefits we imagine eclipse the risks of failure. ICT 'tools' seem more apparent than their precarious nature.

As we approach the new millenium, a simple programming shortcut, reproduced in an unknown number of ICT systems around the world, threatens to expose and possibly fracture some of the precarious foundations of our networked world. We are led to believe that many organisations have invested a great deal of time and money in ensuring that their ICT will not be compromised by the date change. We suspect that there are a fair few which have not. In the UK, the government task force established to help small businesses address the problem, has witnessed a disappointingly low take-up. Perhaps, the target audience believe their systems to be millenium compliant. Maybe they are. Perhaps, compliance is considered unimportant. And maybe, for some businesses, it is. Perhaps, they cannot imagine how their tools could let them down. We do not know. Some large, well-resourced organisations, are reported to have checked their supply chains. We suspect some of these claims to be founded on superficial handling of the 'black-boxed' complexity that must be unmasked and examined. It is impossible to be sure that everything on which one currently depends will continue to function. Usually this does not bother us.

We take for granted the predictability of our day-to-day routines and find comfort and security in them. Our horizons of interest emerge from (and shape) these routines and without them to limit the matters about which we worry, we run the risk of being overwhelmed by complexity (Giddens, 1984). Perhaps, this is why postmodernists' calls for deconstruction are not more widely embraced. Suspending one's capacity for action so that its foundations can be exposed and examined tends to appear unproductive or daunting – one might question where such a project of deconstruction might end. For instance, is it necessary to understand the inner workings of the word-processing package used to write this? Is it interesting that its standard dictionary contains stockholder but not stakeholder?

Inevitably a balance must be struck between ignoring complexity so that one can 'get on' with life, and revealing complexity to reflect critically on what 'getting-on' actually involves. Calls for deconstruction can be seen as a reaction against the increasing tendency to depend on things which are beyond us – things to which Actor–Network theorists draw attention with their notion of 'black boxes' (Law, 1994) and Giddens (1991) highlights as 'expert systems'. In contemporary society, our interests and domains of expertise have become highly specialised and this focus has led to great breakthrough in understanding and technology. We like to think of this as progress, but specialism has come at a price. Most of us now depend on things that are beyond our boundaries of concern and competence. We tend not to think about this. It is distracting. Instead, we place our trust in the things around which our routines are made, assuming such things will either function or be fixed. This is not to say that at some time or other, we have not experienced the frustration of waiting for things to get fixed. Or that we have not coped with the complexity revealed when something broke down. The point is: the scenario of multi-point failure in a highly networked world is alien to most of us. The continuity of our lifeworlds is more familiar than their precarious nature.

In recent years the media has conveyed graphic images of unfortunate others who have lost the stability of routine, refugees who struggle to find anything on which to rely. These representations can invoke a range of emotions – shock, pity, anger, frustration. If we are honest, however, most of us do not empathise. We cannot. We have only limited experience of the break down of things and it is in terms of this experience that we contemplate the future for ourselves and others. We do not imagine that those who would come to the rescue in our hour of need might struggle to be found or would themselves need rescuing. It is hard to think that we and they could be confounded by a web of dependencies that had somehow slipped from view. The multi-point failure scenario focuses attention on such unfamiliar concerns. The question is whether one can actually and usefully prepare for such a future.

It seems sensible to build adaptive capacity in the present for the futures we can imagine. But it is not easy to strike a balance between hoping for the best and preparing for the worst when only limited resources are available. In this paper we have highlighted how images of ICT as dependable tools loom large in the scenarios for the future most of us envisage. We feel it is high time to counter this with an equally strong image that portrays ICT as precarious. We therefore offer the metaphor of Humpty Dumpty. We hope its cognitive force will point out analogies and invite comparisons which cross the boundaries of categories and concepts usually employed to contemplate ICT. Like Gareth Morgan, we regard metaphor as both evocative and tentative – we feel it is important to be circumspect about the knowledge our metaphor generates, but then one must be circumspect with all imagery. Organisations cannot be re-engineered. ICT is not a strategic weapon. The tension between truth and falsehood inherent in any metaphor should encourage healthy scepticism, but it is easy for a metaphor to disappear if it becomes well-grooved in day-to-day discussions about the phenomena to which it refers. For our purposes, the novel image of ICT as Humpty Dumpty draws attention to a dramatic failure scenario and, in so doing, invites some in-depth consideration of our increasing dependence on potentially-fragile 'black boxes'.

Keeping in mind an image of ICT as vulnerable and fragile has implications for the theory and practice of BITM. Those advocating the importance of understanding the social context in which ICT is deployed now caution against their arguments relegating technology from the agenda of concern (Walsham, 1997). ICT can and does mediate social interaction. It 'embodies assumptions that can either invite or extinguish a human contribution' (Zuboff, 1988, p. 182). It can both enable and constrain. It is likely to have intended and unintended consequences. Complex business practices are being built upon it, and one day bits of it could fail.

Our working lives (and many of our other lifeworlds) increasingly depend upon a network of Humpty Dumpties. We raise the complexity with which we must deal if we are alert to that network and its potential for collapse. It may be more convenient to abstract ourselves from the technology, but our chances of being better prepared for failure are greater if we do not (cf. Pirsig, 1974). Whether one is optimistic or pessimistic about the so-called millenium bug, it has raised the profile of risk, dependence and adaptive capacity for those who work with and around ICT. Our alternative metaphor seeks to nurture seeds of doubt that counter the 'dependable tool' image of ICT, thereby setting any assessment of adaptive capacity against a broader range of foreseeable futures. Bringing to life the ideas of 'adaptive capacity' and 'foreseeable futures' in specific business contexts seems vital to BITM in the run up to the millenium and (perhaps more importantly) beyond.

Our words in this chaper are not written as an attack on 'black-boxing' complexity – we have presented it as both convenient and necessary. We wish only to encourage recognition of how the apparent solidity of familiar 'black boxes' belies their fragile and vulnerable nature. To make our point, we have used metaphor as we believe it provides a powerful reminder that things can always appear differently. This is one instance of a sense of 'other' which offers many benefits for BITM.

In raising the possibility that things could be other than they appear, metaphor stimulates both creativity and critical reflection (Morgan, 1996). We see these behaviours injecting useful moderation into the spiral towards increasing abstraction from and dependence upon ICT. This does not mean that the phenomena of 'black-boxing' ICT will go away. It could not. Our call is to recognise that it is happening and work with it, learning to manage and managing to learn in terms of it. To that end, the centrality of 'black-boxes' to Actor–Network theory, has appeal, raising possible avenues for sharpening BITM theory and practice. Like metaphor, Actor–Network theory promotes a sense of 'other'. Yes, actors are network effects, they represent 'black-boxed' complexity. But networks can be found in actors. And actors can be found in networks. Whether through Actor–Network theory, metaphor, or making the relationship between theory and practice a productive one, the tensions set up in trying to develop an acute sense of 'other' provide inspiration for the future of BITM.

Afterword from a five year old:

Humpty Dumpty sat on a wall
Humpty Dumpty had a great fall
He didn't get bruised
He didn't get bumped
Humpty Dumpty bungee jumped !

References

GIDDENS, A. (1984) *The Constitution of Society: Outline of the Theory of Structuration*, Cambridge: Polity Press.
GIDDENS, A. (1991) *Modernity and Self-Identity*, Cambridge: Polity Press.
LASH, S. and URRY, J. (1994) *Economies of Signs and Space*, London: Sage.
LAW, J. (1994) *Organising Modernity*, Oxford: Blackwell.
MORGAN, G. (1996). 'An afterword: is there anything more to be said about metaphor', in Grant, D. and Oswick, D. (eds) *Metaphor and Organisations*, London: Sage, 227–40.
PIRSIG, R. (1974) *Zen and the Art of Motorcycle Maintenance: an Inquiry into Values*, London: Bodley Head.
ROACH, S. (1986) *Macro-Realities of the Information Economy*, New York: National Academy of Sciences.
STRASSMAN, P. (1997) *The Squandered Computer*, New Canaan: Information Economics Press.
WALSHAM, G. (1997). 'Actor–network theory and IS research: current status and future prospects', in Lee, A.S., Liebenau, J. and Degross, J.I. (eds), *Information Systems and Qualitative Research*. London: Chapman & Hall, pp. 466–80.
ZUBOFF, S. (1988). *In the Age of the Smart Machine – the Future of Work and Power*, New York: Basic Books.

Index

315